CRITICAL PRAISE FOR
*A RETURN TO MODESTY*

"The first book of its kind . . . to blaze down the center of the postfeminist battleground between left and right."
—Norah Vincent, *Salon*

"Intriguing . . . [Shalit] writes about . . . how not going through with something can leave a deeper imprint on your imagination than going through with it, and how we have lost the playfulness and mystery of old-fashioned courtship."
—Katie Roiphe, *Harper's Bazaar*

"[An] earnest and serious book. . . . A fascinating subject [brought] to our attention in a fresh way."
—Suzanne Fields, *The Washington Times*

"[An] important book that every thinking young woman (and her mother) should read."
—Maggie Gallagher, *New York Post*

"Brilliant . . . "
—Cassandra West, *Chicago Tribune*

"Wendy Shalit makes a strong case that deserves respectful . . . attention."
—Jonathan Yardley, *The Washington Post Book World*

"The new me was chaste and modest . . . a born-again virgin who went ice skating with her sweetheart and then home to bed. The new me was Wendy, not Ally."
—Amy Sohn, *New York Press*

" Wise . . . "
—Don Feder, *Boston Herald*

"A remarkably mature consideration of the history of manners between men and women. . . . Modesty and sexual shyness are a woman's way of telling the world that what she hides is worth waiting to see. That she is rare, not common. . . . Shalit gives voice to my gut feelings."
—Susan Reimer, *The Baltimore Sun*

"Shalit is a fiercely intelligent and resourceful critic.... We should all pay heed."

—Barbara Dafoe Whitehead, *Commonweal*

"[Shalit] writes well, has read widely, has a keen sense for the fault lines in an argument, and is willing to buck the prevailing tides. Although this is in some respects a young woman's book written for other young women, I wonder if we ought not be recommending it to young men. They might learn from it some important lessons about masculine character and conduct in our culture."

—Gilbert Meilaender, *The Christian Century*

"I can scarcely do justice to this excellent book.... This is a book that should be read by parents and young people alike—yes, boys, too."

—R.S. McCain, *New York Press*

"I find I like Wendy Shalit very much, both as a writer and, even more, as a fierce defender of young women's right to establish boundaries of their own."

—Ariel Swartley, *L.A. Weekly*

"A powerful and witty book that registers all the changes in our social landscape in all their starkness while also illuminating many of the steps that brought us to where we are.... *A Return to Modesty* seeks to reclaim what has been forgotten: that sex is significant.... [P]artly with the aid of expert testimony from earlier and more decorous ages, but mostly through her own preternaturally sharp eyes and mind, Shalit has seen deeply into female nature, and into the malaise of a generation."

—Elizabeth Powers, *Commentary*

"This book is a bombshell.... Her playful, engaging exploration of the richly nuanced concept of modesty is extensively researched and amply supported by evidence drawn from sources as diverse as *Glamour* and last millennium's Talmud."

—Sarah E. Hinlicky, *First Things*

"A heartfelt (and controversial) plea.... A daring book aimed at the core of contemporary gender theory.... It is audacious, and it should not be dismissed."

—*Kirkus Reviews*

"Intelligent. . . . Well-organized, briskly written advocacy."
—Gilbert Taylor, *Booklist*

"Impassioned . . ."
—Jae-Ha Kim, *Chicago Sun-Times*

"Shalit assails a culture in which "scoring" is a virtue, but acting like ladies and gentlemen is not. Old-fashioned? Perhaps. Persuasive? Absolutely."
—Andrea Neal, *The Indianapolis Star*

"When [Shalit] speaks of modesty, she talks about mystery, innocence and sexual reticence, about protecting romantic hope and vulnerability. It's a natural instinct, a lost idea—a virtue found in the Bible that has gone out of fashion, but, of late, finding new adherents. She explains that modesty comes from a sense of self-respect and confidence, qualities she exudes."
—Sandee Brawarsky, *Jewish Week*

"Excellent argument . . ."
—Melinda Ledden Sidak, *The Weekly Standard*

"What makes Wendy Shalit's analysis so refreshing is that she examines and justifies the nature of sexual modesty through rational discourse, rather than relying solely on the increasingly remote influence of religion. . . . While Shalit's assault on sexual promiscuity is not to be taken lightly, she manages to infuse some humor in her discourse."
—Catherine Muscat, *The Dartmouth Review*

"*A Return to Modesty: Discovering the Lost Virtue* is strong evidence that the backlash against Monica Lewinsky will come, not from her elders, but from her youngers."
—James P. Pinkerton, *New York Newsday*

"*A Return to Modesty* shows that its author has read, widely, on the sociology of sex . . . [it] is not a memoir, and Wendy Shalit avoids the embarrassing personal confessions in vogue at present. She tells us almost nothing of her own sexual experience. Is this 'pudeur' . . . ?"
—Dorothea Straus, Baltimore *Sun*

"In this slashing critique of 'the world of postmodern sexual morality,' *A Return to Modesty* surveys a cultural landscape in which people often select automobiles with more passion than lovers. . . . Written with sophistication, wit, and compassion that never becomes preachy . . . "

—Morgan N. Knull, *Campus*

"[Shalit is] outspoken, funny, very bright . . . because she is clever, unafraid, and outspoken, her voice is going to be heard for a long time . . . "

—Andrew M. Greeley, Florida *Port St. Lucie News*

"Miss Shalit . . . wants to change things, and arrives with proposals in hand. . . . [She] deserves credit not only for an important piece of writing but for courage in the line of duty."

—David Gelernter, Author of *Drawing Life*

"In this book Wendy Shalit brilliantly demonstrates how our views of natural modesty have been perverted by ideology. . . . Her book is a tour de force everyone should read and reflect upon. It is a return to first-rate sociology without jargon, an examination of the values of the culture at the end of our century."

—Edith Kurzweil, editor of *Partisan Review* and
author of *Freudians and Feminists*

"Wendy Shalit's invocation of some old virtues is nothing less than a prescription for a new sexual revolution."

—Gertrude Himmelfarb, author
of *Marriage and Morals Among the Victorians*

" Written with style, passion, and plenty of wit, this volume will signal the beginning of a new trend."

—Norman Lamm, President, Yeshiva University

"Wendy Shalit has written a book for all of us—feminists, antifeminists, conservatives, and liberals. By reclaiming modesty, Shalit argues, we might reclaim not only an overlooked but essential cornerstone of a good and stable life, but also a source of merriment and joy—the wellspring for a virtuous and secret eroticism that puts a twinkle in the eye, and shines rather than tarnishes the heart."

—Robin West, Professor of Law, Georgetown University, and
author of *Caring for Justice*.

WENDY SHALIT

A

RETURN

TO

MODESTY

Discovering

the

Lost

Virtue

A Touchstone Book
Published by Simon & Schuster

TOUCHSTONE
Rockefeller Center
1230 Avenue of the Americas
New York, NY 10020

First Touchstone Edition 2000

TOUCHSTONE and colophon are trademarks
of Simon & Schuster, Inc.

Designed by Pei Loi Koay

Manufactured in the United States of America

10

The Library of Congress has cataloged the Free Press edition as follows:

Shalit, Wendy, 1975–
    A return to modesty : discovering the lost virtue / Wendy Shalit.
       p.    cm.
    Includes bibliographical references and index.
    1. Sexual ethics for women. 2. Women—Sexual behavior.
    3. Jewish women—Sexual behavior. 4. Women—Conduct of
    life. 5. Modesty.
    I. Title.
    HQ46.S523   1999
    306.7'082—dc21          98-30489  CIP

ISBN-13: 978-0-684-84316-2
ISBN-10:    0-684-84316-1
ISBN-13: 978-0-684-86317-7 (Pbk)
ISBN-10:    0-684-86317-0 (Pbk)

Lyrics from "Baby It's Cold Outside" by Frank Loesser © 1948
(renewed) Frank Music Corp. All rights reserved. Reprinted by permission of Hal Leonard Corporation and the Estate of Frank Loesser.

*TO MY MOTHER AND FATHER,*

*with love,*

*and to anyone who has ever been embarrassed*

*about anything*

*The two of them were naked, the man and his wife, yet they felt no shame. . . . When the woman saw that the tree was good for eating and a delight to the eyes, and that the tree was a desirable source of wisdom, she took of its fruit and ate. She also gave some to her husband, and he ate. Then the eyes of both of them were opened and they perceived that they were naked; and they sewed together fig leaves and made themselves loincloths.*

—GENESIS 2:25–3:7

*And Isaac went out walking in the field toward evening and, looking up, he saw camels approaching. Raising her eyes, Rebekah saw Isaac. She alighted from the camel and said to the servant, "Who is that man walking in the field toward us?" And the servant said, "That is my master." So she took her veil and covered herself.*

—GENESIS 24:63–65

# CONTENTS

*Modesty, which may be provisionally defined as an almost instinctive fear prompting to concealment and usually centering around the sexual processes, while common to both sexes is more peculiarly feminine, so that it may almost be regarded as the chief secondary sexual character of women on the psychical side.*

—HAVELOCK ELLIS, 1899

My father is an economist, of the Chicago-school variety, so my earliest memories concern Coase's theorem, Stigler's laws, and the importance of buying and selling rights to pollute. Other children played in bundles of blankets and were scared of monsters; I played with imaginary bundles of competing currencies which would float, but really be more stable, and had nightmares that the Federal Reserve Board would ruin the business cycle. The fact that I was a girl never really came up. It was like having blue eyes, just a fact about me. On occasion, I would experience being a girl as a kind of special bonus: it meant getting to be a cheerleader and later, being taken to the prom. It would never even have occurred to me that my participation in these so-called "feminine" activities meant that I was somehow being oppressed, or that such activities precluded my thinking or doing anything else I wanted. When I returned home from the prom, after all, I could discuss anything I chose with my father. To be sure, I had heard of those who claimed that being a woman was not all fun and games, but those people were called *feminists,* and as every budding conservative knows, feminists exaggerate. Indeed, that is how you could tell that they were feminists— because they were the ones exaggerating all the time.

Don't ask me how I was so sure of this, or what this had to do with any other part of my ideology. As anyone who has ever had an ideology knows, you do not ask; you just look for confirmation for a set of beliefs. That's what it means to have an ideology. But life can have a rude way of intruding on theory. Sometimes you have to change your mind when things turn out to be more complicated than you initially thought. Coase's theorem may still be true but it also assumes zero transaction costs, and sometimes, you discover in life, there can be *extremely* high transaction costs.

Perhaps you can imagine my surprise, growing up as I did, to come to college and discover that in fact the feminists were not exaggerating. All around me, at the gym and in my classes, I saw stick-like women suffering from anorexia. Who could not feel for them? Or I would hop out to get a bagel at night and see a student I knew—who must have weighed all of 70 pounds—walk into our corner campus hangout, Colonial Pizza. Oh, good, I would think, she's finally going to eat. I would smile and try to give off see-isn't-eating-fun vibes. No, in fact she hadn't come to eat. Instead she mumbled weakly, looking like she was about to faint: "Do you have any Diet Mountain Dew, please? I'm *so* tired . . . I have a paper, and I can't stay up because I'm so, so *tired* . . . I have a paper . . . and it's due tomorrow . . . any Diet Mountain Dew?" Then in the dining halls I would observe women eating sometimes ten times as much as I and then suddenly cutting off our conversation. Suddenly, um, they had to go, suddenly, um, they couldn't talk anymore. Until that moment I hadn't actually realized that some women really did make themselves throw up after binging.

The bursting of my ideological bubble was complete when I began hearing stories of women raped, stories filled with much too much detail and sadness to be invented.

The feminists were not exaggerating. The feminists were right.

But what was going to happen to young women if the feminists were right? Was there a way out of this morass? I really couldn't see any.

Then I started to hear about the mysterious *modestyniks.*

A modestynik (pronounced "ˈmä-də-stē-nik") is my word for a modern single young woman raised in a secular home, who had hitherto seemed perfectly normal but who, inexplicably and without any prior notice, starts wearing very long skirts and issuing spontaneous announcements that she is now *shomer negiah,* which means that she isn't going to have physical contact with men before marriage, and that she is now dressing according to the standards of Jewish modesty. She is the type of woman who, when you hear about how she is living her life, might cause you to exclaim: "Yikes! What's her problem?!" Hence, among those who do not know her, she is usually known as an *abusenik* ("ə´byüz-nik"), a woman you know has been abused, even though she insists she hasn't been. Otherwise, you figure, why would she be so weird?

I first heard about these modestyniks from grandparents' pictures and hushed voices in the backseats of cars. In my freshman year I became friends with an elderly couple who had retired in our college town. It turned out that they knew my grandpa and grandma from way back, so I saw a lot of them between classes, when I would hear many funny stories about my grandparents. One night after dinner they brought out some pictures of one of their granddaughters, and this turned out to be my formal introduction to the modestyniks. She and her husband were Orthodox Jews, they explained. Then they offered me the first picture—of the granddaughter with her then-fiancé.

What a curious picture. Although the blissfully betrothed were grinning very widely, unlike most engaged couples they didn't have their arms around each other. Here were a young, beautiful brunette and a tall and handsome man standing extremely close together, but they weren't touching each other at all. Indeed, if you looked at the picture closely, you could trace a thin blue line of sky between the two of them. How strange, I thought: If they didn't really *like* each other, then why in the world did they get married?

Fortunately my friends spoke up. "See," said the grandfather, pointing at the photo, "they observe the laws of *tzniut.*" I said, "God bless you!" He said, "No, I didn't sneeze: *tzniut* means modesty. They observe the Jewish laws of sexual modesty."

"Oh," I said, a bit offended. For I was Jewish and *I* certainly didn't know about there being any Jewish modesty laws. I was a bit of a know-it-all, but about Judaism, I figured my parents were Jewish, I was Jewish, and I could recite a few blessings, if pressed. I even insisted on becoming a *Bat-Mitzvah* (subject to the commandments), in a ceremony at the Reform temple my parents belonged to, so there were official people who had actually *seen* me be Jewish once, and they had already given me their seal of authenticity. But no one had ever told me about any modesty laws.

The second picture was of the wedding. This time the young couple weren't looking at the camera but at each other. Specifically, he was gazing down at her and she up at him. Now they were embracing each other *very* tightly. Upon seeing this particular picture, I felt tears float up to my eyes. I hoped the next photo would arrive soon enough to distract me, but unfortunately it didn't quite, and I was left blubbering for an excruciating eight seconds. "I don't know why I'm crying, I'm so embarrassed! I don't even *know* your granddaughter!" Somebody handed me a tissue, and then I was ready for the third and final picture.

In this one the granddaughter was on the beach holding a little baby boy—only now her modestynik smile was twinkling under the brim of a black straw hat. "That's for the head covering," her grandma piped up proudly over my shoulder. "A married woman cannot leave her hair uncovered."

That's how I learned that there are different stages in the life cycle of a modestynik. No Touching, Touching, then Hat. Okay, I figured, I could remember that. I made a mental picture, like that second-grade diagram which helps you remember how a caterpillar becomes a butterfly, and then I knew that I would never forget it. No Touching, Touching, Hat. Got it.

Once I learned how to identify one modestynik, I started to see them all over the place. It seemed every Jewish family had one. And even if a person didn't happen to have a modestynik in his or her family, then at least they knew of one—and more often than not, two or three.

I picked up *New York* magazine, and they were writing about the modestyniks, too:

> *"A teacher of mine told me that if you touch before you're married, a curse is put on your children. But a blessing is given if you're careful," says Chavie Moskowitz, a 20-year-old Touro College student from Borough Park, who with her straight red hair, chocolate-brown suit, and matching brown suede pumps looks more like a young Wall Street executive than like a God fearing bride-to-be. But on this moonlit Saturday night, standing on the outdoor esplanade of the Winter Garden, Chaim Singer, a 24-year-old yeshiva student from Kew Gardens Hills, proposes to Moskowitz, who, bouncing on her toes, gleefully accepts. Instead of embracing her fiancé, she blows him a kiss.*

All around me I started to hear, and read, about young women who were observing Jewish modesty law, not touching their boyfriends and suddenly sporting hats. And all with the same blue line of sky between them and their fiancés. All with the same modestynik twinkle at the end. It was like an epidemic.

I was fascinated. First, because although I had certainly been touching my boyfriends, I wasn't—how I wish there were a more elusive way of putting this—having sexual intercourse with them.

Though boyfriends would occasionally grumble about my "hang-ups," I never gave much thought to what I would come to know as my *sexual repression*. I just assumed it was my peculiar problem, something to be sorted through privately, something of which one is ashamed. When I began to hear about these women, though, I started to think that maybe my "problem," such as it was, was not a problem at all but about something else entirely, something that could even be valued. Could I have been a modestynik all along and not known it?

Alas, I had to conclude that no, I couldn't be. I certainly wasn't shy or quiet, and that's what modesty really means, right? The whole women-should-be-seen-and-not-heard philosophy? That's what I associated it with. Furthermore, I didn't have any hats back in my dorm room. There were only two non-weather-related hats I had ever owned: a purple cone hat, from when I went trick-or-treating as a purple crayon, and a black cap with horns from when I sang the part of a little devil in a Lukas Foss opera. Somehow I didn't think those hats would count with whoever was in charge of the modestyniks.

Nevertheless I was still fascinated, particularly with the way others would react to them. People around me were saying that these modestyniks were really abuseniks: This one was "obviously very troubled," and that one seemed to have a "creepy" relationship with her father. Or the more poetic version, whispered in a sorrowful tone: "She is turning herself into the kind of woman her father could never touch." Or "Maybe she just had a *Bad Experience*." Either way, whatever her problem is, "why doesn't the poor girl just get some counseling already, and then she won't take it all so seriously?"

Now that I knew what was really going on with these modestyniks, I started to worry about them. All these women, and all sexually abused by their fathers! But that's also when I began to get suspicious. If all modestyniks were really abuseniks, I asked myself, then why were they so twinkly? Why did they seem so contented? Why were their wedding pictures so viscerally and mysteriously moving?

I really became intrigued when I offhandedly mentioned my interest in the modestyniks to a middle-aged man at a cocktail party, and he screamed at me, turning almost blue: "They're *sick*, I'm telling you! I've heard of them with their *not-touching*, and they're sick, *sick, sick!*" Someone later informed me that this man had been divorced three times.

I began to perceive a direct relationship between how much one was floundering, sex-wise, and how irritated one was by the modestyniks. After all, if the modestynik is just one more abusenik, she is less threatening, clearly, and isn't that rather convenient, if the poor thing can only be pitied? There is a certain note of wistfulness in the resentment directed against the modestyniks.

By now I have met many women, Jewish and non-Jewish, who grew up in fairly secular homes and have come to find modesty a compelling female ideal. Surely not *all* of them have been abused? They're all such different women. Some are daughters of divorce, others daughters of loving and stable families; some are liberal, others conservative; some are shy and clever, others not so shy or not so clever.

So does the fact that such different personalities are drawn to one idea prove some common childhood trauma, or reflect the truth of the idea? I suppose it could be a childhood trauma, but why do these women then have that undeniable glow about them that is absent, for instance, in our modern anorexic? Fundamentally, they do not seem to be missing anything for not having had a series of miserable romances under their belts. They seem happy. Is this, perhaps, what annoys people most?

In her book *Last Night in Paradise,* Katie Roiphe devotes her final chapter to Beverly LaHaye, founder of the Christian group, Concerned Women for America. After interviewing Beverly LaHaye's press secretary, a young woman who has sworn off sex until marriage, Roiphe allows that she "does have a certain glow," one that "resembles happiness," but she concludes that *really* it owes to "something more like delusion." As for herself, she writes, she is "infuriated" by this woman: "I suddenly want to convert her more desperately than she wants to convert me."

Why? If one may freely cohabit these days, why can't one postpone sex? Why is sexual modesty so threatening to some that they can only respond to it with charges of abuse or delusion? After all, empirically speaking, one woman we know of who *has* had sex with her father is Kathryn Harrison, and she's not exactly observing Orthodox modesty law. (In a 1997 *Elle* profile she wore a lovely, but nonetheless notably short, skirt.)

When I talk to women my age and hear some of the things they're going through, the kind of treatment they put up with from these boyfriends of theirs, the first thing I ask them is, "Does your father know about this?" They look at me as if I'm from another planet. Of course their fathers don't know.

The Marquis of Halifax considered his daughter a "tender plant," requiring the sort of pruning and shelter only fatherly rules could provide: ones "written out of kindness rather than authority." This was in 1688, but when I read that passage I immediately thought of my own father. I'm a much stronger person for having a "paternalistic" father who is always telling me what to do. I know he's that way because he loves me. Also, when a man gives up on me because I won't sleep with him, because he "needs to know if we're compatible," it's easy to doubt myself, and at such times there's really no substitute for a booming male voice at the other end of the line.

But today it is even thought to be sexist for a father to give away his daughter on her wedding day. That, we are told, is a concession to the view that "women are property." Wedding ceremonies, as the scholar Ann Ferguson puts it, can "perpetuate the public symbolic meaning of heterosexism and women as legal possessions of men."

Yet what is really so terrible about "belonging" to someone who loves you? This radical notion that girls shouldn't be too attached to their fathers, because that's the source of all evil, is ironically very similar to Freud's view that girls don't develop an advanced superego because they remain too long in the Oedipus situation. Yet it is typically the girl without a strong relationship with her father who is too insecure to develop a superego. In a sexual landscape without any rules, girls lacking male approval are more often taken advantage of.

After hearing hundreds of stories of self-mutilation from her adolescent-girl clients, psychologist Mary Pipher concludes that "girls are having more trouble now than they had thirty years ago, when I was a girl, and more trouble than even ten years ago." Indeed, "Girls today are much more oppressed. They are coming of age in a more dangerous, sexualized and media-saturated culture." And "as they navigate a more dangerous world, girls are less protected." She is a staunch feminist, but cannot help noticing that "the sexual license of the 1990s inhibits some girls from having the appropriate sexual experiences they want and need."

Mary Pipher's only clients who have escaped the standard litany of self-mutilation and eating disorders are the girls who are not sexually active—usually the ones who come from strict families with "paternalistic" fathers. "Jody," for instance, who is 16, comes from a tight-knit, fundamentalist family. Her mother stays home, and her father even insisted that Jody stop dating her boyfriend, Jeff, in tenth grade, fearing that she would have sex before marriage. Yet in spite of these restrictions which "psychologists would condemn," as Dr. Pipher puts it, Jody seems mysteriously happy. In fact, Jody is the happiest and most well adjusted of all her patients. Since Mary Pipher customarily assumes that paternalism is always oppressive, this observation causes her considerable cognitive dissonance:

> I struggled with the questions this interview raised for me. Why would a girl raised in such an authoritarian, even sexist, family be so well liked, outgoing and self-confident? Why did she have less anger and more respect for adults? Why was she so relaxed when many girls are so angst-filled and angry?

Maybe it's not so terrible, after all, to have someone feel he has a stake in your upbringing. A young woman is lucky, I think, if she has a "paternalistic" father—it can only make her more self-confident. To me the truly abusive fathers are the neglectful ones who seem to feel no emotional stake in how their daughters live their lives. More than half of my friends have parents who are divorced, and some of them hardly see their fathers at all.

But divorce is the least of the problems that have beset most young women of my age and generation. I was born in 1975, and from anorexia to date-rape, from our utter inability to feel safe on the streets to stories about stalking and stalkers, from teenage girls finding themselves miserably pregnant to women in their late 30s and early 40s finding procreation miserably difficult, this culture has not been kind to women. And it has not been kind to women at the very moment that it has directed an immense amount of social and political energy to "curing" their problems.

Why? Naomi Wolf writes in her most recent book that "there are no good girls; we are all bad girls," and that we all should just admit it and "explore the shadow slut who walks alongside us." But for some of us, this is actually still an open question. We certainly feel the pressure and get the message that we are supposed to be bad—we, after all, started our sex education in elementary school—but when everyone is saying the same thing, it makes us wonder: isn't there anything more to life, to love? No More "Nice Girl," as Rosemary Agonito put it in 1993. But don't I have anything higher to be proud of as a woman, other than my ability to be "bad"?

I thought again of the modestyniks, and about why they might be twinkling. Why would so many young women be adopting modesty as the new sexual virtue? I soon became inspired by the idea—not as some old-fashioned ideal that could hypothetically solve some of the problems of women, but as one that could really help me understand *my* life. It explained, among other things, why I never cared for the advice given in most women's magazines and why I was uncomfortable with the coed bathrooms I encountered at college.

During the spring of my senior year at Williams, in our main student center there was a display called "The Clothesline Project." It was a string of T-shirts designed by women on campus who had been victims of sexual harassment, stalking, or rape. "I HATE YOU!" announced one shirt, in thick black lettering. "NO doesn't mean try again in 5 minutes!" read another one, in a red banner. At the end of the clothesline, in plain blue lettering: "How could you TAKE that which she did not wish to GIVE?" The shirt next to it read, "Don't touch me again!" and, beside that: "Why does this keep happening to me? When will this end?"

I was struck, reading these T-shirts, with how polarized the debate about sex is today. Just like on the national level, there were the college Republicans who stopped to snicker and then moved on, tittering about "those crazy feminists," and then there were those who lingered, shook their heads in dismay, and could be heard whispering about the patriarchy.

I want to offer a new response. First, I want to invite conservatives to take the claims of the feminists seriously. That is, *all* of their claims, from the date-rape figures to anorexia to the shyness of teenage girls, even the number of women who say they feel "objectified" by the male gaze. I want them to stop saying that this or that study was flawed; or that young women are exaggerating; or that it has been proven that at this or that university such-and-such a charge was made up. Because ultimately, it seems to me, it doesn't really matter if one study is flawed or if one charge is false. When it comes down to it, the same vague yet unmistakable problem is still with us. A lot of young women are trying to tell us that they are very unhappy: unhappy with their bodies, with their sexual encounters, with the way men treat them on the street—unhappy with their lives. I want conservatives really to listen to these women, to stop saying boys will be boys, and to take what these women are saying seriously.

As for the feminists, I want to invite them to consider whether the cause of all this unhappiness might be something other than the patriarchy. For here is the paradox: at Williams, as on so many other modern college campuses, where there was such a concentration of unhappy women, everything was as nonsexist as could be. We had "Women's Pride Week," we had "Bisexual Visibility Week," we were all living in coed dorms, and many of us even used coed bathrooms. We were as far from patriarchal rules as we could get. So if we were supposed to be living in nonsexist paradise, then why were many of us this miserable?

Perhaps there is a difference between patriarchy and misogyny. Now that we have wiped our society clean of all traces of patriarchal rules and codes of conduct, we are finding that the hatred of women may be all the more in evidence. But why, exactly? I think we might have forgotten an important idea, lost our respect for a specific virtue.

I propose that the woes besetting the modern young woman—sexual harassment, stalking, rape, even "whirlpooling" (when a group of guys surround a girl who is swimming, and then sexually assault her)—are all expressions of a society which has lost its respect for female modesty.

My essay is divided into three parts: the first concerns our culture's view of sexual modesty and some of the problems that this view has created; the second is a survey of the intellectual battle which preceded this state of affairs, and an immodest attempt to reconstruct the lost philosophical case for modesty; and the final third is about women who are ignoring their culture's messages and, for new reasons, returning to a very old ideal.

A thread that runs through all three sections is the story of why this idea happened to captivate me. I would have preferred to avoid this personal thread and hide behind the disinterested sociological, the speculative philosophical. Unfortunately, it didn't work. I simply found it impossible to clear up what I perceive to be some central misunderstandings about modesty without, in some cases, getting very specific. Since I want to recover the idea, to submit what a case for modesty looks like, I have needed to rely on my experience—as well as that of other young women—to fill in the gaps.

Stendhal admits in his short study of female modesty that he is just guessing about it since so much of his argument depends on certain sensations that are necessarily hidden from his male experience. His survey is too vague, he says, and not as good as if a woman had written it. Nevertheless, he predicts, a woman would never write about such things. After all, for a woman to write sincerely about what she truly felt would be too embarrassing for her, "like going out not fully dressed"—and then everyone would point and laugh. For a man, on the other hand, "nothing is more common than for him to write exactly as his imagination dictates, without worrying where it's going."★

Outrageous as this may sound, it cannot be denied that for hundreds of years, it has held true. Though there are many women who conduct themselves "modestly" in their personal lives, no woman has ever attempted a systematic defense of modesty. One has to admit there is a very good reason for this: a woman who is reticent about matters sexual is an unlikely candidate to step forward and squawk, "Hey, everybody, look at me! Boy, am I modest!"

Nonetheless, I think it's about time that a woman proved Stendhal wrong. First, many of the men who have written about sexual modesty have either attacked or defended it for reasons that strike me as false. Was it because they were sexist? Or do we accept the more charitable interpretation—that, as Stendhal says, men can only guess? I don't know. But I have a strong feeling that one of the reasons relations between the sexes have come to such a painful point is precisely that the embarrassed, secretive women usually do not come forward, only the exhibitionists do. And so I think many young women now have a vastly inaccurate picture of what is normal for them to think or to feel. They have been trained to accept that to be equal to men, they must be the same in every respect; and they, and the men, are worse off for it. It is for the next generation of young women that I am writing this book. Perhaps as Stendhal predicted, I will only end up making a fool of myself, but I think the stakes are now high enough to justify the risk.

A friend of mine had an affair with her professor when she was 21. She was in his class at the time and madly in love with him; he had no intention of doing anything other than using and summarily disposing of her. She was a virgin before the affair. As she related the story to me, ten years after it happened, I was struck, not that what had happened had deeply upset her, but that she felt she had to *apologize* for the fact that it had deeply upset her: "And, well, and it didn't mean the same thing to him, and um . . . this is going to sound really cheesy but, um . . . I mean, for God's sake, he took my virginity!" As she struggled to find the words to

---

★The translations of Stendhal's *De l'Amour,* Rousseau's *Lettre à M. d'Alembert sur son Article Genève,* and Madame Renooz's *Psychologie Comparée de l'Homme et de la Femme* are my own, but I've included the original French sources in my endnotes, for those who want to know what the debate actually sounded like as it unfolded.

explain what had happened to her, it occurred to me that in an age where our virginity is supposed to mean nothing, and where male honor is also supposed to mean nothing, we literally cannot explain what has happened to us. We can no longer talk in terms of someone, say, *defiling a virgin,* so instead we punish the virgin for having any feelings at all. Nevertheless, although our ideology can expunge words from our vocabulary, the feelings remain and still cry out for someone to make sense of them. It is to restore this lost moral vocabulary of sex that I am writing this book. And then everyone can come out of the closet about how closeted he or she always wanted to be.

Today modesty is commonly associated with sexual repression, with pretending that you don't want sex though you really do. But this is a misunderstanding, a cultural myth spun by a society which vastly underrates sexual sublimation. If you stop and think about it, you realize that without sublimation, we would have very few footnotes and probably none of the greatest works of Western art. Moreover, leaving aside the whole question of utility, when you haven't yet learned to separate your physical desires from your hopes and natural wonder at everything, the world is, in a very real sense, enchanted. Every conversation, every mundane act is imbued with potential because everything is colored with erotic meaning. Today, this stage in one's life—when everything seems significant and you want to get it all "exactly right"—is thought to be childish, but is it really? Maybe instead of learning to overcome repression, we should be prolonging it.

Many children these days know far too much too soon, and as a result they end up, in some fundamental way, *not* knowing—stunted and cut off from all they could be. If you are not taught that you "really" want just sex, you end up seeking much more. The peculiar way our culture tries to prevent young women from seeking more than "just sex," the way it attempts to rid us of our romantic hopes or, variously, our embarrassment and our "hangups," is a very misguided effort. It is, I will argue, no less than an attempt to cure womanhood itself, and in many cases it has actually put us in danger.

Part One

THE

PROBLEM

# Chapter 1

## THE WAR ON EMBARRASSMENT

*Every blush is a cause for new blushes.*

—*DAVID HUME, 1741*

One day in fourth grade, a nice lady suddenly appeared in our Wisconsin public elementary school classroom. This lady's name was Mrs. Nelson—*"Good morning, Mrs. Nelllllson!"*—and she arrived carrying a Question Box. It was a brown, medium-sized box about the size of a hat, and it had black question marks all over it. The Question Box was our Learning Tool, she said.

I was very excited about the Question Box, because it interrupted, then completely substituted for, the whole math lesson that day.

The class waited in anticipation. Mrs. Nelson opened the top of her box and pulled out a long slip of white paper. Then she read it, cheerily, as if she had just cracked open a fortune cookie: "And the first question is . . . 'What is 69?'" She looked up from the white slip and faced us buoyantly: "What is 69, class?"

Well, that was a good question, because I certainly didn't know the answer. If she had asked what is 69 *plus* something, that would have been easy, but 69 all by itself was pretty philosophical. Some boys in the corner giggled. I immediately shot a glance at our teacher, who was standing up in the back of the classroom with his arms folded across his chest. Usually when the boys giggled, that meant something wrong was going on, and somebody was going to get into trouble. But this time our teacher didn't say a thing; he just looked straight ahead attentively at Mrs. Nelson. This confused me, but before I could try to make anything of it, Mrs. Nelson was speaking again.

"Now remember, boys and girls, there is *absolutely nothing* to giggle about! The first thing we're going to learn in Human Growth and Development is that *no* question is off limits!"

The outburst died down. Mrs. Nelson began again: "69 is . . ." more giggles. Then "69 is, um . . ." I looked back at my teacher, who by now had turned bright red. This was a really strange math lesson.

Finally, after what seemed like 69 attempts to explain the number 69, I raised my hand and piped up, "May I please go to the bathroom?" As I left I could hear Mrs. Nelson was still quizzing: "Doesn't *anyone* know what 69 is? Well . . . these questions were put in by the fifth-grade class. You'll have the chance to fill the Question Box with your own questions."

When I came home I told my mother about my day, about this mysterious number that was very important and shouldn't be off limits. My mother wasn't so enthusiastic. She had me bring a note to school asking for a description of what we would be learning in our special math lessons. I brought it home, and when my mom opened it she was even less enthusiastic. She was also angry, and so was I—but not for the same reason. I was annoyed because she wouldn't let me see the letter. She seemed to be under the impression that what was going on at our special math sessions was not math at all, but something else entirely. But what? She wouldn't let me see.

"If I knew you weren't going to let me *see,* I would have opened it *before* I walked home," I said petulantly.

But my mom wasn't paying attention. She was pacing around the kitchen, fuming. "I can't believe they're planning on teaching you how to masturbate in fourth grade. I can't believe it!"

What was she talking about?

"In fourth grade! Where is your father?" Then to me: "Go find your father."

That was when my mom called Mrs. Nelson. I had a feeling she was going to, so I ignored the directive to find my father. I remember, a few minutes later, my mom putting her hand over the phone and saying to me, in a high, extra polite voice, "Mrs. Nelson would like to know if I want you to be whispering in the locker room." Then she asked me, very gravely, "*Do* you want to be whispering in the locker room?" I thought about it, and said yes. I liked whispering. Whispering about stuff is exciting.

"Yes," my mom had returned the phone to her ear. "Yes, I've asked her, and she says she *does* want to whisper in the locker room." I found this terrifically funny, that adults could disagree over whispers. "I get to whisper in the locker room!" I called, jumping up and down.

"Yes, I'll have her bring another note. Goodbye."

From that day forward, I sat out sex education in the library. I always felt bad for the girls who didn't have this escape because after each sex ed session, as the lockers slammed and everyone prepared for the next class, the boys would pick on them, in a strange, new kind of teasing.

"Erica, do you *masturbate?*" one boy would say to one poor pigtailed victim as she struggled to remove her books as fast as she could. Then another boy would say, closing in on her from the other side, "It's really *natural,* you know." Or sometimes just "why aren't you masturbating *now,* Erica? It's normal, you know."

Then, "Shut up! Shut up! Shut up!"

"Why aren't you developing, Erica?"

"It's time for you to be developing, didn't you hear? Weren't you taking notes in class?"

"Shut up! Shut up! Shut up!"

"Well, *I* was paying attention, and you're really behind your proper growth and development!"

"Shut up! Shut up! Shut up!"

"You may be a treasure, Erica, but you ain't got no chest!"

And so on. Invariably, just before the moment when the girl would burst into tears, I noticed that she would always say the same thing: "Mrs. *Nelson* says that if you *tease* us about what we learn in *class,* then you haven't understood the principle of *respect."* Respect is a very important doctrine in sex education class. Sex ed instructors often use Respect, a puppet turtle, to teach elementary school children about their "private places." As it happened, Mrs. Nelson was usually gone by the time the teasing began, so no one really cared about what they had learned from Respect the Turtle.

My public school wasn't unique. In 1993 more than 4,200 school-age girls reported to *Seventeen* magazine that "they have been pinched, fondled or subjected to sexually suggestive remarks at school, most of them . . . both frequently and publicly." Researchers from Wellesley College, following up on the magazine's survey, found "that nearly two-fifths of the girls reported being sexually harassed daily and another 29 percent said they were harassed weekly. More than two-thirds said the harassment occurred in view of other people. Almost 90 percent were the target of unwanted sexual comments or gestures." School officials do very little about this, the study also found. One 13-year-old girl from Pennsylvania told them: "I have told teachers about this a number of times; each time nothing was done about it."

More recently, psychologist Mary Pipher reports in *Reviving*

*Ophelia* that she is seeing an increasing number of girls who are "school refusers," girls who "tell me they simply cannot face what happens to them at school." One client, Pipher says, "complained that boys slapped her behind and grabbed her breasts when she walked to her locker." Then "another wouldn't ride the school bus because boys teased her about oral sex." Pipher concludes that the harassment that girls experience in the 1990s is "much different in both quality and intensity" from the teasing she received as a girl in the late fifties.

When I was in college, a mother who owned the local deli persistently brought up in conversation how much her daughter was being sexually taunted by the boys at her school. The girl couldn't even concentrate on her homework when she was at home: all she did was dread returning to school. The mother was visibly distraught. She grew up in the fifties, she told me, and "this kind of thing *never* happened to us. Sure, the boys would flirt and tease us, but they were shy and nervous about it. They never ganged up on the girls like this. I'd never heard of a bunch of guys assaulting a girl verbally and physically."

For some reason, no one connects this kind of harassment and early sex education. But to me the connection was obvious from the start, because the boys never teased me—they assumed I didn't know what they were referring to. Whenever they would start to tease me, they always stopped when I gave them a confused look and said, "I have no idea what you guys are talking about. *I* was in the library." Even though I usually did know what they were talking about, the line still worked, and they would be almost apologetic: "Oh, right—you're the weirdo who always goes to the library." And they would pass me by and begin to torture the next girl, who they knew had been in class with them and could appreciate all the new put-downs they had learned.

All across North America, sex educators are doling out such ammunition under the banner of enlightenment.

Sex education instructors in Massachusetts, New York, and Toronto teach the kids "Condom Line-Up," where boys and girls are given pieces of cardboard to describe sex with a condom, such as "sexual arousal," "erection," "leave room at tip," and then all the kids have to arrange themselves in the proper sequence.

New Jersey's *Family Life* program begins its instruction about birth control, masturbation, abortion, and puberty in kindergarten. Ten years ago, when the program was first instituted, there was some discomfort because according to the coordinator of the

program, Claire Scholz, "some of our kindergarten teachers were
shy—they didn't like talking about scrotums and vulvas." But in
time, she reports, "they tell me it's no different from talking about
an elbow." In another sex-ed class in Colorado, all the girls were
told to pick a boy in the class and practice putting a condom on
his finger. Schools in Fort Lauderdale, Florida, get a head start on
AIDS instruction, teaching it in second grade, four years earlier
than state requirements. In Orange Country, Florida, second
graders are taught about birth, death and drug abuse, and sixth
graders role-play appropriate ways of showing affection. "I think
that's too young," said one parent, Steve Smith. He would prefer
his kids to "be learning about reading and writing." New York
City Board of Education guidelines instruct that kindergartners
are to be taught "the difference between transmissible and non-
transmissible diseases; the terms HIV and AIDS; [and] that AIDS
is hard to get." This, we are informed, fulfills "New York State
Learner Outcomes: 1,2."

And yet, as they confidently promote all this early sex education, our school officials are at a loss when it comes to dealing
with the new problem of sodomy-on-the-playground. It's hard to
keep up with all the sexual assault cases that plague our public
schools in any given month. Take just one reported in the New
York *Daily News* in 1997:

> *Four Bronx boys—the oldest only 9—ganged up on a 9-year-old
> classmate and sexually assaulted her in a schoolyard, police charged
> yesterday. . . . [The girl's mother] said she is furious with Principal
> Anthony Padilla, who yesterday told parents the attack never hap-
> pened. . . . The girl's parents and sisters are also outraged that when
> the traumatized third-grader told a teacher, she was merely advised to
> wash out her mouth and was given a towel wipe."*

The associative link between the disenchanting of sex and
increased sexual brutality among children works like this: if our
children are raised to believe, in the words of that New Jersey
kindergarten teacher, that talking about the most private things is
"no different from talking about an elbow," then they are that
much more likely to see nothing wrong in certain kinds of sexual violence. What's really so terrible, after all, in making someone
touch or kiss your elbow?

I wanted to tell the other girls that they didn't have to put up
with all this, that they could come to the library with me if they

wanted. The library was cool and quiet, and there were old year-books with funny pictures of our teachers—from when they were younger and still had hair. Sometimes there was even a bowl of pretzels. But I didn't say a word. I still feel kind of guilty about it. I was afraid if I spoke up I would get into trouble and that I wouldn't be allowed to escape to the library anymore.

However, now that I'm older and know that some things are more important than your fear of getting into trouble, I'm quite willing to share my views on sex education. But first I needed to confirm when it started. I called up my old elementary school and learned that when I was there, it actually started in kindergarten as part of the personal hygiene unit, but in fourth grade someone is brought in from the outside.

At my school sex education was given in kindergarten to ninth grade, but I was excused from fourth grade on. The first time I was conscious of any real sexual desire was the summer after ninth grade, about age fourteen or so. One shouldn't extrapolate from my own case, which may be abnormal, but generally speaking I'm struck by the way my generation's sex education ended around the time that natural desire usually begins. I guess the theory is that this way we know everything before we start, and can do it properly, but I think what happens instead is that we end up start-ing before we feel, because we think it's expected of us. Usually when adults start shoving condoms in our faces, we would much prefer to giggle.

A 23-year-old friend of mine recently reported the following story about his younger sister:

> My 13-year-old sister went to the family doctor for a checkup. He's been our doctor for a good eight years. Not particularly bright, but good for a referral. At the end of the examination he says, "If you're sexu-ally active, you should be using condoms." And he offers her some. Upon hearing the word "sexually," my sister burst out laughing. This annoyed the physician, who felt she wasn't taking her reproductive health seriously. He began chastising her, at which point my grand-mother came in—at which point all hell broke loose.

## BECOMING EMBARRASSED

During the time in which I was excused from class, I was con-ducting my own education of sorts. Since I was always given a general directive to acquaint myself "with the mechanics" and not "to be embarrassed," I decided right away that I would strive to avoid the mechanics and be as embarrassed as possible about as many things as I wanted to be embarrassed about. I just didn't know where to begin, though. There was so much to be embarrassed about, and so little time.

Even though we live in an age that prides itself on being beyond gender role stereotyping, young girls are still the experts on embarrassment. Everyone tells us not to be self-conscious, but we always are. It's as if the world's embarrassment passed through us, from generation to generation. It's as if girls had some special responsibility to keep embarrassment alive and also to teach others how to diffuse it. A letter-to-the editor of *American Girl* reads, "Dear *Help!*, I'm *SO* embarrassed! At recess I was doing gymnastics near some boys. While I was landing a handspring, my shirt flew up! The boys began to laugh because I didn't have anything on underneath. Now they won't let me forget it." She is *"Miserable in Virginia."* The editors reply: "Dear Miserable: They'll forget it themselves eventually. The joke will get old, they'll tease you less often. In the meantime, be patient, ignore them, and tuck in your shirt."

"There's a blush for won't, and a blush for shan't and a blush for having done it," wrote Keats. There's also a blush for a million other things. *American Girl* magazine was fielding so many questions about embarrassment in 1997 that it eventually had to come out with a whole book on the subject, to advise girls on how to deal with it. *Oops!* the book was called, because "There are some things that make a girl cringe, and horribly humiliating moments are among them."

*American Girl* considers the plight of a girl who forgets to go to her friend's birthday party, and then a girl who wets her pants in public. "What *do* you do when you're so embarrassed you could die?" asks *American Girl*. It's a very important question in the life of a girl. Today, embarrassment is something to "overcome," but maybe if so many girls are still embarrassed, even in an age when we're not supposed to be, maybe we have our embarrassment for a reason.

The natural embarrassment sex education seeks so prissily to erode—"Now remember, boys and girls, there is *absolutely nothing* to giggle about!"—may point to a far richer understanding of sex than do our most explicit sex manuals. Children now are urged to overcome their "inhibitions" before they have a clue what an inhibition means. Yet embarrassment is actually a wonderful thing, signaling that something very strange or very significant is going on, that some boundary is being threatened—either by you or by others. Without embarrassment, kids are weaker: more vulnerable to pregnancy, disease, and heartbreak.

### FAILING TO TAKE RESPONSIBILITY FOR YOUR SEXUALITY

If "overcoming your embarrassment" is the first mantra of sex education, "taking responsibility for your sexuality" is the second. The health guidelines for the ninth grade in the Newton, Massachusetts, public schools, printed in the *Student Workbook for Sexuality and Health,* inform us that not only do "Sexually Healthy Adolescents . . . decide what is personally 'right' and act on these values," but also they "take responsibility for their own behavior." Grown-ups get the same advice. "What does undermine feminism is women . . . refusing to take responsibility for their sexuality," says Karen Lehrman. "Every woman must take personal responsibility for her sexuality," warns Camille Paglia.

Fine, but if you're a child, you're not sure what taking responsibility for your sexuality entails. I certainly didn't want *not* to be taking responsibility for something, whatever it was. I thought I knew what they meant. It's like when you steal a cookie from the cookie jar, and then you've got to face up to it, take responsibility for it. I got the impression that somehow I had done something wrong, that the reckoning was going to come soon and so I would have to know what to apologize for. Well, then, I determined, I was going to figure out what all the fuss was, and then— I was no coward—I would take responsibility for it.

So I kept up with the material, even though I was excused from "Human Growth and Development." The teachers gave me weekly worksheets so I could see what my peers were learning. I looked them over dutifully, tried to understand them on my own. I only remember two of these worksheets, the two that confused me the most. One said that an "orgasm is like when you have to sneeze, and then you sneeze." I remember thinking—Why would I want to sneeze more than I already sneeze? I hate sneezing! Then I learned that an orgasm was a *positive* sneeze. That still baffled me. A few months later, my class was on to more advanced conceptualizing: "Try to imagine that an orgasm is like an extended tickle. You like being tickled, don't you? Well, adults like to tickle each other too, to share warm feelings." I don't know which text this came from, but Planned Parenthood's book *It's Perfectly Normal,* by Robie H. Harris (Penguin Books), recommended for kids age 10 and up, reminds me of ours: It features illustrations of nude, playful boys and girls as they masturbate on beds and heterosexual and homosexual couples as they have intercourse in different positions.

Yes, *it's perfectly normal.* But what was perfectly normal? I still felt that I was missing something. Sometimes when things aren't comprehensible to children, there's a very good reason. Mostly I just skimmed these worksheets. Thanks to my mother's note, I wasn't going to be tested on the material. They basically set me loose in the library. The only requirement was that I periodically turn in book reports to "demonstrate proficiency" on the subject matter. I had to show them, essentially, that I knew what was going on. Of course, before I could do that, I had to find out what was going on.

It was a daunting subject for a nine-year-old, particularly since the books they had at our grade school library were so disappointing. After thumbing through six *Sweet Valley High* books, I decided right away that I was going to have to go to the public library if I was going to do the thing properly. My teachers were beginning to get worried that I was missing out on so many important sex-ed sessions and, specifically, that I wouldn't "know what to do" as a result. To tell you the truth, I was starting to get worried, too. I "had to take *responsibility* for [my] sexuality," they said.

It was there where I first opened the encyclopedia and peered under the "Sex" entry.

I read about three lines, glanced behind me, then shut the book quickly. How embarrassing.

I had higher hopes for the next book I came across. It was a pale blue book with a nice cover of a hugging couple—the title was *Choosing a Sex Ethic,* and, if memory serves, it was written by a rabbi named Borowitz. This seemed appropriate for me, being Jewish, and also the title was very intriguing since I would have thought that ethics were precisely the things you couldn't choose. But, apparently, you could. Well, then, I would just have to choose the best one. The sweet-looking guy on the blue cover was hugging a smiling woman in such a tight, affable way that I was thinking a) *she* certainly looks happy and b) maybe if I choose the right ethic, someone nice will hug me, too.

I opened to the table of contents and my eye immediately leaped to something called "the ethics of orgasm." I turned to that chapter first, because that looked like the most interesting one—containing that mysterious sneezing and tickling concept—but after that one I was just too embarrassed to read on. I think that time I must have gotten it.

This was going to be harder than I thought.

But somehow I ended up figuring out the facts anyway. Could it have been the condoms and dental dams all the adults were dangling in my face everywhere I turned?

In 1997 Alexander Sanger, president of Planned Parenthood of New York City, penned an Op-Ed in the New York *Daily News,* "Sex Ed Is More Than Just Saying No: Teens Need All the Facts." Contends Sanger, "In a perfect world, teenagers would wait until they're older and wiser to have sex. But the fact is, 75% of American teens have sex before high school graduation. In New York, more than 54,000 teens, ages 15 to 19, become pregnant each year." Therefore, he concludes, "teens need all the facts."

Where does he think all this high school sex and all these pregnancies are suddenly coming from? Doesn't he find it even a *bit* curious that the more we do what he prescribes, the more such behavior goes on? Most studies find that knowledge about AIDS or HIV does not decrease risky behavior. A 1988 study in the *American Journal of Public Health,* which examined exactly the year when public health information about AIDS grew, found that no increased condom use among San Francisco's sexually active adolescents resulted. A 1992 study in *Pediatrics* conducted a broader investigation and ended up warning, "It is time to stop kidding ourselves into thinking that our information-based preventative actions are enough or are effective." This shouldn't be so surprising. The few studies that show that instruction on condom use changes the behavior of students conclude it is only likely to make them more sexually active. This cult of taking responsibility for your sexuality is essentially a call to action.

But beyond this, how does Alexander Sanger imagine he was born, if his parents were never given "the facts"? I am sure he intends no harm, but the ground in dispute was never *whether* we would get the facts—the question is how and when. Do we get the opportunity to seek out the facts when we are ready? Furtively? Or do we have them forced upon us when we're not ready, when we're inclined to yawn about the whole thing and conclude it's no big deal? It's really not very complicated why so many kids are getting pregnant these days, now that we have so much sex education on top of a wholly sexualized culture. It's because sex is not a big deal to them and because they think this is what they are expected to do. They are just trying to be normal kids, to please people like Alexander Sanger and prove that they are "sexually healthy."

We're not flocking to Jane Austen movies because we want the facts, but because we're sick of having the facts shoved in our faces all the time. One is entitled to imagine that there might be something more to hope for than all this dreary crudeness—this view of sex as something autonomous and cut off from obligation, whether familial obligation or obligation to one's "sex partner" (as the locution has it).

So in a funny way, the facts about sex conceal the truth.

Or so I conclude, in hindsight. Actually, I hadn't given my fourth-grade flight to the library much thought until around ten years later, when I began to detect a difference in the way I dated, compared to how other kids my age "hooked up," and in a million other things that just seemed foreign to me, and didn't to them, and then I started to put some of the pieces together. In retrospect I can see that, more than anything else, it is the fact that I escaped sex education which separates me most from other kids my age. It doesn't matter whether they're liberal or conservative— if they're around my age and they've had my generation's sex education, it's very hard for us to understand each other in some fundamental way. I'll never forget the president of my college's Republican club, who told me that of *course* he was in favor of sex education since, unlike me, he had "a *healthy* attitude towards sex."

The mindset that concerns me is not political but cultural. Anyone who's been through the mill of my generation's sex education has trouble understanding why I'm concerned about the things I'm concerned with—indeed, to have my kind of concerns, I'm told, is "unhealthy"—and I for my part cannot understand how they can be so *unconcerned*, so cavalier. When I hear the words that they use, "hang-ups," "hook-ups," "check-ups," for example, it's as if we lived in different worlds.

# Chapter 2

# POSTMODERN SEXUAL ETIQUETTE, FROM HOOK-UP TO CHECKUP

*Here, I think, is a task for sex research: an objective inquiry into the short-term and long-term effects on men, women, and children of emancipation from sexual repression, from feelings of sexual shame and guilt. Sweden and Denmark, where convalescence from Victorianism appears to have progressed the furthest, are favorable sites for such an inquiry; but much might also be learned from a comparison of the inhibited and the emancipated here in the United States or anywhere else.*

—EDWARD M. BRECHER, 1969

Along with his wife Ruth, Edward Brecher was a key figure in popularizing and promoting the work of Alfred Kinsey, William Masters, and Virginia Johnson. He was on the forefront of trying to save his culture from Victorianism, what he saw as a "debilitating sexual disease . . . also known as Puritanism, and as the Judeo-Christian ethic." And yet, as the above passage reveals, even as he railed against the last remnants of sexual repression and that diseased Judeo-Christian ethic, he did not know what sex would be like without shame and guilt. There were no liberated societies to study nor any empirical data to collect because there had always been shame, guilt, and various taboos, even in the most primitive of cultures. By his own admission, then, he was just guessing. He enthusiastically set us on a path, without any reservations, and guessed that it would be good.

Thirty years later, now that we do live in a condition of "emancipation from sexual repression, from feelings of sexual shame and guilt"—indeed we are actively urged to overcome such feelings in the classroom—we no longer have to guess.

So welcome, Mr. Brecher, to the world of postmodern sexual morality. In some respects it has turned out more horrifying than even the "inhibited" might have imagined, but in other crucial respects the experiment turned out to be a great tribute to the human spirit.

We may not have the old Judeo-Christian rules, but we do have an extremely detailed and tangled system of postmodern sexual etiquette—fashioned not out of any wealth of stored wisdom, traditions, or familial advice, but simply out of necessity, broken hearts, and the discovery that maybe we are human, after all.

The question, I guess, then becomes, Is our guerrilla etiquette as good as the older rules?

### STAGE ONE: THE HOOK-UP

About a decade ago, the late Allan Bloom surveyed the college sex scene, and found it unsettling that the young rarely said "I love you"—and certainly never "I'll always love you." Rather, he found, most lived together because it was convenient, "with sex and utilities included in the rent," and then often "le[ft] each other with a handshake and move[d] out into life." This was called *having a relationship*. As Bloom famously, scornfully, put it: "Did Romeo and Juliet have a *relationship?*"

The answer to his rhetorical question, of course, was that Romeo and Juliet had something slightly more profound than a relationship, but even a relationship is closer to what Romeo and Juliet had—when we compare it to what we have now. For ten years later, we are very lucky if we can find a young couple capable of sustaining Bloom's much-maligned relationship. What we have now, mostly, are *hook-ups*. Here is *Sex on Campus: The Naked Truth About the REAL SEX Lives of College Students*, 1997:

> In recent decades, the students at small colleges seem to have moved away from the whole concept of dating. . . . The favored approach is just to play it cool and wait until you see the person again to develop your relationship further. . . . Hooking up: You were almost certainly acting on physical attraction, not a well-formed emotional attachment, and there was no risk to either of you. You're under no obligation to date each other or call each other—nor should you expect to be called or dated. . . . Ball-and-chain rating: 1. . . . you should never get so drunk that you do something you didn't want to. In reality, however, a great many college hookups occur when both parties are sloshed. Sometimes it's no problem at all and everyone can have a good, sloppy time. . . . [But] if you realize almost immediately after you finish having sex that this will definitely be a one-time-only event and you really don't want to pursue any relationship—even a purely physical one—with this person, try not to sleep through the night with the per-

*son. It may seem awfully awkward and it may be late at night, but get up, get dressed, say, "Thank you for a wonderful evening," and go home. . . . Leaving someone with whom you've just traded bodily fluids can seem strange, rude, and inconsiderate, but at least you'll have the knowledge that you were being honest, and it will make things less complicated down the road.*

*Hook-up* is my generation's word for having sex (or oral sex) or sometimes for what used to be called "making out." The hook-up connotes the most casual of connections. Any emotional attachment deserves scorn and merits what *Sex on Campus* calls a dangerously high "ball and chain rating." ("A ball-and-chain rating of 0 or 1 would mean that you should be able to go on about your business without much worry.") Without embarrassment, there cannot be any surrender. We can only hook up.

In context, the typical exchange is, "I hooked up last night." "Yeah? Me too." Above all, it is *no big deal.* Indeed, hooking up is so casual, and the partners so interchangeable, that sometimes it's hard to discern a pattern in all the hooking and unhooking. It seems almost arbitrary. Hence, a 1998 issue of *YM* magazine takes up the question: "Q: Why do guys dump a girl, then try to hook up with her again?"

For the full answer, here is NBC's report from the University of Michigan: "Dating takes a lot of time," as one male senior puts it, "it costs a lot of money, and also I think out of the little time that you have, you want to kind of maximize what you get out of it." Sums up the NBC reporter: "Dating . . . is a practice which on this campus and others is history." Why date, when you can just hook up, then unhook? And perhaps later, hook back?

It's such a strange expression, hooking up, like airplanes refueling in flight. Not just unerotic but almost inanimate. Where did this idiom come from?

I looked everywhere for the origin of the expression, but couldn't find "hook-up" anywhere. First I checked the Bible. Nope, wasn't there. Then I looked in Samuel Johnson's *Dictionary of the English Language,* but it wasn't there either. I won't bore you with the rest of the search. The end of the story is that after months and months of research, I finally tracked down the first use of the expression ever recorded. It turns out that the "hook-up" originated with Nena and George O'Neill's 1972 tract, *Open Marriage.* Here is how it was first used:

*Your Hook-up Points: . . . So there you are, a person, a particular identity, with your unique pattern of hook-up points. And there next to you is your mate with his own particular identity and his own unique pattern of hook-up points. You become joined together because you find that numerous, perhaps even a majority of your hook-up points match. You grew up together, you speak the same language, have the same values, both like potted plants . . . but however many hook-up points you share, there will be others that you do not, simply because you are unique individuals.*

As for "those hook-up points you and your mate cannot match," you can just go ahead and match them elsewhere:

*Whether they are actual needs that your mate cannot meet, or unrealized potentials that your mate cannot stimulate to further growth, they are part of you. And if they are not used, if they remain untouched, unvalidated or unfulfilled, they will become brittle from disuse. Eventually, to continue the image of these hook-up points as external antennae, they will become so deadened that they will simply drop off, making you a diminished person with fewer points of contact. These lost hook-up points leave you less of a unique person, less than you once were or could in the future be. If one of these hook-up points has roots deeply imbedded in your personality, stemming from a major need, it may be impossible to simply shed it like a porcupine's quill. Instead it will fester where it is. . . . In our closed marriages, we allow only those hook-up points that match those of the mate to be fulfilled.*

So see ya later, alligator—you didn't hook up all my hook-up points. In this light, it is not very surprising that so many date-rape charges should fly after these "hook-ups." At every turn our romantic hopes are quashed by the words once used to rationalize faithless marriages. Our sexual landscape is already soaked in the language of betrayal before we've even begun.

Which brings us to the one minor problem with the hook-up: women have been known to be less enthusiastic about these hook-ups than men. A 1993 study of college women, in fact, found that 69.8 percent of the women surveyed reported they had been "verbally coerced" into having "unwanted sex." For the past 15 years or so, feminists and conservatives have been locked in a bitter struggle over whether retroactively claimed "unwanted sex" constitutes rape. Totally unaddressed is the fact that, whatever it's called, most women are not happy with these "hook-ups." Why? The advice given by *Sex on Campus* provides us with a clue: "And if the person asks the dreaded question, 'Will I ever see you again?,' respond with a platitude of some sort, like 'I really enjoyed spending time with you tonight, but I'm not into having a relationship.'" Then "Comfort yourself with the knowledge that, as long as you're not in Texas, gunplay is unlikely." Translation: it's okay to treat women like prostitutes, because nobody cares anymore.

Consider the following advice given in a 1997 issue of GQ magazine: "Q: I've just had a one-night stand with a woman I really like. I don't want a relationship, but I don't want to look like a cad, either. What's the etiquette here?" Comes the reply:

> *Don't presume that (1) all women are living in the 50s and (2) all women want to cultivate a relationship with every Tom they meet. Good news for both genders: It's 1997, and chicks like unencumbered sex as much as men do. We just like it polite. So, here's the rule: The seemly thing to do after you've shared a poke is to call . . . yes, you can leave a message on her machine. All that's needed is a two-minute base touching: "I really had fun with you. It was nice. Thanks for a great date." Keep it sweet, simple and sincere and women will understand. It's called closure. Do not allude to a future when none is intended. And no matter what you say, never, ever trot out the "I'll call you" line when you know you won't.*

Well, if "chicks" like "unencumbered sex" so much, then why is it so important that the man call after the hook-up? And why is it so important that he not give the woman false hope about the future?

In any case, that's stage one in postmodern sexual etiquette: you should be hooking up on a regular basis. If you're like me and a bit disgusted with the very idea of a hook-up, you may simply refuse to hook up with anyone. You can explain to the men you date that you are just particular and simply have too many hook-up points. But be forewarned: avoiding the hook-up is no guarantee that you won't get your heart broken.

### STAGE TWO: THE DUMPING

There is very little etiquette surrounding the actual dumping itself, because it either happens or it doesn't, and when it does, that's usually it. I have heard of three cases in which women tried to postpone their dumping. That is, when they heard someone beginning to disentangle himself, they did not urge him to reconsider, but rather, tried to prevail upon him to dump them *later*. As in: "Okay, but this week is really hard for me since I have this deadline at work. Couldn't you dump me next week instead? I mean, have some consideration!" This doesn't seem to make much sense. The moment you know he wants to dump you, what are you buying yourself another week for?

It's much better to accept your fate and move right on to Turning a Negative Into a Positive. For here is where we can observe one of the clear advantages to living in postmodernity. Although being dumped in postmodernity is just as unpleasant as in premodernity, in postmodernity instead of killing yourself you get to consider it a Learning Experience. As long as you Learn a Lesson from it then you Shouldn't Kill Yourself. As Sharon Thompson puts it, "Even when love goes badly, those brave enough to learn from romantic experience will find they've been well served."

How true. For example, if we did not endure the considerable pains of the dumping, we could never experience the joys of the post-dumping checkup.

### STAGE THREE: THE POST-DUMPING CHECKUP

Explains Lesley Dormen in "Breaking Up: A Protect-Your-Heart Plan," "Once the breakup has taken place . . . and you have the capacity to listen and speak calmly, talking things through" with your ex-boyfriend is ideal. According to psychologist Bonnie Jacobson, Ph.D., author of *If Only You Would Listen,* post-breakup conversations "can be an outstanding clinic for healing and learning how to love better." Oh, really?

A 45-year-old woman told me the following story about her son: He called home from college two weeks ago, very confused. He and his girlfriend had broken up, and it seemed she wanted to remain "friends," but he didn't. They were living in the same dormitory, which made it all very awkward. "Mom?" he asked her, his voice sounding suddenly faraway and boyish. "Mom? Is something wrong with me? I'm not sure I want to be her friend." I feel like I know his ex-girlfriend already, because she or someone like her has just written a letter to the magazine lying on my coffee table: "My ex and I were getting along great," moans 20-year-old "F.G." in a 1997 *Mademoiselle,* "and then he called me up and said he didn't want to be friends anymore! What *happened?*"

I'll tell you what happened, F.G. It's called human nature. You're concerned, I know, because you're not getting all the post-dumping checkups you were promised. I understand what you're going through: You're feeling kind of left out and strange. If your ex doesn't call you, how in the world are you going to get your "outstanding clinic for healing and learning how to love better"? But don't worry about it, F.G. It's not you who's strange; it's this post-dumping checkup that's strange.

A brief explanation for those who are not familiar with the art of the post-dumping checkup. Apparently, if you've hooked up with someone—or if you haven't technically hooked up but were going out for more than a month or so—and then dump this someone, it's considered poor manners not to calmly "check up" on your ex-girl- or boyfriend later on. It's the new etiquette: One may dump shamelessly, but one must always be friends and check up! You know, just so that they should find out how you've been doing ever since they decided they didn't like you. And if you are a really well-behaved 90s man, you're expected to be tolerant of all your girlfriend's ex-boyfriends who are religiously performing their post-dumping checkups on *her*. Dave, 23, told *Cosmopolitan* in 1998 that of course "My girlfriend talks to her ex-boyfriends." Why? "They were part of her life before she ever met me, and I'm not going to try to intrude on that."

The same year, Daryl Chen in *Mademoiselle* gave her readers pointers on how they could increase the likelihood of receiving their post-dumping checkups: "He's no longer a lover. It's even possible you can't stand the sight of him. But if you follow our timetable, you can still recycle him as a confidante, mentor, handyman and fan." If he hasn't called after three months, "you may be ready to make that initial phone call and set up an exploratory meeting." We were advised to "keep conversations short," and only say extremely clever things, such as "'fallen under a bus? Just checking.'" Then after six months, "it's safe to go back to the movies" with your ex. And finally, "By the two-year mark and later, you and your ex should be incorporated neatly into each other's lives ... you know you can look forward to a long and eventful future spent in the comfortable orbit of each other's existence."

Since I had been seeing my boyfriend for a year before we broke up and then never heard from him again, I was definitely not in the comfortable orbit of my ex's existence. My friends told me I was most assuredly not getting my proper post-dumping checkups. When I first heard this I instinctively defended my ex: Well, since ours was a long-distance thing and we didn't really see each other all that often, maybe ours is a special case and the checkup rule doesn't really apply here. No, they explained gravely, shaking their heads, even long-distancers are supposed to check up.

What *was* this checkup business? I wondered. To me it seemed so ridiculous, but everyone else was acting like it was perfectly normal. My friends would proudly tell me things like, Yes, *my* boyfriend checks up on *his* ex-girlfriends *all* the time. Or they would brag, I'm *best* friends with all the guys *I've* hooked up with. At first I felt kind of bad that I wasn't getting my proper checkups. But then the more I thought about it, the more I was glad my ex-boyfriend wasn't calling me because, really, what in the world would we *say*?

> *"Oh! It's you—it's really you. I was hoping you would call. I've missed you so much."*
>
> *"Yes, it's me. Don't get too excited, though. I'm just calling because it's time for your checkup."*
>
> *"Oh. Well, still that's awfully considerate of you. I have so much to tell you. . . ."*
>
> *"Hmm. Not too much, I hope, because remember, this is only a checkup."*
>
> *"Yes, that's true, I forgot that for a second there. Sorry."*
>
> *"That's okay. So anyway . . . how's life?"*
>
> *"Oh, you know, just the same old stuff. College. How are you?"*
>
> *"No, how are you? I'm worried about you. Indeed, that's exactly the purpose of this call: to check up on how you are."*
>
> *"Oh, really—don't worry about it. I'm fine."*
>
> *"Gosh, I just feel terrible. And so guilty."*
>
> *"Well, you shouldn't you know, because* at least *you're calling, sweetie."*
>
> *"Don't call me sweetie!"*
>
> *"Sorry, sweetie! I mean, sir. It's just that it's—it's been so long, I . . . I completely forgot—"*
>
> *"No, it's too late now. This will have to conclude your checkup."*
>
> *"Oh no!"*
>
> *"Yes, I'm sorry. Checkup's over."*
>
> *"Oh, well. So anyway, talk to you next week, then? I ho——"*
>
> *Dialtone.*

Did I really need this checkup? No, thank you. A checkup would not have made me feel any better. It would have just been another opportunity to humiliate myself. I'm grateful to my ex-boyfriend who didn't check up on me. At least if you feel sadness, disgust, anything on a sliding scale to mutual loathing, at least then you know you're human. All those bad feelings we are too enlightened to feel nowadays—such as resentment, jealousy, betrayal—also signify the capacity to lose yourself in the first place, to fall in love with someone other than yourself. They presuppose that there is a soul to protect, that there are hopes to be shattered, a lost love to guard, even if now only mentally and futilely. No hard feelings? I'm advocating a return to precisely that: hard feelings. At least then you know you're a person, that you have a heart. Whereas this checkup business is like a computer backing itself up automatically. A farce.

But my girlfriends simply couldn't understand how I couldn't want my checkups. I should get a lawyer and sue for them. I had a *right* to my checkups, so that we could be "good friends." The first 20 times I heard this I smiled politely and nodded, but I finally had to speak my mind: Look, he should live and be well, of course, but what could be gained by hearing from him? I don't want to be fakey friends with him. Well, sure, not now, they nodded nervously, but someday . . . someday! I had no clue what they were talking about, and they had no clue to what I was talking about. So I was lost in grand, dramatic thoughts, such as, What is this prudish, morbid stake society now has in making everyone stay fakey friends? In insisting on eroding the natural barriers which protect the self, the ones which also hold out the possibility of true friendship? In launching a pre-emptive strike against any real emotions which might, God forbid, surface and remind us we are not robots? At least the advice a young woman would get a hundred years ago—"let no half courtesy continue, but break at once"—permitted room for a sense of tragedy or dignity. That's what my thoughts settled on, eventually: where is our dignity? But that particular pompous thought lasted all of five seconds because then they told me something which assured me that, indeed, we still had our dignity.

We just called it something else.

### ADVANCED TECHNIQUES: THE PRE-HOOK-UP CHECK FOR PRIOR-POST-DUMPING-CHECKUP-INTERVALS

"The best predictor of someone's future behavior is their past behavior," warns *YM* magazine in 1998. This is what used to be known as a *reputation*. All the questions a woman might wonder

when it comes to the man she's about to become involved with—
Is he moral? Is he good? And does he know what it means to be
a man?—have been reduced to this. For we are not supposed to
care if he's moral (who knows what's moral?), or if he's good (who
knows what's good?), and above all we are not allowed to ask if
he knows what it means to be a man. That, of course, would be
extremely uncool because that would be sexist. One cannot ask
about male honor because male honor is supposed to be oppressive to women. Every woman of my generation knows this—we
learned it with our ABC's.

So instead we conduct the Pre-Hook-up Check for Prior-
Post-Dumping-Checkup-Intervals.

That is, before you become involved with a man, you're supposed to ask: Excuse me, but are you on good terms with all of
your ex-girlfriends? And excuse me, but if you dump me, will you
be checking up on me regularly? And if so, at what intervals? You
can't get it in writing, I'm told, but it's still important to find out
the answers to these questions. To quantify how often a man
checks up on his ex-girlfriends and, by implication, how often he
will check up on you. Because you might miss him. Because it
might be hard for you to unattach so quickly.

To be concerned with male honor, of course, is wrong because
it implies that a woman might want to be a little bit less casual
about sex than a man. And nobody wants to generalize. You can
get in serious trouble for generalizing. But why, then, does modern woman employ the Pre-Hook-up Check for Prior-Post-
Dumping-Checkup-Intervals?

Unfortunately, as with many things, the desiccated rule simply
doesn't work as well as the richer notion. It expresses the need,
without guiding it in any way or helping a woman glean any
meaningful information.

For if a man scores extremely well on the Pre-Hook-up Check
for Prior-Post-Dumping-Checkup-Intervals, he could be any
number of things. He could be just a nice guy, a gentle soul, or he
could be a rather passionless fish just doing his checking up
because it's expected of him. Or he could be selfish and just covering his tush so that in case his little dumpee commits suicide,
he won't be held liable: "Your Honor! I swear I checked up on 'er
*quite* regularly! I was a *wonderful* ex-boyfriend!"

Worst of all, there could be something quite suspicious going
on. What really goes on during all these checkups? That's what I'd
like to know.

And if a man scores extremely poorly on his Post-Dumping-Checkup-Interval? Let's face it, there are really only two possibilities: he's either the most passionate man in the world, so enthralled by the sweetness and light that was your time together, so convinced he made the biggest mistake of his life, so filled with self-loathing at dumping you that he couldn't possibly check up—not even once—because he'd just fall apart, *or,* alternatively, as Susan, 21, put it, "You could have, like, just been involved with a completely callous schizophrenic psychopath. *Gross!*" There's simply no way to know. Oh, well.

Of course, a woman could always play it safe and just try to *optimize* the Pre-Hook-up Check for Prior-Post-Dumping-Checkup-Intervals, but then she could just wind up with a mushy person, and no one wants a mushy person.

### YOU WILL HAVE MANY MEN—OR ELSE!

As long as you seem to be "hooking up" on a regular basis, no one has a thing to say to you, but if you're alone, people become very concerned and start to give you lots of advice. I listened carefully to all of it when I was alone, but I had to conclude—without wanting to seem ungrateful—that the advice young women were getting was just appalling. I was stunned by the way my friends reassured me. You will have many men in your life, they all predicted. Your body's not so bad, your face not so ugly. You'll see, you'll see. You'll do very well on the market. Trust us. Just "maybe put on a shorter skirt or something," stop "hiding" yourself, stop "taking things so *seriously,*" and "you'll see how the men will . . ."

I tuned out at this point, my mind whirring over this *You will have many men* business. Was that a compliment, I wondered, or a life sentence? It's a life sentence if you're like me, one who hopes for—dare one even say it?—not many men but just one. *You will have many men.* Well, thanks for the generous offer, but am I allowed to decline?

More irritating advice: *"Baby, you're just getting started!"*

Amy, 19, with whom I discussed this at the time, nodded, "I know what you mean," and offered, after glancing behind her, this explanation: "I think if I came out and said I only wanted one man, people would say, of course *you* do, you could only *get* one man anyhow. You know what you always hear—'she's too pretty to be alone, she must have a boyfriend' and everything. So I guess I sleep with these men to prove I'm not ugly, I'm normal, I'm 'mature,' and I have this sex life so people won't, you know, make fun of me or think there's something wrong with me . . ." At this she started laughing and added quickly, "That probably sounds stupid."

But in fact, it makes a lot of sense. At one point or another in every young woman's life, maybe at sixteen, maybe nineteen, maybe twenty, she advertises to the world that it is time for her to decide how to live, what to "expect," and she is often given the comforting assurance, "you're pretty, you'll have many men." This compliment is innocent enough. These days it's just a thing people say, akin to nice day, isn't it? But to her, crucially, it sounds normative. To her it comes out, "if you do not have many men, *you're not pretty.*"

The language my peers use is very revealing. In the age of the hook-up, young women confess their romantic hopes in hushed tones, as if harboring some terrible secret. Amy, revealingly, spoke of "coming out" and "admitting" she just wanted one man, as if her true desires were out of the boundaries of acceptability. She was torn by a need to be accepted by society and a fear of coming forward and learning that there was something horribly perverted about her, after all. These women have learned their cultural lessons well, and they know what is not permissible.

If in a different time, a young woman had to avoid giving public evidence of sexual desire by living with someone out of wedlock, today she must avoid giving evidence of romantic desire. The Spring 1998 edition of the teen magazine *YM* contains a "Pool of Love" test. The goal is the "Diving Area: Out for a Good Time" part of the pool, where "You'd be looking for lots of Mr. Right Nows!" If you're too romantic, you tread water at the "deep end" where "your intensity could scare off some potential candidates." Any girl who scores too high on their romance test *YM* labels a "Deluded Dreamstress."

If you have any dreams at all, you are deluded and need to be reeducated. You have a long path ahead of you. Consider some more advice I got, this one from a letter which was meant to be kind: "You stand at the beginning of a long and painful process of becoming a woman." But what if I'm already a woman and I don't think I have to go through a lot of pain to prove it? Maybe being a woman isn't painful, but actually a good thing. I see so many young women around me spending half of their time sleeping with all these men, and the other half telling me how heartbroken they are, and I wonder who gave them the idea that this is what they had to do in the first place?

Anne Roiphe writes in her latest book, *Fruitful,* that when she saw that her child was a daughter, she immediately was sad and thought, "God help my baby, she was female like me." I don't want to have to gaze down at my daughter someday and have to tell her ah, what a terrible and painful process it is to be a woman—God help you. I want to be able to explain to her why being a woman is wonderful, why she doesn't need to pretend she's a man, and why she's just fine the way she is.

Simone de Beauvoir talked so much about how one "becomes" a woman, and then it turned out her ideal woman became most womanly when she rejected being a wife (a "parasite"), being a mother ("a discontented woman"), and being in love ("a paranoiac"). Maybe to think of womanhood in terms of *becoming* at all is entirely to misunderstand it, and all this talk of becoming a woman is all a way of trying to avoid being a woman.

Yet the desire to avoid being a woman is a perfectly understandable impulse, given the obstacles that today's woman faces.

# Chapter 3

# THE FALLOUT

*Where the Victorians' sensual longing was veiled, ours is aggressive to the point of violence.*

—JAMES ATLAS, 1997

It is no accident that harassment, stalking, and rape all increased when we decided to let everything hang out. A society that has declared war on embarrassment is one that is hostile to women.

The human need to veil sensual longing dates to long before the Victorian Era. In Orthodox Judaism, sexual relations between husband and wife are absolutely prohibited under the following conditions: coercion, confusion, strife, intoxication, or famine. If either husband or wife is intoxicated, they can't have sex. If they have been fighting and haven't made up yet, they can't have sex. If either husband or wife isn't sure, they can't have sex. Intercourse without consent was once thought to be a very serious crime—even when it took place within marriage.

Tocqueville, who famously wrote that the "chief cause of the extraordinary prosperity and growing power of [America] was ... due to the superiority of their women," also observed that the virtue of the American woman was protected by punishing rape by death—

*American legislators, who have made almost every article in the criminal code less harsh, punish rape by death; and no other crime is judged with the same inexorable severity by public opinion. There is reason for this: as the Americans think nothing more precious than a woman's honor and nothing deserving more respect than her freedom, they think no punishment could be too severe for those who take both from her against her will. In France, where the same crime is subject to much milder penalties, it is difficult to find a jury that will convict. Is the reason scorn of chastity or scorn of woman? I cannot rid myself of the feeling that it is both.*

This is why "In America a young woman can set out on a long journey alone and without fear." How strikingly different is our present state of affairs, when young women are cautioned not to set out alone, lest they be treated to a whole host of indignities.

## STALKING & RAPING

In any given month, scores of articles on stalking appear in the women's magazines: we learn how to protect ourselves against stalkers, when to file a restraining order with the police, and what to do when the restraining order is violated. A 1996 issue of *New Woman* reports that all 50 states have anti-stalking laws, but "they are often ineffective." One Connecticut woman's stalker was arrested "many times over six years," but "didn't spend one night in jail"; the law required "proof that he intended to cause her fear or alarm," and this was almost impossible to produce.

A year later, Jeffrey Toobin writes that "Given the law-enforcement options, you'd better hope that no one becomes dangerously obsessed with you." When one woman, "Mary," reported to police that her neighbor had been regularly leaving abusive messages on her answering machine, trespassing, and even interfering with her mail, she was told by one officer to "leave the guy alone." She eventually moved, but her stalker doggedly turned up at her business, too. Then Mary had to close down her retail shop, but since she was never killed, she is considered a "success story." As Toobin notes: "despite all the attention and effort that stalking has received, law enforcement remains largely powerless to address the concerns of victims."

Meanwhile, in a recent survey of Rhode Island teenagers who were asked to give their opinion about whether a man "has the right to have sexual intercourse with a woman without her consent," 80% said it was okay if the couple were married, 70% if they planned to marry, and 61% said it was okay if the couple had had prior sexual relations. In another study, 65% of the boys replied that it was acceptable to "force sex" on a person after dating her six months, and one-fourth of the boys said it was acceptable to force sex on a date when you've spent money on her.

With this mentality, it is not surprising that today rapists are given, on average, five years in prison. Instead of punishing rape by death, as in Tocqueville's time, we now prefer to take the rapist's perspective on things. On July 11, 1997 two women tried to explain why their lives had been ruined by being raped. They described the humiliation as Damon Freeman, 17, and Walter Ward, 18, held their boyfriends at gunpoint and forced them to watch, how every day is a struggle for them, how they live in fear. "You took something from me I could never get back—you took my pride, my dignity, along with my heart," one woman said.

But then, dignity and heart—we don't really go for that stuff anymore. As Camille Paglia has explained, if rape "is a totally devastating psychological experience for a woman, then she doesn't have a proper attitude about sex." Rape is just "like getting beaten up. Men get beat up all the time." Both women pleaded that the rapists be given the maximum they could be ordered to serve, of the 12½–25 years open to the judge (confessions were detailed, there were eight felony counts). Justice Felice Shea of Harlem gave them six years. Then Justice Shea explained to the rapists that she was "considering where you're coming from." The rapists had a history of depression, and when you're depressed, that's what you do nowadays, apparently—you go out for a little rape, and then you feel better. In 1993, Glen Ridge, New Jersey, boys Christopher Archer, Kevin Scherzer, and Kyle Scherzer were found guilty of first-degree aggravated sexual assault for brutally raping a retarded girl with a baseball bat. The judge could have sentenced them to forty years in prison, but instead gave them "indeterminate" minimum terms of imprisonment at a young adult offenders institution.

A member of the Spur Posse, those fourteen high school athletes from Lakewood, California, who were on trial for "scoring" with girls as young as ten, complained that "The schools pass out condoms and teach us about pregnancy, but they don't teach us any rules." Well, that's not entirely true. We do teach our children that if they rape, they must do so, at the very least, *safely.* Before the gang rape of a 14-year-old girl at August Martin High School, reported *The New York Times,* "two of the suspects went to a guidance counselor's office for condoms. When the girl was in the empty classroom, one of the teenagers held her down as the other three raped her, the police said."

Other than stranger rape, then, we have this newer variety: classroom rape and, of course, date rape or "acquaintance rape," which has been the subject of searing national controversy ever since Mary Koss published her 1985 study of 3,187 college women. After Koss found that 15.3 percent of women had been victims of rape, 84% of whom knew their attackers, feminists immediately rallied to her defense and started date-rape awareness-raising campaigns, while most conservatives trivialized her findings and held that feminists were trying to "criminalize" normal heterosexual sex. One of Koss's ten questions was worded vaguely, critics said, and seemed to expand the definition of rape. This was the one that went, "Have you ever had sexual intercourse when you didn't want to because a man gave you alcohol or drugs?"

Much was made of this single question. Katie Roiphe and Christina Hoff Sommers use this question in their books to indict the so-called date-rape hysteria. Conservative Mary Matalin wrote in a *Newsweek* article that 73 percent of the rape victims "affirmed they had intercourse when they didn't want to because a man gave them drugs or alcohol."

But in fact, this 73 percent figure is a distortion of Koss's original findings. Only 8 percent of the women in Koss's survey said that they had had sexual intercourse because "a man had given them alcohol or drugs." The main finding of Koss's data—that 84 percent of the women tried to reason with their attackers, 70 percent put up some form of physical resistance, and 64 percent were held down—went ignored.

Presumably, conservatives should have something to say to men who cannot have sexual intercourse with their dates without physically restraining them. Attacking feminists for expanding the definition of rape seems a distraction from the harder but clearly more necessary task of socializing our males.

"God forbid," Henry Fielding reportedly wrote to Samuel Richardson after reading *Clarissa* in 1748, "God forbid that the man who reads this with dry eyes should be alone with my daughter when she hath no assistance within call." Notice what Fielding did not say. He did not say, "God forbid that my daughter should be alone with the man who reads this with dry eyes, because then she will get what she deserves."

In Frank Capra's *It Happened One Night* (1934), Clark Gable tells Claudette Colbert, through gritted teeth, "You'd better go back to your bed," when she professes her love for him. She was engaged to marry another man at the time, and so she was off-limits even when she threw herself at him. A man who is alone with a woman is not thereby excused from acting morally. The date-rape crisis is not feminist hysteria, as conservatives say, nor is it a sign of the patriarchy, as the feminists say. It is one more indication that we have failed to socialize our males in the specific way that Fielding and Richardson took so seriously.

Our pursuit of androgyny, though, has not aided the task of socializing our males. It's rather difficult to turn around suddenly and try to teach men to be gentle around women, when we have been training them all along to assume that women are the same as they. If men are brought up, as today's boys are, believing that girls always want the same thing *they* do from sexual encounters, and that it's evil and sexist to assume otherwise, then they are that much more likely to be impatient and uncomprehending of a woman's "no." Female modesty gave men a frame of reference for a woman's "no." Without that frame of reference, but instead taught from day one that women are always as ready to receive advances as they are eager to make them, the modern male always takes a "no" as a personal rebuke. That is why women today must link arms, charge down campus in their anti-date-rape rallies, screaming *"No means no!"* Before, it was a woman's prerogative to say no—she didn't have to join some political rally to enjoy this right—while now it is a man's prerogative to expect sex.

The effect that the attack on modesty has had in making rape more acceptable is nowhere clearer than in the astonishing House of Lords case of *Regina* v. *Morgan*. A woman was sexually assaulted by three men who had been out drinking with her husband, and the assailants defended themselves with the explanation that the victim's husband had *told* them that they could have sex with his wife. Here's my wife—help yourself, he said. So they attacked the woman while she was sleeping, held her down while each of the three raped her in turn. The men admitted to the court that she had protested, but they claimed that her husband had already prepared them for this very possibility. She had kinky tastes, they had been told. While Lord Hailsham affirmed the men's convictions, he opined bizarrely that since "rape is nonconsensual sexual intercourse, and . . . the guilty state of mind is an intention to commit it," an "honest belief" that a woman is consenting should really preclude conviction because it "clearly negatives intent."

In an accompanying statement, Lord Fraser of Tulleybelton added: "No doubt a rapist, who mistakenly believes that the [married] woman is consenting to intercourse, must be behaving immorally, by committing fornication or adultery. But those forms of immoral conduct . . . are not now considered appropriate to be visited with penalties of the criminal law at all. There seems therefore to be no reason why they should affect the consequences of the mistaken belief . . ." Here we can explicitly observe the connection between the loosening of modesty's sanction and the acceptance of rape. Since we don't take adultery seriously anymore, it's no longer such a big deal if a man tells his friends to help themselves to his peacefully sleeping wife. So what if they have to hold her down after she wakes up, goes this theory—we're not prudes around here anymore.

In pursuit of a unisexual society in which we deny that men are physically stronger than women, drunks (and sober opportunists) with total disregard for women will simply have more chances to prey on them. All our unisexual society has achieved is precisely this greater opportunity for women to be taken advantage of. Equal-opportunity rape, stalking, beating and equal opportunity death.

In some elite circles, many actually celebrate this equal-opportunity brutality as a hallmark of women's true liberation. In 1996, TV talking-head Bonnie Erbe defended the equal-opportunity beating of a female illegal alien in Riverside, California, on just this basis: "if women want equality in society, can you then say, well, beating a man is terrible, but beating a woman is horrendous?" If we are ever going to take seriously the notion of civilizing our males again, we have got to leave off this absurd idea that brutalizing women is somehow something to be shrugged off.

The best protection against rape, stalking, and domestic violence is to raise men who both understand that women are different, and would never dare take advantage of this difference. Specifically, though they are physically stronger and may be capable of forcing a woman to have sexual intercourse, they should not because this is not how it's done in civilized society.

### STREET HARASSMENT

Women who are sexually harassed at work can now hold their employers liable, but who can be sued for harassment on the street? No one. That is why respect for modesty once protected women far more than any lawsuit.

Take Karen, 22, who has just moved to New York, and lives on the Lower East Side. She is slight, with dark blonde hair and blue eyes. We went out for brunch, and afterwards I bought the Sunday paper. She waited for me outside the store, and when I returned I could see she was very upset. Did something happen? I asked. "Yes," she wailed, "Some guy just said I had pretty eyes!" I started to laugh. She does have pretty eyes. I objected and told her she shouldn't be upset; that wasn't vulgar, that was a nice compliment. "No, no," she continued, insisting, "it was like an attack." I wasn't there, I didn't understand. He came really close to her, right up to her face, and spat it out like an accusation, *you have pretty eyes!* He almost knocked her down. I hate when strangers do that, she says, now almost chanting: *I hate it, I hate it, I hate it!* Her cheeks flush and I feel a kind of burn pass through me, too. If he really came that close to her, then maybe it wasn't right. Maybe it was an assault on her privacy. I end up agreeing with her and apologizing for not being sympathetic. She feels better now that I understand, calms down a bit, and then becomes more thoughtful. "It's weird," she says, trailing off, "when I'm with my boyfriend I don't feel this way at all, walking down the street."

I wonder what you make of this young woman. Do you think she was overreacting, or do you think she was justified? Maybe if you're a conservative, you think that she was overreacting, and that boys will be boys. Maybe you think she should be grateful that she's in a position to field compliments. Or maybe, if you're a feminist, you think that her reaction was entirely justified, but that she is wrong to look to her boyfriend to protect her, since her boyfriend is more accurately seen as contributing to the problem. Maybe you think that the patriarchy, of which her boyfriend is a member, is responsible for the treatment she just received, and she should therefore break up with her boyfriend instead of wanting him to be around more.

Or perhaps you just think she could benefit from psychological help.

I want to propose a different explanation—this woman does not need to have psychological counseling, nor does she need to have her consciousness raised. When I saw her burning face, it was clear to me that some natural boundary had been violated. I don't see why she should have to work to suppress this innocent thermometer. Something *was* off, and I think it's good that she instinctively sensed this. I would prefer to ask why this individual man was so presuming—why wasn't he more respectful of her? Why didn't he admire her from a distance?

At college, I would often spot the "You Didn't Choose To Be Harassed" poster, which always contained this anecdote:

*I live in the city so I'm used to it. Men walk by and try to shock me, frighten me with gross statements; once on the subway, a man mastur-*

*bated in front of me and I couldn't move away. I'm always being asked "Hey, baby, where are you going?" as though it's their right to know. You can't let your guard down for a second.*

Sara McCool, age sixteen, writes that she is tired of being hassled on the street, and observes, "I have never seen a pack of girls get together around some boy and yell at him how much they want to have sex with him."

You might ask, as Hillary Carlip does in her recent book *Girl Power,* but "what do young women who have lived less than twenty years have to be angry about?" Well, "Angela," one frustrated young woman who joined a "Riot Grrrl" group, wrote that she hates having "to prove herself worthy of respect." She was not alone in this. "From the majority of the girls' writing," Carlip concludes, "it is clear they feel continually disrespected, especially by acts of violation and humiliation. These acts come in many forms, including harassment; mental, physical and verbal abuse; and rape. Sexual harassment is a daily concern, considering that most girls don't even feel safe walking down the street alone."

Tocqueville said that a woman in America could walk anywhere alone without fear, so great was men's respect for their modesty. Women then didn't need their boyfriends to protect them, nor have to "prove themselves worthy of respect," because men respected all women as ladies, not only their girlfriends. Today we are taught that this "every woman a lady" idea was sexist, that it made women into property, but sometimes it seems as if abandoning it has made women all the more into property. Because men no longer treat all women as ladies, my 22-year-old friend needed her boyfriend on the street to give off everyone-stay-away-she's-mine vibes, as it were. Maybe treating all women respectfully was not subordinating, after all, but precisely a way of conveying that they were not mere property—that they didn't have to be "owned" by one man to deserve respectful treatment.

In the 1966 movie, *Walk, Don't Run,* Samantha Eggar has nothing to fear from the two men renting her place. Indeed, when she catches her boarders just *speculating* about her as a sexual prospect—Cary Grant and Jim Hutton peek at her underwear, and try to extrapolate her sexual history—the men feel terribly ashamed and ply her with presents and apologies for the rest of the movie.

Respect for modesty made women powerful. When the creepy Mr. Slope of *Barchester Towers* "contrived to pass his arm round

[Eleanor's] waist" when it was unwanted, he was stigmatized for the rest of the novel. This freedom from sexual harassment, so to speak, was the direct consequence of a society that valued female modesty. As Trollope stated in his *Autobiography,* one of the aims of his writing was to teach the men to be honest, and the girls, "That modesty is a charm well worth preserving."

This wasn't just in fiction. Consider the 1909 man, so concerned about losing the favor of a young woman that he wrote to *The Ladies' Home Journal:* "Q: May I call upon a young woman whom I greatly admire, although she had not given me the permission? Would she be flattered at my eagerness, even to the setting aside of conventions, or would she think me impertinent?" "A: I think that you would risk her just displeasure and frustrate your object of finding favor with her. The proper way is for you to request [a mutual friend] to ask the young woman's permission."

We still are concerned with the same things, of course, although our vocabulary has been impoverished. Instead of men adhering to conventions, today women constantly complain of their personal discomfort. Hence, "I hate it when someone I'm not very close with, like a first or second date (or even a colleague or acquaintance) kisses me hello and good-bye. How can I politely duck out of it without seeming rude?" A: "Stick out your hand to shake theirs before they try to kiss you. You're right not to want to do anything that makes you feel uncomfortable." That exchange, from a 1997 issue of *Cosmo,* is not unlike that in a 1905 *Ladies' Home Journal:* "Q: What do you do when a man persists in holding your hand despite all that you can say?" "A: No man who is fit to be welcomed in your home would refuse to release your hand if you asked him as if you meant it." Yet the difference is also profound: In 1905, a man who was too presuming wasn't "fit to be welcomed" in society, while in 1997 the problem is the woman's. Now it is up to her to invent various arbitrary maneuvers to alleviate her discomfort, whereas before it was the man's job to demonstrate he was worthy of her.

Women my age were told that these demonstrations, rules, and codes of conduct were sexist, and that's why our mothers got rid of them. So why, then, do we find ourselves facing more harassment in the public sphere? If we took care of the problem by abolishing male courtesy, then why do we hear so much about how women are "objectified" by the male gaze? Why is the problem worse, and not better? It is odd that a woman today must always have a man around her to feel truly secure in public, whereas before she did not. Which woman was more independent? Lovers are now desired not necessarily to give one's life meaning, but rather in the way you might desire a zoo keeper. Might this explain why the clarion call of modern woman is "you don't have to love me"? It's supposed to be a sign of liberation that women are having sex with men who do not love them, but sometimes I wonder if it isn't more an admission of being enslaved to men. You don't have to love me; please just keep the other animals *off* me.

My own experience with sexual harassment is pretty unremarkable, just your basic street vulgarity. One incident deserves special mention, though, because it was so bizarre. During my senior year in college, one of my male professors asked me if my independent project (yes, it was about modesty) was going to be entitled "Modesty: an Outsider's View," since I was so provocative. No, I'm not, I protested, I always keep my raincoat on, even in class (a strange response, but then I wasn't really prepared for such a conversation). No, you're still very provocative, he insisted. Once I saw you in the gym, and you were wearing a tank top! Well, I returned, I have to fulfill my physical education requirement in order to graduate! Eventually we agreed not to have personal conversations, since at this point I still respected him as a professor. But then in class, when I would offer my opinion, he would say, in a hostile way, "You *would* think that." When I saw him during office hours to get my essay topic approved, five minutes into the discussion he burst out with: "Look, I think there's something wrong with you, and I'm not the *only* one who thinks it!" He kept agreeing not to make personal remarks, but he couldn't seem to control himself. I had never experienced anything like it in my life. Finally, after about six such outbursts, he sent me an e-mail message saying that if I didn't want to attend his classes anymore, that was fine with him, he understood. (The only advantage to having unpopular views: your professors tell you that you don't have to attend class.) Was this sexual harassment? Was it ideological harassment? I don't know. It was certainly very unpleasant.

During the time in which I was excused from his classes, though, I thought a lot about that passage in the *Communist Manifesto* where Marx talks about the sentimental veil being torn away. That's exactly how I felt at the time—that a veil had been torn, and I was seeing too much.

Maybe the purpose of the "sentimental veil" was really not so silly and sentimental, after all. Maybe a little illusion sometimes is good. In some sense you could say that men on the street are more honest today because they leer and make crude remarks instead of tipping their hats and observing "artificial" proprieties. I guess you could also say that all romantic love involves a kind of deception about what is really being sought. Yet if lovers really believe the words they say to each other, and strangers believe in the proprieties they observe, personal interactions don't have to be so crude. Maybe the biggest illusion of all was thinking that we could ever succeed in tearing down the sentimental veil. Too many of us still secretly yearn for it. We can't seem to help ourselves; it's just in our nature.

The rule in Samuel Richardson's *Clarissa* was: "Talk not to a lady in a way that modesty will not permit her to answer."

Maybe that wasn't such a bad rule, after all.

## THE NORMALIZATION OF PORNOGRAPHY

One of the "100 Most-Asked Questions About Love, Sex, and Relationships" is the following: "My husband and I have an ongoing battle about his habit of constantly reading porno magazines. I feel like it's wrong, and that he shouldn't need them now that we're married. He says all men do it, that it's 'no big deal,' and I'm overreacting. It's starting to ruin our sex life, because I feel so angry and turned off to him. Should I just try to accept it, or should I take a stand?"

This may be one of the "most-asked" questions about sex, but it is not the most answered one. Most talk about pornography today has been reduced to a ping-pong game over censorship, with the feminists and conservatives crying yes, and the civil libertarians volleying back their no's. What rarely gets attention is how much our view of pornography has changed, and what this shift means for the ordinary lives of men and women.

When Victor Hugo's play *Hernani* opened at the Comédie Française in 1830, it almost sparked a riot. Around a hundred and seventy years later, Elizabeth Berkley took everything off for the movie *Showgirls,* and the public was incredibly bored. Juliann Garey notes that the number of strip clubs in America has doubled since 1992, and that now "strippers have become part of our visual vocabulary—a sort of cultural wallpaper." In fact, "Strippers are showing up with such frequency . . . that they're no longer shocking—and that's the problem. What once provoked some kind of response—embarrassment, outrage, anxiety, titillation—

now seems routine." A year after *Showgirls,* Dennis Rodman issued the book *Walk on the Wild Side,* where he announces his affairs with transsexuals and his plans to change his name to "Orgasm." All one reviewer could say, devastatingly, was "Yawn."

"Yawn" is putting it mildly. When Baudelaire wrote his poem "La Charogne," where he says to his love, after passing a carcass in the road with its legs in the air, "You will be like that carcass/ Star of my eyes!"—it was subversive, a *Fleur du Mal*. Compare this with the reaction that greeted Sally Mann's *At Twelve* series of photos in 1988. In one, a 12-year-old girl is standing with v-shaped carcasses all around her. Mann tells the girl to spread her legs, the girl complies, and Mann snaps the picture. It's more explicitly rendered than Baudelaire's poem, actually involves a living girl, but now instead of being a *Fleur du Mal,* the whole setup "could lead viewers to think about their feelings on the subject," according to critic Wendy Steiner.

None of this is intended to suggest that we should censor Sally Mann, but I am interested in the way that pornography is now taken to be positively therapeutic. What does it mean that Mann's *At Twelve* series "could lead viewers to think about their feelings on the subject"? What is the content, exactly, of this injunction to think about feelings? Do all feelings suffice? Mann photographs another twelve-year-old girl facing away from us, one who does not realize that thousands of viewers will see her naked breast through the gap in her tank top. Do you think that's fair? What are *your* feelings on the subject? As long as you develop feelings on the subject, you know, and use this girl to come to terms with your feelings, then it's all perfectly kosher.

Next, consider *The End of Alice,* a 1996 novel written from the perspective of a sexually deviant man with a taste for raping little girls. The author, A. M. Homes, told reporters that her pedophile, well, "he's a person we haven't heard from before. I think he's smart . . . he has a certain moral center." For instance, though he rapes one of his twelve-year-old victims with a spoon, stabs her sixty-four times, decapitates her, dips his lips in her blood and kisses her repeatedly, then continues sexual relations with her dead body, he refuses—absolutely refuses—to use a fork in the proceedings. Yes, that's right, no fork: see page 263. Look, a guy's gotta have some standards. The *Boston Book Review* said *The End of Alice* was "full of tantalizing ideas," the *Chicago Sun-Times* said it contained "highly seductive prose," and Gregory Crewdson of *Bomb* added that it was really "at its center a romantic, and even moral, tale." Only Cathleen Medwick expressed doubt. But what, she asked A. M. Homes in an interview, does writing a novel from the pedophile's perspective do to what we think of abused children? Our novelist mused: "I think that young girls do play with that kind of power."

*"I think that young girls do play with that kind of power."* This time one is really at a loss to describe one's feelings on the subject. Is the proper response, At least Nabokov, in *Lolita,* was a little ambivalent about it? Or, At least he didn't go for stabbing, decapitation, and necrophilia! No, that doesn't seem quite right either. Of course young girls play with their attractiveness, but one isn't supposed to take them up on it and then stab them sixty-four times. What is horrifying is not so much that someone wrote a sympathetic portrait of one who does, but that everyone else found it "tantalizing," "seductive," "romantic," even "moral."

At the same time, a *U.S. News* poll of February 1996 found that 88% of Americans think incivility is a serious problem, and 78% think incivility has worsened over the past ten years. We all seem to long for the advantages of a more moral, less crude society, but we want it without having to judge anyone else or draw any lines in the sand. Nobody wants to be accused of being a prig, to be the one to say, Excuse me, but this isn't "tantalizing," this is just sick.

Which brings us to a related question—how pornography has coarsened the relations between the sexes.

In a fascinating article in *Mademoiselle* magazine, a Miss Jennifer Silver tells why it bothered her that her boyfriend kept copies of *Playboy* around their apartment. Her boyfriend had explained that men are just "visually stimulated," that's all, to which she replied: "Oh. Well. Then you won't mind if I start going out for coffee with some of the men from my writing class? You know, it won't mean anything—I'm *conversationally stimulated,* that's all." He did mind, of course, but the magazines kept coming. Our young author was "taken aback by how furious it made" her, since "I've never been uptight about porn." Why, then, she asks, "was I feeling so threatened?" She wasn't sure, and began polling her friends. That's when she made a surprising discovery: Though "many of them agreed they'd be outraged if their boyfriends got *Playboy,*" they were all, like her, "slightly abashed by the vehemence of their feelings about porn. It didn't feel 'cool' to get so upset; it felt prudish." Yet, Miss Silver added, "we knew we weren't prudish, and our visceral reaction was baffling to us."

Though it is not cool to be against pornography in a pornographic culture, many other women, Miss Silver found, privately feel the same way as she—instinctively. She searched for a logic behind this natural reaction, and came up with what to me seems an eminently reasonable one:

> *The real reason I hated* Playboy *was that the models established a standard I could never attain without the help of implants, a personal trainer, soft lighting, a squad of makeup artists and hairdressers, and airbrushing. It's a standard that equates sexuality with youth and beauty. I didn't want my boyfriend buying into* Playboy's *definition of sexuality. I was planning a future with this man, and I wanted to feel secure in the knowledge that, even after two kids and 20 years, he would still find me sexy. After sorting all this out in my mind, I leveled with my boyfriend. I told him that he wasn't doing something bad, but that it made me feel bad. Rational or not, justified or not, I didn't like having* Playboy *in my house. . . . When he understood how I felt, he kindly and graciously canceled his subscription.*

Accompanying this essay was *Mademoiselle's* query-box: "What if *Your* Boyfriend Read *Playboy?*" Reading some of the interviewees, I was struck by the fact that in every case, the younger women were more likely to share the author's visceral reaction. Were the younger women more upset because they were naturally modest, or were they simply more childish, pouting over nothing?

In the original article, the women's responses were not listed in chronological order, but I am arranging them this way to illustrate a point. The youngest, "Elizabeth," was 22 and the fiercest: "I'd be severely upset," she told *Mademoiselle,* "because it would make me think I'm not enough stimulation for him." Anne, who was 24, was also offended, but more philosophical than emotional: "I think *Playboy* is demeaning to women," she said, "and I'd tell him that. Also I'd reevaluate whether he was a good boyfriend, because it would show me he had a complete lack of respect for my gender." Margaret, a little bit older at 25, was also just a little bit less offended: "I wouldn't necessarily think he was a misogynist, but I would think he wasn't a cool person." Danielle, who came in next at 26, still wanted her boyfriend to throw out *Playboy,* but wouldn't judge him harshly at all. She would just "feel sorry for him." By the time we hear from Susan, who was 27, the *Playboy* got to stay—"I wouldn't mind too much"—but you can still hear her ambivalence in the way she would want her boyfriend to read the magazine: "I'd look through it with him and say, 'She's gross, she's gross, that's gross . . ." And finally, Sue, at 30, was the oldest of those interviewed and also the most blasé: "It wouldn't make me feel insecure—they're just pictures. . . . Besides, you can't control a guy's life."

Interestingly, though the oldest woman seems the most secure, it is the youngest woman's visceral response that seems to be supported by findings in a recent study. According to psychologist Douglas Kenrick's research, men shown pictures of *Playboy* models do later describe themselves as less in love with their wives than do men shown other images.

This is a fact that tends to get lost in the debate over pornography, now that it has been normalized. Most intellectuals seem more interested in toying with arguments about pornography—twice or three times removed from what is actually going on—than in addressing how pornography affects the lives of men and women. In his book *Sex and Reason,* for example, Richard Posner argues that the feminist and conservative arguments against pornography undermine each other. For if what Irving Kristol says is true, and pornography does provoke a regression to infantile sexuality, then Posner claims it could not at the same time also promote rape, as Catharine MacKinnon argues, since rape and masturbation are "substitutes." To be specific, a man masturbating all the time would presumably be too busy to go out and rape someone. As Posner concludes, "The feminists fear that pornography causes rape; Kristol that it causes the substitution of masturbation for intercourse. Since rape is a form of intercourse, Kristol must believe that pornography reduces the incidence of rape, while feminists must believe that it reduces the incidence of masturbation."

This argument is clever, but it does very little to defeat Kristol's position. The regression to infantile sexuality that pornography encourages is totally compatible with raping a woman. To put it in Posner's terms, rape and masturbation are not substitutes, they are complements: both are expressions of a man who doesn't want, or is incapable of sustaining, an adult sexual relationship with a woman. It is precisely the infantile personality which is likely to be impatient and take by force that which a woman will not give. Indeed, this is just the state of affairs we seem to have now.

Camille Paglia says that "what is *needed* now . . . [is] *more* pornography, *better* pornography. Pornography everywhere!" But in interviews she is often described as walking down the street with her two bodyguards, a detail that to me is fascinating. She promotes pornography, safe behind her bodyguards, while the rest of us have to live in a pornographic culture without bodyguards. We who cannot afford bodyguards depend on men to treat us well on the street when we are walking alone, not to rape us or stalk us. We depend, in other words, on male respect for the fact that we probably want to be more sexually discriminating than they. A respect for female modesty was a woman's natural body-guard, invisible and free of charge. Thanks to the attack on modesty, and the attack on male respect for it, now only rich or famous women can feel safe.

More significantly, a culture in which pornography has been normalized has certain expectations of its girls, expectations that are often hard to meet. *"I think that young girls do play with that kind of power,"* as A. M. Homes puts it. If our culture always expects young women to be playing with their sexual power, always at the ready for the advances of anyone, this means they never have the right to say "no."

### GIRLS WHO CAN'T SAY NO

A high school girl, Abigail, is teased by a friend for being a virgin. "For what reasons are you still a virgin?" pressures Elena. "I don't want to do it with some random person," Abigail replies. "Are you going to wait till you get *married?*" Elena continues. "Well, not till I get married," she avers. "Have you ever had the opportunity to have sex?" "Yeah." Suddenly their conversation, recorded by Nancy Jo Sales in *New York* magazine, takes a surprising turn. Elena asks softly, quizzically: "How do you handle it when you don't want to?"

How do girls today handle it when they don't want to? Not very well at all. A young author explains why she had first inter-course at 13: "Why not, since everyone seems to think you're a slut anyway, just prove them right? Why not flirt and f——— around with strangers?" She writes that she had sex with married men in the back of buses just because she had "nothing to say" to them "that wouldn't be rude." She "endlessly found [herself] in identical situations where it was easier to just f——— them than to say no."

Fourteen-year-old "Courtney" from Reston, Virginia, doesn't want to lose her virginity yet and is baffled that her parents allow her to be alone so often with her boyfriend. No parental super-vision makes it "difficult for Courtney to draw the line." She complains to journalist Patricia Hersch that her parents aren't helping her at all by giving her so much freedom: "'They let me go over to my boyfriend's house when they know his parents aren't home. That is weird. I am surprised they let him come over all the time.'" So she pretends that she has her period, but this only delays her boyfriend a week. He becomes increasingly aggressive, and soon Courtney is "running out of excuses." After two and a half months of dating Nat, "'I just did it because he really kept bothering me about it.'" But she insists that she be permitted to keep her sweatshirt on. Covering up doesn't seem to make it any easier, and the next morning she "wakes up feeling totally humiliated."

To appreciate the peculiar bind of a nineties girl who wants to say no to sex, first consider the 1948 song, "Baby, It's Cold Outside," by Frank Loesser. In this fuguelike tune, a woman, "the mouse," begins each phrase, and her suitor, "the wolf," chimes in relentlessly, but sweetly, behind her. The man has a hundred reasons why his date should not "hold out"—including, but not limited to, the fact that it is very cold outside. If his poor date were to leave, argues our Wolf, she would freeze, catch pneumonia and die. That, of course, would cause him "lifelong sorrow." If she allowed him to "move in closer," on the other hand, then they would both be nice and warm. Our mouse has her own reasons for begging off, which she scatters between his invitations:

> *My mother will start to worry . . . And father will be pacing the floor . . . The neighbors might think . . . My sister will be suspicious . . . My brother will be there at the door . . . My maiden aunt's mind is vicious . . . There's bound to be talk tomorrow . . . At least there will be plenty implied.*

Now this song is very stereotypical because certainly not all men are hungry wolves and not all women reticent mice. Indeed, I've known quite a few hungry women and mousey men. However, the simple fact remains that a young woman in 1948 had a hundred and one reasons to say no to sex, *if she wanted to say no,* and those reasons were credible. The story we are told today is that all these reasons, such as a father waiting up for you, were oppressive to women. And yet in their absence we can appreciate how an earlier generation of girls was made powerful by them. A father waiting up for his daughter gave her room to stand on. Unmarried women who wanted to have sex have always managed to go ahead and do it regardless. The only thing that has

changed today is that a girl who wants to say no now has no support. Before she could say, "The neighbors might think," "My
maiden aunt's mind is vicious," or "There's bound to be talk
tomorrow."

A girl today who tried to use any of these excuses would
induce a hysterical fit in her male companion. What is the significance of this shift? What does it mean, exactly, for an individual girl
to have this floor of excuses pulled out from under her? For one
thing, to the extent she has no social support in her decision to say
no, when a girl for whatever reason wants to say no to sex, today
she is always making a personal comment on her date: that he is
ugly or in some other way unappealing. This is very hard to do. We
know from Carol Gilligan that girls are pretty eager to please, and
put great stock in their relationships with others. The social support for modesty was a counterweight, balancing out this desire to
please and enabling young women to test men's character, in order
to choose a suitable partner. Without this support, a woman who
doesn't want to sleep with a man is insulting him. Thus, she is perceived as having "hang-ups," being "screwed up," or not having "a
healthy attitude towards sex." Failure to sleep with someone is now
an act of hostility, whereas it was once understood to be part of the
natural process of searching for one's mate.

One of the purposes of the laws of family purity in Judaism,
according to Tehilla Abramov, is that "the separation of the *niddah*
period [when the wife is menstruating, and for seven days after]
teaches a couple to develop a love of friendship and harmony
which finds physical expression in the dynamic and active happiness a couple experience when the woman is *tehorah*." Beyond
the importance of developing non-sexual intimacy, though, having a time of mandatory separation gives a woman and a man a
right to privacy. When one's advances are rejected it is always easy
to take this personally, but if the separation is not subject to
choice—because it is dictated by God's law or by social mores—
then one does not take it personally.

As long as premarital sex was not expected of them, our single
girls enjoyed a similar right to sexual privacy. This had implications in the public sphere as well: many etiquette books, in both
England and America, stressed a woman's prerogative to greet a
man on the street first, particularly if he was not a close friend. If
she chose to greet him, he was obligated to respond in kind, but
if she passed him by, there was absolutely nothing he could do
about it.

But now, since all rejections, whether in public or in private, are taken as ad hominem attacks, one often sees these kinds of letters cropping up in women's magazines: "I've been dating a guy for a month (we haven't done it yet), and he asked me to go on vacation with him. This means he wants sex, right? Would he hate me if I went with him and still said no?" This was from a 1997 issue of *Mademoiselle*. A few months earlier, the same magazine ran the piece, "How to Turn Him Down Without Turning Him Off: The Fine Art of Sexual Rejection," by Ellen Tien. And a year earlier, a woman as old as 24 wrote in: "How can I keep a man from pressuring me for sex before I'm ready to be with him?" A young girl spends "the rest of the night crying and bleeding" after she loses her virginity to a guy she barely knew. "I wish I had been strong enough to overcome the pressures," she regrets. The 1995 Sex in America survey found that while 13 percent of young women used to say peer pressure made them have sex for the first time, now that number is over a third.

What does this inability to say "no" mean for your average girl? Mary Pipher sees a "deadness" in her girl clients' demeanor "that comes from inauthenticity, from giving away too much." Many of her girls don't know how "to set limits with others." One of her patients, "Casey," was abusing alcohol "as a way of deadening her anxiety so that she could have sex, and also of killing her guilt feelings afterward." So they rehearse a little speech that Casey will give, to help her say no: "I'm someone who likes to start slow and get acquainted before I get too physical. So let's go out a few times and become closer friends. Later we can talk about whether we want a physical relationship."

Notice that Casey announces the problem is her own. "I'm someone who . . ." is, essentially, a weirdo. Hi, my name is Casey, and I'm a weirdo! It's not you, really, it's me. I'm weird. I'm one of those really weird *slow* people. Let's talk about sex later, if you haven't dumped me by then because I'm so peculiar.

This is rather hard to say. I'll bet Casey never gave that rehearsed speech. But she may learn to deal with her "saying no" problem in other ways.

# Chapter 4

# NEW PERVERSIONS

*My anorexic body was a confused statement directed more at the world than at my father . . . an apology for being a woman.*

—MARYA HORNBACHER, 1998

I came to college thinking that eating disorders were invented by elite white feminists, but after spotting dozens of women on campus whose legs were half the size of my arm, I now know otherwise. My conclusion is that feminists are right to draw our attention to the problem, but that they misunderstand the nature of it.

I was introduced to the world of eating disorders, strangely enough, not by a woman, but by a man. I was eating dinner in our main dining hall during my freshman year in college, then left to go to the bathroom. It happened to be Eating Disorder Awareness Week. When I returned for my books, the young man sitting at my table was wearing a very worried expression. He greeted me very seriously, looked at me with intensity. "Hi," he breathed.

"Is something wrong?" I asked him.

"Well, when you notice a girl going to the bathroom after a meal, you know, you have to ask her, do you have a problem?"

"I beg your pardon?"

"C'mon, you can tell me," he said, leaning forward in his chair, reaching for my hand. "My last girlfriend was one."

I was still clueless, and trying to formulate a delicate way of explaining how, after you drink a lot of Diet Coke . . . but then his meaning hit me. "Oh, you mean that . . . that your ex-girlfriend was . . ."

"Yeah, *bulimic.*"

Wanting to seem sympathetic, but also wanting to keep my appetite for dessert, I tried to make a face that was nonjudgmental, but also conveyed I was grossed out. It must not have worked because he continued, brightening, "Actually, bulimia is a very effective form of weight control."

*"What?"*

"Yes, but it's also gross. Once I caught her," his voice was low as he leaned forward for emphasis, *"eating chocolates in the bathroom."*

"You *didn't!"*

"I *did!* See, that's a sure sign."

Right. The chocolates-in-the-bathroom problem.

Not exactly Romeo and Juliet, but then this is the nineties. "We follow thee, Juliet, the county stays/ Go, girl, seek happy nights to happy days/ Without any chocolates in the bathroom."

What do we know about anorexia and bulimia? What is not in dispute is that ninety percent of eating disorder sufferers are women, and that most cases occur at the onset of puberty or when a young woman begins to negotiate with the men who appear in her life. Having an eating disorder, I would submit, is the only way our culture allows a woman to find order in a sexually chaotic landscape. In a culture that permits food hang-ups but not sex hang-ups, it's become the new way for a girl to express her modesty, to restore distance between men and herself.

In 1998, a young woman who suffers from anorexia and bulimia writes that casual sex has been effortless for her. Yet hugging was "difficult," since "the idea of being cared for in a non-sexual way was not something I could understand." The conflict between what she was doing and what she needed, emotional connection, left her "perpetually nauseated" and even more self-conscious. Later, in boarding school and then in college, she learned she was not alone. The girls she met—many of them from unstable homes like hers—would "brag of the careless use of our bodies, our common disdain for the boys or men. 'I didn't feel a thing,' we'd say with pride." Yet at the same time, the "dorm bathrooms rarely worked because the pipes were perpetually clogged with vomit."

Sixteen-year-old Heidi, one of Mary Pipher's patients, explains her preference for binging over being with boyfriends this way: "Sometimes I want him to take me home so I can binge. I'll make up an excuse to end our date. . . . I hate to say this, but I'd rather binge than make out." I hate to say this, meaning, I understand that I'm offending the cultural sensibility, but if this is what it takes to get a little privacy around here. . . .

In her memoir, *Drinking: A Love Story,* Caroline Knapp describes her years struggling with anorexia this way: "When I was starving, I couldn't think about . . . the fact that I was young and scared and sexually threatened and angry."

"If I was at my ideal weight I'd feel really in control of my life," says a college anorexic to researcher Sharlene Hesse-Biber. Another anorexic student tells her, "I think my issue was wanting to control my life."

I hear so much about how young women today want *control,* and I wonder—why? Some tell us that the answer is "patriarchy," but in an era of greater patriarchy, this was never a problem. Why are none of my grandma's friends anorexic? Why do none of them need seminars to be taught how to be "comfortable with their bodies"?

When modesty was given a sanction, woman not only had the right to say no to a man's advances, but her good opinion of him was revered. Today, on the other hand, when our popular culture tells us that women should lust equally to men and feel comfortable about putting their bodies on display in coed bathrooms, on coed beaches—coed everything—women seem to be reporting that they feel only more at the mercy of male desire. The anorexic disfigures her body to become unwomanly because if she no longer has the right to say "no," at least she has her body language at her disposal.

So natural modesty has a way of reasserting itself, even in desperate and neurotic fashion.

### PERVERTED SHAME

Hamlet, when considering the motives for his mother's hurried marriage to his father's murderer exclaims, "O shame! where is thy blush?"

When someone behaves badly, we tend to assume that shame has departed for good. But that rarely happens. When I was deciding between schools and visited Swarthmore College, I was very surprised when, around 11 PM, the nice girl with whom I stayed shoved a towel under her door, and then returned to reading quietly at her desk. She was very kind to have put me up for the evening, and so I didn't want to ask too many questions. Still, I was dying to know, "What's that for?" "Oh," she replied casually, "it's nothing, everyone does that. It's so people can't tell that you're studying." *Huh?* "Yeah," she laughed good-naturedly, then shrugged. "People are very competitive here, but you're not supposed to advertise that you study because that's threatening."

I thought of that towel incident a few years later, when I was rummaging through the salt-and-sugar package bin at the end of a deli's checkout counter, and the cash register lady called out to me: "No, *no! Don't* put salt on that! Because there's already *cheese* on your sandwich, and if you put salt, too, it's gonna be *way* too salty!" Everyone in the deli looked over at me. I dropped the salt package like a hot potato, and fled the store. I felt as if I had a scarlet S on my raincoat.

I don't think we live in shameless times. We are human beings, and we always are ashamed of *something.* We've just mixed up the proper objects of our shame. We are ashamed of smoking, but not see-through clothes for young girls. At college, we are to be ashamed of wanting to learn. The administration is shy when it comes to the core curriculum, but it is always glad to inculcate the delights of hard-core sex.

Take Yale. In the fall of 1997, five Orthodox students asked to be excused from Yale's requirement that they live in coed dorms, and the administration denied the students their request. This is the same administration, incidentally, which approved a Bisexual, Gay, Lesbian, and Transgender Cooperative, an African-American cultural studies house, and a Latina/Latino cultural center. Apparently diversity ends where religious morality begins.

Yale's official response to these Orthodox students spoke volumes. In a letter to the *Times,* Richard H. Brodhead, the Dean of Yale College, enjoined us to remember that "Yale College has its own rules and requirements, which we insist on because they embody our values and beliefs." Do they ever. At least now they admit as much. Thirty or so years ago, when colleges all over the country abandoned *in loco parentis* in favor of *in loco libidinis,* they claimed that they were just being "neutral," that they were going to let the students decide for themselves what their sexual morality would be. Dean Brodhead's remarks prove otherwise. Yale's requirement that the sexes live together, he wrote, "embodies our belief that . . . when students enter this community, their daily interaction becomes a continual scene of teaching and learning: a place . . . to learn to work with others across lines of difference."

In such elevated rhetoric it's easy to forget that this common learning we are all supposed to be doing is not Plato or Aristotle, but living in an appropriately promiscuous fashion. Well, at least we have *one* eternal verity.

But buried at the end of *The New York Times*'s 24-paragraph report on the "open living arrangements that have been the vogue on campuses for years," we learn that, by the way, there are actually some non-Orthodox students who aren't terribly pleased with today's dormitory arrangements, either. The final paragraph ends with this whispered cavil: "But some quietly confessed that the permissiveness of residence life sometimes made them uncomfortable." Quietly confessed.

Chris Thacker, a non-Jewish senior at Yale at the time, explained the living situation to me: "Freshman year it's all mixed, sophomore year you might get lucky and have a single-sex floor, but it's never enforced or anything. You really don't have a choice. It's usually mixed floors, mixed bathrooms. It's the same for the rest of the years. I'm a senior and I have my own room, but I have to share a bathroom with three women. I'll be in there brushing my teeth and then you know . . . they'll come in and it's, well, it's kind of weird."

At one point not so terribly long ago, universities used to be on the side of those who wanted to study, and defended them against the pressures of sex. If students did have sex, it had to be furtive. You had to sneak into someone's room or car. Now when your roommate is having sex, *you* are the one expected to sneak around, *you* are the exile (or "sexile," "as the official *Yale Daily News* "Yale lexicon" has it, someone who is banished from your dorm room because your roommate is having more fun than you."), you are the one who should be ashamed of yourself for not being sufficiently libertine. You are the one who must "quietly confess" your taste for sexual modesty, as if admitting some depravity. The objects of our shame have become so mixed up that modesty is now what is taboo.

But it isn't the only postmodern taboo. Today's girls are also to be ashamed of being shy and romantic.

### WICKEDLY SHY WOMEN AND ROMANTIC GIRLS

In 1899, Edward Sandford Martin wrote: "There is nothing the matter with girls. No large, general mistake or miscalculation has been made about them. They are a good invention of the kind, and the kind is indispensable and has never been beaten. If you don't think so, there is something the matter with *you*."

Today many in our culture would disagree with Edward Martin's statement.

I listen to people, male and female alike, gossiping about young women, and I find fascinating what upsets them most. It's never

that a girl is too promiscuous, or that she has had an affair with a
married man. What really annoys people nowadays is if a young
woman is too shy. So-and-so is too shy, what do you think is
wrong with *her?* She really needs to get to the root of the problem and overcome it. Everyone agrees, and then it's on to more
interesting topics. Well, so much for poor so-and-so. Her only
hope is to pick up *Cosmo's* May 1997 "Shy Girl's Guide to Making Man Contact."

I hate to sound like a party pooper, but maybe there's nothing
wrong with so-and-so at all. Maybe there's something wrong with
our telling her she cannot be the way she is.

Let's see, was she dropped on her head as a baby? Since she
could only have been abused, was it by father or by boyfriend? Or
maybe she was poisoned, ate something funny. What do you think
it was, then, animal, vegetable, or mineral? What's *your* guess? How
do you think she came to be contaminated by such shyness?

If a new baby is a girl, one of the first things parents are worried about nowadays is that their daughter might turn out to be
a shy so-and-so.

"My husband and I have two teenage daughters who can be
strong and assertive, but who act the opposite around boys . . .
how can we encourage them to speak out. . . ?" runs a letter in a
1997 issue of *New Woman* magazine. Comes the reply: "The
behavior you describe is normal (that is, the norm) among
teenage girls. And your daughters will have to find their own way
in a world that may pressure them to silence their own authentic
voices at every turn."

What is a young woman's "authentic voice?" Is that she feels
and acts differently around boys necessarily to be corrected? The
May 1997 *Mademoiselle* teaches us "How Not to Die of Embarrassment." A year earlier in *Mademoiselle* (April 1996) we learned
not only "Risk-Free Seduction Tips for the Sexually Shy" but also
how to "Give Stage Fright the Hook." The January/February
1998 *Mirabella* teaches us "How to Overcome Shyness."

But what if it were okay to be shy?

The second chief fault our experts find with young women
today is that they are too romantic. Meet "Cayenne," who lost her
virginity at 13 in a darkened party and sighs at 15, "I wish it had
been more romantic." Is she right or wrong? Our cultural consensus is that she is wrong. Mary Pipher writes that if girls were
less romantic and more like the boys, "more androgynous," they
would have "the ability to act adaptively in any situation regard-

less of gender role constraints." Amy Erickson puts the case more starkly: "romantic ideals were simply a means of maintaining male dominance at a time when overt demands of submission were no longer acceptable."

A 1994 survey by Roper Starch in association with SEICUS (the Sexuality Information and Education Council of the United States) finds that "Girls and boys differ in many of their attitudes about sex. They found that "Girls are more likely to say they 'should have waited until they were older' to have sex" (62% vs. 48%), and "Girls are much more likely to say they were in love with their last sexual partner (71%) compared to boys (45%)."

Sharon Thompson's more recent study, *Going All the Way: Teenage Girls' Tales of Sex, Romance, and Pregnancy,* also agrees that this notion of "love" is causing girls a lot of trouble. The only reason these girls are so unhappy with all the casual sex they are supposed to be having is that they are still "condition[ing] sexual consent on romantic expectations." There is Deana, for instance, who "attribut[ed] enormous gravity to her romantic loss." The point being, of course, that one shouldn't attribute gravity to one's romantic loss.

Then "Tracy" was a girl so distraught over her first premarital sexual encounter that she vowed not to have sex until marriage: "until I'm sure that relationship means as much to him as it does to me and until it's positively proven that it does." Does Ms. Thompson support Tracy in her decision? No, she concludes that Tracy "had gone back . . . to the very same convictions that had set her up to become a victim of love in the first place." It's much better not to expect too much: "having serial expectations help[s]." For then you can never be disappointed. Liza, for instance, "did well. She had many lovers."

This view that pining for one's beloved is more properly understood as a problem to be cured is certainly not a new one. For Freud, the pressure of undischarged romantic expectation induced anxiety neurosis. But today's romantic girls are irritating the intellectuals for a different reason. A young girl tearful about a failed romance does not merit our sympathy, according to Ms. Thompson, for she is engaging in calculated "bids for sympathy and absolution based on assumptions about gender differences so conventional that whole genres turn on them." Specifically, "Even granting the [romantic] genre's dramatic conditions, and Tracy's wish to make a future out of love, her distress seems disproportionate." Without this inconvenient and clearly disproportionate distress, Tracy would be able to "play the field" like a good bad-girl should, and then this thing called "love" would not be her "downfall." For "the more a narrator took the romantic equation apart, in contrast, anticipated and understood pleasure," or "accepted love as ephemeral, the more likely she was to be realistic, even humorous, about romance."

And so, just as the ideal young woman would in 1631 progress from "Honour" to "Estimation," today the ideal young woman is expected to outgrow "Victim of Love" (Chapter One of Thompson's book), and spiral downward to "Playing the Field" (Chapter Two). If she is a particularly good bad-girl, she will learn to sink all the way to Chapter Three, "Infinite Possibilities of Doing: Sexual Opportunity and the Capitalized Self."

But wait: something is wrong. In the same book where she enjoins girls to outgrow their romantic hopes, Thompson concedes that "sex . . . for teenage girls . . . seems more dangerous than ever now." And, finds Peggy Orenstein, the bodily harm girls do to themselves just keeps getting worse. There is not only the usual gorging and purging, discussed in chapter five of her recent study of schoolgirls, but now also something called "delicate self-cutting," which is the disturbingly common practice among girls today of slicing themselves up with razors. Mary Pipher's book is crammed with examples of this practice, for instance:

> *Tammy [seventeen] came in after her mother [Alice] discovered her cutting her breasts. Alice had awakened around three and noticed a light on in Tammy's bedroom. She went in to check on her and found her sitting on the bed surrounded by bloody newspapers, a razor in her hand. Alice woke [her husband] Brian and they drove Tammy to the hospital. The doctor stitched up the deeper cuts and made an eight o'clock appointment for the family with me.*

In her interviews with Tammy, who used to make the honor roll every semester and was a twirler in the high school band, Dr. Pipher gradually uncovers why she came to mutilate herself in such a grotesque way. "Are you sexually involved with your boyfriend?" she asks her. Tammy "nodded miserably." Dr. Pipher presses: "How do you feel about that?" Tammy says: "I don't know," and then it all comes rushing out: "She spoke softly but rapidly. 'Martin's really into sex. This New Year's Eve, he had a party and rented porno videos for all the couples to watch. The guys liked it, but us girls were really embarrassed. We didn't want to watch.'"

In her first ten years as a therapist, Pipher continues, she never saw a client who mutilated herself. "Now it's a frequent initial complaint of teenage girls." The trend, she says, is "particularly disturbing because most young women who have this problem think they are the only ones." She ends by wondering: "What cultural changes have fostered the development of this widespread problem?"

To be sure, moralism about being good was annoying, but one put up with it because, it was thought, one was *supposed* to be good. But why all this moralism about being bad and "playing the field," particularly when it seems to be making our girls so miserable? Why, if our girls are so liberated, are we telling them that they don't really know their own minds? If they tell us they don't like casual sex, why do we tell them that they need to be having more of it?

As our reluctant reporters testify, we seem to have spawned a generation of girls whose thwarted feminine nature is reasserting itself in grotesquely distorted forms—in food hang-ups (that culturally acceptable way to create social distance), in self-mutilation (often, and poignantly, directed against the feminine, most unacceptable, parts of their bodies), or in charges of sexual harassment and date rape. Perhaps we're learning after thirty years of trying harder that a young woman's hopes are simply very hard to suppress. That the search for love cannot be so easily condescended to.

"Romantic love," wrote Kierkegaard, "presents an analogy to morality by reason of the presumptive eternity which ennobles it and saves it from being mere sensuality." So if we tell girls that they need to get over their romantic hopes, we shouldn't be surprised when they allow boys to treat them immorally. Or, as Kant put it, "sexual love makes of the loved person an object of appetite; as soon as one has the person and the appetite has been stilled, the person is cast aside as one casts away a lemon which has been sucked dry." Without love, sex "taken by itself . . . is a degradation of human nature," because the young woman, instead of being treated as an end in herself, is treated as an object. Instead of telling our girls that they are right to want to wait for love, we tell them that they are wrong. We are turning them into lemons which boys cast aside, and then everyone wonders why they are so sour.

We also encourage them to dress in a manner appropriate to their role.

**IMMODESTY IN DRESS**

A 23-year-old man told me his 15-year-old sister called him a few weeks earlier, wanting him to intercede on her behalf with their grandmother, who was "chewing her out for dressing like a slut." He said to her, "I'll have to side with her on that one," and she protested: "But I've stopped dressing like a slut at home. I don't *want* to dress like a slut. It's only when I go to school. *I have to. All* the girls in school dress like sluts."

Tammy, a blond mother in her mid-forties, told me, laughing, an almost identical story: "My daughter says she doesn't like wearing tight clothing all the time, but she says all the girls at school dress like that, so she's always saying 'Mom I *have* to!'" Parents with adolescent daughters or brothers with young sisters often talk about the "I *have* to" problem. If these girls wear clothes they are more comfortable with, they will stick out and will probably be ridiculed.

For many, it's the mothers themselves who are the ones to instruct their daughters in the ways of immodesty. As the lovely sixteen-year-old actress Natalie Portman glumly admitted to *W* magazine, "My mom was telling me the other day, 'I wish you were a little more outgoing with the way you dress." Yet as she explained to reporter Merle Ginsberg, she stubbornly refuses, to her mother's great irritation: "I [still] dress very conservatively— skirts to the knee, three-quarter-length sleeves, little coats."

Of course, talking about modesty or immodesty in dress is tricky because it's not clear that revealing clothing necessarily signifies immodesty. Take Hiram Powers's *Greek Slave* (1846), a great example of how a woman can be naked and still quite capable of preserving her modesty. Indeed, because her downcast gaze was said to indicate modesty but not shame, this naked slave was a real favorite among Protestant ministers of the time. Bathsheba's immodesty was typically conveyed by depicting her enjoying the spectators, particularly King David, at her bath. Many fifteenth century woodcuts show Bathsheba sometimes dressed and sometimes not. It was something entirely independent of dress, namely her desire for spectators, which betrayed her immodesty. Just like the naked woman in Manet's *Le Déjeuner sur l'Herbe* (1863), whose bold stare conspires with the viewer to *épater le bourgeois.*

"Many races that go absolutely naked possess a highly-developed sense of modesty," Havelock Ellis noted. For instance, there were the women of New Guinea who turned around if they noticed anyone was paying close attention to their bodies (they also refused to climb the fence to go to the "wild pig enclosure" when a man was present); there were the women of the Pelew Islands who had the right to punish men by fines or even death if they passed without permission while the women were bathing; there were the women of the South Sea Islands who refused the advances of explorers by saying simply, 'tirra-tane, I am married'; there were the Mandurucu women of Brazil who were very careful to avoid any "indecorous postures;" and there were

Greek Slave *by Hiram Powers, 1846. Courtesy of the Corcoran Gallery of Art, Washington, D.C.*

the Andamanese, whose "women are so modest that they will not renew their leaf-aprons in the presence of one another, but retire to a secluded spot for that purpose."

And in all of these societies, the women (and the men) were either totally naked or wore nothing more than a leaf apron, or in some cases, just a "triangular garment of skin suspended between the thighs." As long as there is "consciousness of perfect propriety alike in the subject and in the spectator," Ellis concludes, "nakedness is entirely compatible with the most scrupulous modesty." When subject and spectator do not agree, then there is trouble:

> *A. Duval, a pupil of Ingres, tells that a female model was once quietly posing, completely nude, at the École des Beaux Arts. Suddenly she screamed and ran to cover herself with her garments. She had seen a workman on the roof gazing inquisitively at her through a skylight.*

So it all depends on the context.

In Western societies modesty in dress will manifest itself differently from that among the Andamanese, and within Western society different things will be immodest at different times. But that doesn't mean we can't establish what immodesty in dress is. When a culture becomes immodest, it is immodest with respect to the conventions that have gone before.

We still draw our lines, and it is revealing where. Even a 1997 issue of *Cosmo* admits, "Yes, it is possible to look too sleazy. Does your skirt run up to your crotch when you sit down? Is your cleavage bouncing out of your blouse? On dates, avoid racy leather miniskirts and fishnets . . ."

Then in the *Irish Times,* Frances O'Rourke reports that "in a season of bare midriffs and short skirts, many parents worry that their daughters look too sexy for their own good":

> *Even fears for a child's safety are complicated by our modern feminist consciousness, our belief that women cannot be held responsible for sexual attack because of the clothes they wear. Modesty isn't a virtue kids see illustrated much on MTV: how do you explain that dressing a certain way can send out all the wrong signals, without appearing to have a dirty mind?*

We are concerned that if we discuss the correlation between immodest dress and street harassment, such a discussion will end up blaming the victim of the harassment. But it's not clear that this is the only conclusion to such a discussion. Many women report that when they dress extremely provocatively and step out on the street, they simply get too much unwanted attention. It feels oppressive, as if they are wading through a jungle. What should one make of this?

A feminist could argue persuasively that women should get to wear what they want, and that the problem is the boorish men. An economist could counter, perhaps somewhat less persuasively, that it's more efficient for one person to change her dress than to try to change all the boorish men in the world. Both answers have some truth to them. But there is one thing that complicates the question, and that is that even if construction workers did not behave like boors, many women would still be uncomfortable when too provocatively dressed. It feels "false" to them. Caroline Knapp writes,

> The world's absolute-worst dress was a scrunchy black minidress made of Lycra that looked like a long tube sock when you held it up in front of you. Julian saw it in a women's clothing store on Newbury Street shortly after we moved in together, and he took me to see it one weekend. "You'd look great in that," he said. I tried it on and came out of the dressing room feeling half naked, like I was wearing a small, slippery black towel.
>
> "I don't know . . . ," I said.
>
> "It looks great," he said.
>
> So I bought it. I wore it to a New Year's Eve party a few weeks later and I looked like a cheap imitation of a Victoria's Secret model. The dress had a wide scoop neck and long sleeves and if you stretched it way down it came to about mid-thigh, but it was made of really tight, elastic material so it kept riding up higher than that. I spent the whole night clutching my wineglass and tugging at the hem. . . . I stood there teetering on my black high heels and tugging at the damn hem and feeling exposed and if I hadn't had a lot to drink I probably would have burst into tears or lain down on the carpet and died of shame.

Author Jenna McCarthy becomes a "Slut for a Day"—that is, she is dared by one of her friends to dress up in a leather microskirt and an off-the-shoulder, skintight black T-shirt. At first she feels good about it, she reports in *Mademoiselle*, because she is "exercising her right" to look sexy. Then Miss McCarthy steps out of the house. First, at 9:30 A.M., she is offended by the guys who gape at her breasts. She thinks: *"They're just breasts, for God's sake. Don't you people get any cable-*

*access channels?"* Then at 9:45, a man on a loading dock says he would like to, as she puts it, "do something unmentionable." "Sick bastard," she thinks. At 4 P.M., she doesn't like the way a man is grunting at her at the laundromat, so she gives "him my best up-yours look." At 9 P.M., another man says something obscene to her at a pub, and then in a failed bid to peek up her skirt, he falls off his bar stool and knocks it over. As her article concludes:

> *I'm torn between feeling sorry for the schmuck and wanting to deck him. . . . Yes, it's a free country. Yes, I should be able to walk around in whatever I damn well please. But I practically have Sure Thing tattooed on my forehead. If I were just out to get laid, this is pretty much the getup I'd wear. How's he supposed to know the difference?*

Brenda Polan in the *Daily Mail* reaches a similar conclusion about the Wonderbra: "a good percentage of the recently purchased Wonderbras are gradually being eased towards the back of the drawer." Why? Many women, she writes,

> *confess that actually leaving the house with these proud protuberances aggressively to the fore is beyond them. One who did reflected that a woman likes to choose the occasions upon which her breasts become the centre of undivided attention. She likes to choose the payer of attention, too. And that rules out the bus queue in the rush hour. "I went all the way to work with my arms folded miserably across my chest," she remembered.*

Which brings us to a related problem.

### FEMALE SELF-CONSCIOUSNESS

I notice that whenever I'm in a car with women who are wearing extremely short skirts, what they say, nervously adjusting their skirts and desperately gripping my shoulders is, "Do I look OK? Do I look OK?" No amount of reassurance can satisfy them, because they feel at their very core exposed. "Do I look OK?! But are you *sure* I look OK?!" Louder, more plaintive this time. Of course you look OK, I say, you look more than just OK—you look *beautiful*. And they do look beautiful, and I wish I could give them something that would reassure them of that. Like their modesty back, for example.

So here, is the great irony: Modesty in dress, which today is considered evidence of being "hung up" about sex, actually permits women precisely not to be hung up about sex. It allows me to be taken seriously as a woman, without having to be desperate about it or on the other hand, having to pretend to be a man. It gives me the freedom to think about things other than *Do I look OK?!*

My purpose is not to suggest to provocatively dressed women that they need to cover up. That would be absurd. This book is for the woman who is forever asking herself in public "Do I look OK?" Who cannot think or talk of anything other than *"Do I look OK?"* There may be a very good reason she is asking this. Maybe this is a sign that she is presenting herself in a way that does violence to who she really is. Maybe her dress, in other words, is not in line with her hopes. If you are practically naked in front of people you hardly know, your self-consciousness might be your natural thermometer telling you that something is off.

Take the November 1995 *Cosmo,* for instance, where Carolynn Hillman instructs us on "Overcoming a Negative Body Image When You're Making Love." "Do you cower under the covers, insist on sex with the lights out? Time to toss off bedroom inhibitions, revel in *naked* passion!" Then there is *Cosmo* of March 1996: "Coping With Shame," by Pamela Margoshes, and my all-time favorite headline, from *Marie Claire* in October 1995: "Sex Hang-Ups Solved! Go From Neurotic To Erotic With These 8 Sensuous . . ." You get the picture. If so many women are this uncomfortable, well, instead of trying to fix them and chiding them to "get over" their discomfort, maybe we should be listening to them and taking their discomfort seriously. Maybe we should be asking why they are so uncomfortable.

As Kurt Riezler pointed out in 1943, "The further role shame plays between two sexual companions depends on love. Mutual love banishes shame. In a sexual intercourse that we imagine to be the mere satisfaction of a biological urge and without a tinge of love, shame insists on being present; without love, the companion becomes the observer."

Therefore, if so many women report that they cannot bear their lovers to even look at their naked bodies, if so many women regard their companions as their critical observers, then maybe this should tell us something. Nervous "Sandy" tells *Cosmopolitan:* "When I'm with someone for the first time or just getting to know him, I'm very self-conscious in bed. I'm sure he's going to bolt when he sees my cellulite."

Why in the world does she feel she has to go to bed with someone who makes her feel so uncomfortable?

Trying to pretend that we are perfectly comfortable in situations where we are clearly not only makes things worse. And nowhere is this clearer than in the case of adultery.

### INFIDELITY

*The New York Times* informs us that "TV has turned more realistic in its depiction of adultery, making a pessimistic comment on marriage." Reporter Caryn James has found that "the infidelity cuts across sexual lines: the married Greg Medavoy and the single Donna Abandando on 'N.Y.P.D. Blue,' or the married Jeanie Boulet and the single Peter Benton on 'E.R.' In those high-profile plots from recent seasons, all four characters were depicted as realistically flawed people who made understandable mistakes." As our reporter concludes: "This is a great improvement over the days when television defied reality and insisted that marriage was a constant state of unblemished monogamy." So she ends simply by gushing in admiration, "Where did all these grown-ups suddenly come from?"

Where did all these *grown-ups* come from? Yes, in case you missed it, having an extramarital affair is now a sign of maturity. TV used to be afraid of even hinting at sex between husband and wife—Dick VanDyke and his wife slept in separate beds, you'll recall—but nowadays it's the faithful couples who are looked upon as oddly childish.

Dr. Annette Lawson's 1988 study *Adultery* reported that 78% of British husbands had committed adultery, and a similar proportion in the United States (up from 47% in 1965). Lest anyone think that the increase is anyone's fault in particular, we learned from *Time* magazine in 1994 that it's actually the genes that are doing all the cheating: "Infidelity: It May Be In Our Genes," as Robert Wright put it. But whatever the cause, it doesn't matter anyway since luckily, "Affairs can support a marriage," as Chicago-based sex and marital therapist Jennifer Knopf explains in a 1997 issue of *Elle*. Cheating is not only acceptable, but equal-opportunity, too: in the same year, *Glamour* applauded that "women are cheating, and not feeling guilty."

The somewhat less than cheery side of this advice can be observed usually in the very same magazines. Over 1996, Kelly Squires in *The Complete Woman* teaches us a variety of different techniques to "Spy on Your Man." First, we are told how to sift through "The Magnum P.I. Wanna-Be" and hire the best private detective. If you cannot afford this, her "guide for anyone who suspects a partner is cheating" also includes some less expensive tips, such as being on the lookout for new-fangled sexual positions or a quirky diet and exercise plan. One must be ever-vigilant. It all sounds very tiring. And it's also confusing, because if marriages are so improved by infidelity, then why is all this secrecy necessary? Why not just ask, Honey, have you been trying to improve our marriage lately?

Half of the articles in women's magazines are devoted to advising the reader on what to do when your "significant other" doesn't want to commit, how to spy on him after he commits, what to do if he isn't faithful, and so on. Then the other half of the articles are devoted to How to Seduce a Married Man. Odd, but I think I understand the theory: We're not supposed to be little wives-in-training, because that's sexist. Instead we're all supposed to be little adulteresses-in-training, which to me is much more insulting.

Helen Gurley Brown encourages us to keep "a married man or two"—not to fall in love with them, mind you, "just keep them as pets." As she explains in a recent interview, "I do not feel that marriage is a sacrament between a man and a woman." Then in the same breath, she stresses the importance of being "very good in bed . . . being so enjoyable that [your lover] will never want to leave you—making him so happy in bed, making him think that there's nobody in the world like you." To me this philosophy just seems desperate and sad. Instead of living with constant anxiety in one's own life, and spoiling other people's lives, wouldn't it be far easier if we simply did *not* keep married men as pets?

If women want men to stop behaving badly, to be faithful and devoted to us, we are going to have to leave off How to Seduce a Married Man. When men are unfaithful, they are unfaithful, usually, with other women. That is why, as Laura Gowing points out, women were responsible for maintaining some degree of opprobrium against adultery: they did so not because they were evil or deluded or wanted to oppress other women, but simply to preserve the sanctity of their own marriages.

Essentially, feminists hope to change the behavior of men without the women having to change. That will never happen. They want the men to be gentlemen without having to be ladies. Conservatives, mostly men, for their part, want the women to be ladies while still getting to do whatever they want, and clucking "boys will be boys." That will never happen, either. Everybody wants the other guy to change and to be nice to him, without having to change his own behavior. If women want the men to be good, they have to want to be good too. If men want women to be ladies, they have to start acting honorably.

So this is the terrain so far. Girls who can't say no, anorexic girls, girls who are mutilating their bodies, girls who are stalked or raped, many who never see their fathers—and from the Left, the advice we get is, "Whatever you do, don't be romantic," and from the Right, "Whatever you do, don't become a feminist." Meanwhile, we're not allowed to ask any questions—not any really important ones, that is.

### FORBIDDEN QUESTIONS

A writer calls me on January 12, 1998, to warn me that I'm "going to get into a lot of trouble when this book comes out next year." I ask, "Why?" "I'm telling you this as your friend," he says. "The world is cruel. Everyone is going to make fun of you." I remind him that he hasn't even read my book. He replies, "But you've told me about some of the things you want to discuss, and certain things, well, you're not supposed to talk about . . ."

There are certain things we are not supposed to talk about these days. Take Holly, the college sophomore who is featured naked in a 1998 *Playboy* spread: "Ever since I was a kid looking at my dad's *Playboy*s, I've wanted to Playmate," she gushes in the caption below, "But when I told him that I was Miss April he got very upset. I said, 'But Dad, I got the idea from you!' He's OK with it now and of course, I'm ecstatic."

The fact that we *can* pose for *Playboy* doesn't tell us if we *should,* and it doesn't explain why we might not like our daughters to pose for *Playboy.* Yet if anyone asks us to articulate why, we cringe.

What kind of women do we want to become? And, for that matter, what kind of men do we want to become? These are not questions you're supposed to ask nowadays, and certainly with good reason. In a free society, nobody wants to interfere with anyone's business. Being told how to conduct one's personal life is extremely irritating. So everybody wants everybody to be able to do everything, to be whatever they want to be, with whomever they want. The interesting thing, however, is that in our own lives we usually cannot be every kind of woman or every kind of man—we usually have to make a choice. We have to decide what to do in this particular car, bedroom, or hotel, with this particular person, at this particular time.

Our well-justified fear of interfering in other people's business has resulted in a sad, and little-remarked-upon reality: that a girl, when she is making this choice—when she is deciding what kind of woman she will become and how to handle the men who appear in her life—can expect virtually no guidance. She will be utterly alone when it comes to what may be the question of utmost importance in her life. And when it comes to teaching the boys how to treat women, they for the most part will be left alone, too.

In his 1995 book *The Stalking of Kristin,* George Lardner recounts the horrible story of how his beautiful daughter Kristin was stalked and eventually murdered by her ex-lover, Michael Cartier. She was a 21-year-old art student, he a troubled and jealous bouncer at a club. Her father, an investigative reporter at the *Washington Post,* recounts all the restraining orders that were filed and tells how the justice system failed his daughter. It's a powerful story because, as it turns out, this man who shot Kristin three times in the head had a criminal record. Cartier should have been in jail at the time he killed Kristin. He was violating another restraining order at the same time and the police did nothing.

Yet another story emerges from this book, a story which to me is even sadder than any police captain's bungling. Her father was always proud of the way his daughter "was rebelling against being a girl, or at least against what society still expects of 'a young lady.' Kristin didn't want to be 'sweet,' or quiet or submissive." This is certainly admirable, but it also meant that when she told her friend Kevin that a man was beating her up, she would never admit that she was afraid. Her father recounts this anecdote approvingly: "Her mother and I can attest to [her not being afraid]. We wanted all the children to be independent minded, to think for themselves." When Kristin called home and confessed to Mom and Dad that there was a man in her life who had killed her cat, they advised her to get rid of him. Then she told her brother, who also advised her to get rid of him—but nothing more. Then she told her friend Brian that Cartier repeatedly kicked her in the head and legs, and threatened to kill her, and he too did nothing. When gently questioned by her mother, Rosemary, why she was putting up with this man, Kristin replied that "she wanted to have a boyfriend, 'just like everyone else does.'"

In our well-intentioned effort to keep our daughters "independent-minded," we have grown too afraid to give them any advice, to step in on their behalf. I think the death of Kristin Lardner is not just the fault of some police department in Massachusetts—it should weigh on all of our consciences. The justice system can only do so much. In any given month, typically four or five articles on stalking appear in the women's magazines. How to protect yourself against stalkers, how to file restraining orders with the police, what to do when the restraining order is violated, and so forth. The tragedy of stalking, we are learning, is that there is so little the police can do about it. On the cover of a typical issue of *Glamour* screams the headline: "STALKED! WHY THE NEW LAWS WON'T PROTECT YOU."

We are finding out, essentially, that the kind of men we raise matters very much.

Kristin Lardner and others like her are the casualties of a very specific and sickening silence, the cost of maintaining a very peculiar sensibility. If we admitted that women can be physically more vulnerable than men, that would be sexist and compromise their independence. So what should we do? Should we step in, and risk being called sexist, or should we respect their independence and risk their death? Too often these days, we seem more afraid of being called sexist than we are afraid of a woman's death. Yet in the end, which is really more "subordinating" for a woman—a little advice, a friend stepping in on her behalf—or being raped or killed?

On April 11, 1996, 7-year-old Jessica Dubroff took off during a driving sleet storm, trying to fulfill her parents' dream that she become the youngest pilot ever to complete a cross country flight. "Never mind the fact that she can't reach some of the cockpit pedals—she's in the driver's seat anyhow!" trilled CNN's anchorman, Martin Savidge. "Now the 7-year-old girl from Pescadero, California, is taking her independent spirit to the sky," gushed the *San Francisco Examiner*'s Eve Mitchell. This stunt came to a predictably tragic end when Jessica took off at too sharp an angle, the plane stalled and took a sickening dive. Mother Lisa Hathaway said her daughter "had a freedom which you can't get by holding her back." Jane Pauley agreed: Jessica may have "lost her life, but she'd had her freedom."

Her freedom to . . . what? Since we know that the trip was Jessica's father's idea, and the decision never to teach "negative words" such as "risk" or "danger" her mother's, it wasn't exactly Jessica's decision to make. Still, even if it had been, a 7-year-old cannot understand the significance of this tradeoff. It is up to her parents, and all of society, to protect her from making just such a choice.

But we don't protect our girls anymore. "Cayenne," a 15-year-old girl who is suffering from herpes, blames her parents for not "keeping her safe." But we don't really believe in keeping girls safe anymore. We believe that their independence is more important.

They are not even girls anymore—they are *women*. They are women and already "independent" at age 7. As Jessica Dubroff's cap read: "Women Fly." If her cap had read instead "Little Girls Fly," perhaps the media would not have been so eager to rubber stamp her mission.

But there wasn't time to reflect, because it was on to the next casualty. Now on the covers of all the magazines was little Jon-Benet Ramsey, a baby wearing the painted heavy caked-on make-up of an aging starlet. Before she died a mysterious death at age 6, her parents liberated her by stuffing her into tight, provocative outfits.

After the JonBenet Ramsey killing, many who were not aware of the "beauty queen" industry for toddlers were genuinely disgusted and shocked. Yet almost all of our department stores peddle see-through white tops for girls as young as age five, and nobody says a thing about that. Fashion is fashion. People should be able to wear whatever they want to wear, dress their children however they want. *De gustibus et coloribus non disputandum,* one should not argue about tastes and colors.

But are tastes and colors really just tastes and colors? Sometimes, as in the JonBenet Ramsey killing, the tastes and the colors are so disconcerting that they become allegorical. The dangers besetting girls have grown steadily more extreme, the situations we force them to endure ever more ridiculous, and still we dare not ask the questions we are not permitted to ask.

Maybe it's time to give the advice we are not supposed to give, to ask exactly the questions we are not permitted to ask. What, if anything, do we want to protect our daughters from? When is it too much, too soon? What does it say about *Playboy* that its regular readers are horrified at the thought that their own daughters would appear there? What kind of men do we want to raise our sons to be? Why, after years of telling men what to do, does the behavior of our men seem worse than ever? How do we make our choices, in love and in life, and how are the sexes' choices related to one another? Are they related at all? What does our society value most in women, and what in men? Is what we do value in line with what we should value?

These questions seem to be inadmissible these days. If you ask them, you'll get into trouble. As that friend of mine warned me: *"Everyone will make fun of you."* But if you add up all the women, and all the men, and all the stalkers, and all the rapists, and all the prostitutes, and all the adulterers and adulteresses, and all the bedrooms, and all the hotels, and all the marriages, and all the children, and all the divorces, and all the paths taken and not taken, some of which can never be retraced, then it seems to me that the question of what kind of women, and what kind of men, we become is a pretty important question, even if it is an admittedly risky one.

"I'm so determined that I meet a man," confesses actress Alicia Silverstone to *Premier* magazine. Then she immediately corrects herself: "Um, a person," she means. As she continues, apologetically, "I say man because I'm attracted to men—but it could be a woman, for all that matters."

We are privately "determined," and in public we pretend it all doesn't "matter." In private we know exactly why these things are important to us, but to others we must be cavalier.

There is such a disparity between what is really important to us and what we are permitted to discuss, that each one of us has become a kind of closet anthropologist in his own tribe. We don't have to travel to a distant land any longer to peer out of our window and wonder, is it just me?

"Are You Normal?" runs a headline in *Women's Own* magazine. We'll never know what's normal until we resume talking publicly about the things that are important to us privately. Until we start asking a few of these questions we are not supposed to ask. How does a woman decide whether she will live with her boyfriend? That's between a woman and her boyfriend, we're told. How does a girl of 13 decide if she should go on the Pill? That's between a woman and her doctor. Privacy is privacy.

So because it's nobody's business, because we're not allowed to discuss what goes into such a decision, she will decide it all on her own. Better that some girls are harmed, rather than discuss the things we're not supposed to discuss.

Don't you ever wonder why, if we live in such liberated times, we have all of these doors so tightly shut?

Don't you find it curious that, on the one hand, everyone seems to agree that things are not right, and how, on the other, we have all of these doors so tightly shut? Don't you ever wonder, if we peeked behind the right door, whether we might be able to flip everything around?

Female modesty is one of those ideas we are not supposed to entertain seriously anymore, one of those taboo subjects, one of those locked doors. Perhaps it seems threatening because it doesn't just ask the question, "what kind of women do we want to become?"—it provides a very specific answer. And maybe, just maybe, modesty is the answer which could, with all due modesty, flip everything around.

Part Two

# THE

# FORGOTTEN

# IDEAL

# Chapter 5

# FORGIVING MODESTY

*I have two teenage sons, and I'm married to a man who is very comfortable with nudity, very comfortable in bikini briefs—this is real embarrassing! And he feels that it's O.K. to walk around in front of our sons with me being in the room? I find that very embarrassing. I'm a very modest person!*

—ANGUISHED CALLER ON THE "SONYA LIVE" SHOW, DECEMBER 17, 1993

There are two very different kinds of modesty, of course. There is, first, modesty in the sense of being humble. We say that monks who lead an ascetic existence lead a "modest life," or that the person who says he doesn't deserve a compliment is being "too modest." Then there is sexual modesty, the kind we associate with the Medicean Venus or a Muslim woman's *chador*. The French have two words to keep them straight: *modestie* is the humble kind, and *pudeur* the sexual kind. There are also two words for the virtue in Latin: *modestia* means a respect for decency, restraint (the opposite of *superbia,* or haughtiness), and *pudor* refers to a consciousness of what is decent regarding sexual behavior or dress. And the ancient Greeks? Not only did they have *sophrosyne* for self-restraint and *hagneia* to refer to a concern with purity or chastity—that one popped up often on the Stoic lists of virtues or good emotions— but there was also *aischunē* for the shame in dishonoring man-made codes and *aidōs* for shame or awe in sexual matters.

We have only one word, which at first seems like we have less fun because we have fewer toys to play with, or that we aren't as clever because we're not capable of making such fine distinctions as the French or the Greeks. Yet having one word has its advantages: it underscores what the two kinds of modesty have in common and leaves open the question of how they might be related.

My dictionary defines the humble kind of modesty as "having moderate estimation of one's abilities or worth," and the sexual kind as "the damping down of one's allure." My inquiry is concerned mostly with the latter kind because that's the one I think has been seriously misunderstood, even by the experts who write our dictionaries.

Why did so many women dress modestly for thousands of years if this is all modesty is about? What woman wants to damp down her allure?

If you think that women are basically stupid creatures, then you can easily accept this definition because it means that for thousands of years women were behaving and dressing in ways that made them unappealing, and they are so dim, they didn't realize it until very recently. If you accept this definition, then you assume that for 99% of world history, the basic drama with women was this:

> "Hey, you over there—woman!"
> "Yes, my lord?"
> "Damp down your allure over there! You've got too much allure going on over there!"
> "Okay, I'm damping, I'm damping, my lord! Please don't hit me!"

But if you think that women are smart, then you know that there has to be more to the story of modesty than this. If you give women credit for being intelligent creatures, you trust them and assume that they wouldn't have put up with dressing and acting in a certain way for so many thousands of years unless it had some meaning for them. Exactly what, though? That is what I've been trying to figure out for a long time.

### THE RETURN OF THE REPRESSED

When I asked the prepubescent girl I babysit for what she thought of modesty, she offered, exuberantly, "Modesty? I know what you mean. That's like that 'You-Ain't-Never-Gonna-Get-it' song, right?"

Well, not quite. It's much more like "Come, Kate, we'll to bed," as Petruchio says at the end of *Taming of the Shrew.* Modesty isn't about snubbing men, but about postponing sexual pleasure until the time is right. When it *is* right, female modesty is more like, "Come, *Petruchio,* we'll to bed."

How do you know when it's time to forgive an old friend? Perhaps you are reminded of her by the daily problems you face, when you remember how she would minister to you. Suppose for a moment, though, that your parting was so horrid you can't even bear to think about this person, much less speak her name. In such cases is reconciliation even possible?

Modesty is like that lost friend. Though as a culture we have officially excommunicated the idea, it is still here, though we may call it by a different name. We are, for example, consumed by solving what we deem the "self-esteem problems" of teenage girls. At a certain age we find they start to get a bit shy around boys, but today we chalk it up to sexism.

"Kate" and "Joe" on a recent "Love Connection" dating show proclaim themselves "comfortable with their bodies." So naturally on their first blind date Kate arranges for—what else?—a double massage. Joe enjoys it, but Kate tells us she was "mortified," and also that "he saw much more of my body than I would have liked." She even disapproved of the way Joe breathed while he was getting his massage—too heavily, it turns out.

Channel-surf around the talk shows, whose life's blood is a veritable circus of immodesty, and you will find that even the proudest exhibitionists are not free of modesty's natural claim. "Marilyn" is proudly hosting a show on women who hire male prostitutes, and excitedly asks her guest what a male prostitute will do for her that nonpayers won't. The woman smiles. She's on national TV! She very excitedly begins to boast of her exploits, but suddenly her voice catches and she becomes unhelpfully vague: "We just do, I dunno . . . *stuff.*" Marilyn giggles sympathetically and tries again, more conspiratorially, "No, but I mean *what* do you do?" The woman turns bright pink. She knows this was why she was brought here, and yet she can't go through with it—only keeps repeating numbly, "I dunno, you know . . . *stuff.*" Who would have thought a woman who hires an escort would get an inconvenient attack of modesty just when she makes her national debut? As the woman shifts uncomfortably in her seat, you can see Marilyn growing more irritated—for *this* she flew the woman here, and bought her a free hotel room? Her smile freezes as her eyes calculate the drop in ratings.

To begin to understand where modesty has gone we must start with this, our frustration with modesty when it does—in spite of everything—manage to surface. A woman who is suddenly shy or wants to cover up is taken as a standing rebuke to some of the most treasured sympathies of our age. She "just doesn't get it," is in need of a lesson or two, for she has committed what is for modern woman the cardinal sin: not being *comfortable with her body*. This charge is the way our guardians of the status quo pre-empt any genuine discussion of female modesty. I first discovered this in my freshman year at college when I told my dormmates that I didn't much care for the idea of sharing a bathroom with male students. Immediately one girl smiled condescendingly and wrapped her arm around my shoulder, explaining that she, too, once thought she wouldn't like coed bathrooms, but then "I became *comfortable* with my body." So would I someday learn to put away childish things.

It is the perfect *ad hominem* attack: targeted well enough to sig-nal that this sort of thing is no longer discussed in polite society, but also clean and neat, hiding under the guise of concern for your interlocutor's psychological well-being. Anything you say will only harden the boundaries of the tautology. Smug sympathy usually follows.

"But, I *am* comfortable with my body!" you may protest. "I am just not comfortable with strange men seeing me coming out of the shower," you may sputter. Until you realize that the more you speak, the more evidence you're offering for the sad fact of your benightedness. You feel the sting, and though you don't quite know what hit you, your instinct is to retreat. There is nothing more to say, and the discussion is over before it began.

In the wake of a sustained attack on modesty—which has found its full flowering in our age, but which is actually more than two centuries old—a strange thing has happened. In elite circles, one is discouraged from even discussing the notion seri-ously. I learned this during a philosophy class at college, sopho-more year, when we were discussing Luce Irigaray's *Ethics of Sexual Difference*. The class was having a lively discussion, which is to say, everyone was nodding and agreeing with what everyone else said. Yes, woman was "place" and man was "not-place." Yes, "mucus should no doubt be pictured as related to the angel," as Irigaray puts it. Yes, yes, this was a defining work of post-Kantian philosophy.

Well, after about a half an hour of placing, not-placing, and angel-mucus, I had to admit that I just didn't get it. All these post-Kantian gender theorists wanted to construct ethics of sexual dif-ference, but they never talked about *real* sexual differences, the biological ones. Why? If they didn't want to talk about sex differ-ences, that's fine, but why write books about differences and then proceed to ignore the most basic ones? It was like some kind of joke. So I blurted out, "If you want an ethics of sexual difference, let's talk about Rousseau's *Emile*. In the fifth book you've got Sophie—she's modestly waiting for her beloved and collecting flowers; you've got Emile going around performing charity work to prove his worth because Sophie rules over him; and after Sophie collects enough flowers, and Emile swears he won't masturbate, they marry and seem quite contented. True, in the sequel, *Emile et Sophie*, Emile abandons Sophie after she is seduced by a mean Parisian fellow and that is somewhat less poetic, but one can still find the fifth book of *Emile* very compelling. No wonder the novel was one of the most influential works of its time. Now *there's* an education in the ethics of sexual difference."

The class was silent. That's when I learned that I was an *essentialist*. I didn't know what that was, but it sounded delicious. What is an essentialist? I asked my classmates. "It's someone who believes that there are differences between the sexes," they explained. But aren't there? *"No,"* they chorused, quite firmly. The earnest boy behind me tried to help me out, clarifying that "the whole point is that we're supposed to try to *transcend* essentialism." But even if I wanted to transcend essentialism, I asked them, shouldn't we first find out what the differences are, so we know what we're supposed to be transcending? No, even to mention "real differences" is itself essentialist, no matter what your intention is.

I did some research after this class, and my classmates were right. Robert S. McElavaine defines "essentialism" as the "heresy" that "there are biological differences between males and females." Judith Butler from Johns Hopkins University, another well-regarded "antiessentialist," criticizes "feminists" for even claiming to support the "fictive" category called "women."

So there was nothing more to say. I was chastened. I was an essentialist, and that wasn't allowed. It was as if the class had accused me of being racist. No one entertained my view, no one wanted to talk about Rousseau, they just rolled their eyes. So I was quiet, while the rest of the class chatted happily on about "place" and "not-place." Then we saw a film about Simone de Beauvoir, who was, of course, "place," but her sweetheart, Jean-Paul Sartre, though he was "not-place," was placing his not-place-ness in way too many places, which must have made her feel quite displaced.

At any rate, the really interesting thing that happened that day was not during class, but after it, when my professor took me aside and said, bemused, that if *his* daughter came home from college and proposed to take the fifth book of the *Emile* seriously, he would be just *horrified*. He grew up in the sixties, he explained, smiling. So I asked him, would he be equally horrified if his daughter returned from sex-education class prepared to embark upon a life of promiscuity? He said, that's different, and I walked back to my dormroom very confused.

I never intended to take the fifth book of Rousseau's *Emile* seriously. My father is a free-market economist, so as far as I knew Rousseau was tainted because he was that socialist fellow. But as soon as someone told me that I couldn't take him seriously, I began to wonder, What is so horrifying about a little female modesty? Why were those in charge so threatened by the idea? There it was, the *Emile,* right across the room. I had only to pick it up and try it. I felt the way someone in the sixties must have felt upon suddenly discovering a free bag of LSD in their room. No one else was looking. I would reread the fifth book and try to keep my mind open.

Could this be true?

Could female modesty be natural?

And was Rousseau right that the best sex education for women was an education in the ways of modesty?

The more I thought about how my male professor understood that I took the *Emile* to be a kind of ideal, and found that laughable, the more I came to feel that there was a certain misogyny behind the sexual revolution. Yes, dear, you can be a bitch, you can be a slut, you can sleep around as much as you want, and you can pretend to be a man, but you're not allowed to be *this*. He grew up in the sixties. Inspire him? I had to be kidding.

But surely modesty must get a fairer hearing outside the academy? Actually, no. Pick up the October 1996 issue of *Harper's Bazaar* and find, eerily, an almost identical exchange to the one that took place in my college dormitory. Two women write in because they were offended by the August cover, which featured a model wearing a see-through blouse and no bra. Both letters demand immediate cancellations of subscriptions. One writes that an exposed breast and nipple is just too "outrageous" to be on the cover, another wonders simply, "What happened to elegance and glamour?" No matter that one of these women has subscribed to

*Bazaar* since the 1950s; the editors feel no need to condescend to engage her point, which they dub "Nipple Ripple":

> *The barely revealed breast on our August cover wasn't meant to offend. It was meant to celebrate the beauty of the female form.* Bazaar *believes that women should feel* comfortable *with their bodies [my emphasis], and toward that end we've printed "Breasts: An Owner's Manual," on page 272. Nipple-watchers beware: It's an eyeful. October is National Breast Cancer Awareness Month: we sincerely hope that all our readers will take a good, long, unembarrassed look.*

So if you do not like seeing nipples on covers of national magazines, the solution is to bombard yourself with a greater number of such images until you are numbed to their power. The letter writer's question about mystery and elegance is never addressed. Presumably a desire for it is something one outgrows. Notice that if you object to their cover because you buy fashion magazines for "elegance and glamour," you are not simply mistaken: there is something fundamentally wrong with you. The clever twist here on physical—not merely psychological—health is truly the touch of a master, for it suggests that the letter writers hold not merely unnatural views beyond considered judgment, but potentially life-threatening ones.

Is modesty really so toxic?

In the April 1997 journal of *Ethics,* the philosopher G. F. Schueler penned an article on modesty, and discusses why the sort of modesty we associate with humility could be a virtue. It's an engaging article, but curiously, sexual modesty is relegated to a footnote at the bottom of the page: "There is also," he notes, "the use of 'modesty' in which, e.g., someone who refuses to wear skimpy swimming suits is said to be modest. This use of 'modest' will be discussed below." Then when you get to the "below" part, near the end of his article, he says only this: "At the same time it is hard to see that a desire to deflect attention from oneself (i.e., shyness) by itself would be a virtue."

How has it come to pass that sexual modesty, what many thinkers once did think was a virtue, what for most of recorded history was thought to be a virtue, could be totally dismissed in a major philosophical journal? Equated with mere "shyness" and tossed aside? It's not G. F. Schueler's fault. Among intellectuals, sexual modesty is simply *verboten*. Nobody, if they want to be taken seriously in academic circles, is allowed to take the idea of sexual modesty seriously.

Fortunately, Dorothy, we're not in academia anymore.

### THE ARMOR OF HOPE

I begin my little philosophical reconstruction not with the philosophers, but with the women themselves. At a party I went to, a recently married 29-year-old woman told me: "I slept with four men before I was married, but now that I am, I wish my husband was the only one. Once you meet someone you really love the other ones don't mean a thing, and then you're sort of disgusted by them." I've never heard a woman regret too little sexual experience, but I often hear women regret too much.

A 1998 issue of *Glamour* reports that 49% of women wish they had slept with fewer men, compared with 7% who wish they had slept with more men and 44% who are happy with their number as it is. Those who were happiest were generally those who, like Nina, 30, had one partner—her husband: "I honestly feel sorry for women who haven't experienced the thrill of having only their spouse as a sexual partner." As for the majority of women who were unhappy with their sexual experiences, they were for the most part like Ellen, 29, who said: "I wish I hadn't given so much of myself—I feel that some of my experiences thinned my soul, and such an effect takes time to undo." She had 23 partners. The response to this article was tremendous: a 21-year-old woman from Montreal wrote in that she had 17 lovers; the reason was that she was really "looking for comfort in my first year of college." A woman from Providence, Rhode Island, with four new partners in the last five months was "worried I was losing my real self." Another woman, from Bowie, Maryland, wrote that "between my two marriages, I slept with 20 men; now I'm infertile, and my health-care provider and I suspect I may have had chlamydia." She wishes, she writes, that she'd had "a little less independence and a lot more peace of mind."

Here's another puzzle to add to our soup: David Buss and David Schmitt's 1994 sex survey found that men say they would sleep with a woman after knowing her only a week, while women report that they would need at least several months. What's more, while men projected that they would ideally like 6 sex partners over the next year, and 8 over the next two years, women responded that their ideal would be to have only one partner over the next year. And over two years? The answer, for women, was still one.

The first thing sexual modesty seems to protect is a certain vulnerability. Today girls are generally brought up to assume that they have no special vulnerability, because that would be sexist. Our cultural coaches drill into our heads sayings like "Equality means equally bad as well as equally good." Being as promiscuous as any man is taken to be a badge of one's liberation. But why, then, do so many young women end up sounding like victims today? Though now it is considered "sexist" to admit that women are naturally more vulnerable in any way, it seems it is precisely denying a woman's special vulnerability and stripping her of her natural way of compensating for it that is the height of true misogyny. The impression one gets from touring the sad pictures of my college's Clothesline Project—where women hung up T-shirts that read, "I Hate You!" and "Don't Touch Me Again"—is that these women, far from being equal, seem at men's mercy. Women had a special vulnerability in the past, we are told, only because there was a risk of pregnancy. Now that we have the Pill, all vulnerability is abolished. But we seem to be learning that there is more to sexual vulnerability than the risk of pregnancy.

Kate Potter, 25, a respondent featured in a 1997 issue of *Marie Claire,* is touted as the most sophisticated of those interviewed. *Marie Claire* introduces her as "a production assistant who has one-night stands." The woman elaborates,

> *I made love last night. I met a guy at a concert who knows a friend of mine. I finally approached him. I asked if he wanted to hang out after the concert, and we drove back to his hotel. We were all over each other at every traffic light. We planned to have drinks once we got to the hotel, but we were naked by the time room service arrived. . . . The biggest plus of casual sex is that you get rid of sexual frustration. The worst thing is that there's no guarantee you'll see the person again. I try to be as detached as men are, but it doesn't always work that way.*

She tries "to be as detached as men are" because she has been told that being the same is proof of her equality, but since she finds it hard to be detached, her one-night stands only leave her feeling more vulnerable than before: "There's no guarantee you'll see the person again."

Even the most enthusiastic pro–casual sex articles are not immune from such outbreaks of vulnerability. A gushing article,

"Women Who Have Sex with Lots of Men," in *SexLife* magazine, for example, reports admiringly of our "more freewheeling sisters": "Some women really do want that guy with the perfect triceps and the endearingly dumb stare to take them home, lick them all over like a lollipop and disappear the moment the passion is over. These women can enjoy sex for sex's sake even when there's no romantic backdrop, no promise of love or talk of commitment."

One can only say *mazel tov* to all of these remarkable women. How brave and strong they must be, to be so cool that they need "no romantic backdrop." And then on top of that, it just so happens that they long most for the men "to disappear the moment the passion is over"? Well, how convenient for them that they are made this way. Just think: in case men actually *do* disappear the moment the passion is over, they will then have had their greatest fantasy fulfilled. I read on, to learn how I can become like this admirable breed of tough lollipops, but unfortunately the author of the piece just can't seem to find enough women who fit into this category. Soon we are hearing stories only of women who once tried casual sex, and were disappointed. "Even women who enjoy casual sex can go through periods where they feel let down by it. At 21, Candace had just broken up with her first love. Shortly thereafter, she had her first experiences sleeping with men she didn't know. 'It was a random process. We'd be the last two people at a party, and all of a sudden we'd be in bed together,' she says. 'I wasn't doing it for the right reasons,' she says. 'I thought I'd get a boyfriend.'"

Then we meet "Michelle," who "also had sex for the wrong reasons after she lost her virginity at the age of 16." Next, there is "Peggy," who "ultimately called a halt to her casual sexual encounters" after being hurt by someone named "Victor."

Well, so much for our "more freewheeling sisters." We really want to believe that there are all these women who enjoy "sex for sex's sake" because it's consistent with our androgynous project, but the stories of real women's lives keep intruding and stubbornly pointing to a different reality. I don't see how we do young women any service by ignoring it. It seems to me that we only create situations where they can be hurt more often.

The younger the girl, the more obvious this sexual vulnerability. My sophomore year in college I tutored a seventh-grader whose appearance was very jarring: tight jeans; nose ring; stringy, dirty blond hair; and heavy caked-on makeup. Yet she had an innate gentleness, and was forever reassuring me "I'm fine, I guess." She wrote me a letter on blue-lined stationery notifying me that "My boy friend dumped me and I'm feelen a little upset now. But I'll be fine, I guess."

Why do young women today feel the need to hide their vulnerability? Why do they pretend they're tough when they're not? Why do they say they're "fine" when they're not? Why was Kristin Lardner so ashamed to admit that she was afraid of her ex-boyfriend? And why did everyone around her admire her "independence" instead of confronting the jerk who was stalking her?

In the tale of Pandora's Box, hope is the one thing that "remained within." This is a fitting allegory for our present dilemma. Perhaps we flee from discussion of feminine vulnerability because we are afraid it will lead to a dead end—to victimization, nothing more. But if we could allow ourselves to consider for a moment a young woman's hopes, it is also possible that we might make their fulfillment more likely by being honest. Then we could protect these hopes instead of barking at girls to suppress them. And maybe, as with Pandora's Box, hope is the one thing that still "remains within," and if we listen to it we might be in a better position to get some of our other problems back in the box.

It's always hard to separate what you really want from what you're supposed to want, but try it as a thought experiment. Women, when no one else is around, do you secretly long for a whole series of men; to arbitrarily marry one of them and then maybe have affairs, maybe not—to be cool and wait and see if anyone better comes along, and then divorce—or do you long for one enduring love? That's a loaded question, but still, if you could be guaranteed that no one would laugh at you, would it be the latter? If your answer is yes, why do you allow your culture to shatter your hopes? Why is it that you feel so dictated to, when you were supposed to be, above all, independent?

Nowadays, if a young woman loves a man, she is a pathetic loser. Donald Kratz, a 25-year-old software developer in Boston, complains to *Cosmo* that his girlfriend is starting to say "things like 'If we ever broke up, I don't know what I'd do' or 'I waited all last night for the phone to ring, and you never called.' She's sweet about it, but sometimes I wonder if she's stable." *Cosmo* hurriedly marshals the expert opinion of Judy Seifer, Ph.D., president of the American Association of Sex Educators, Counselors, and Therapists, who cheerily warns women, "to avoid sounding unbalanced, keep your expectations in check. Realize that this wonderful man

had a very full life before he met you and that this life will continue. Yes, you're a part of it, but you're not the only part of it. . . .
Show him that you're an independent person. . . ."

Be independent. Don't count on anyone. Have the low expectations you're supposed to have. Be independent. Don't ask any
questions. Don't demand more than what we say you can have.
Don't feel anything you're not supposed to feel. Do as you're told.
Be independent! Don't embarrass yourself by loving someone
other than yourself. Remember, don't trust anyone! *Show him that
you're an independent person.* After all, this could be you: "A woman
once bought me a plastic photo frame that let you record a message; when I pushed a button, I heard her voice say, 'I love you.' I
know this could make me sound jerky, but I thought it was a
cheesy gift; I would have appreciated something I could use or
wear. I told her I'd keep it at the office, which I did—in a drawer. When we broke up, I erased her voice and gave the frame to a
co-worker for Christmas." That was gentle 29-year-old David in
*Glamour,* responding to the question: "What's the best (or worst)
gift a woman ever gave you?" Of course, if this woman had only
taken *Cosmo's* advice and "shown him that she was an independent person," this kind of unfortunate occurrence could have
been averted. If she had never said "I love you," there would have
been no voice to erase.

Meanwhile, women all around the country, women who have
already had numerous sexual affairs, are descending on nineteenth-century period dramas—at the cinema, on PBS, anywhere
they can catch a glimpse of Jane Austen's Emma or Elizabeth—
with a kind of religious seriousness that would be comical if it
weren't so poignant. While we may confess to each other our
romantic hopes, we dare not go public with our thoughts. We are
so afraid of being thought "unbalanced."

But why should you care, and why is it any of your business?
The answer is that in modern society, the main way a young
woman could protect her hopes has been ripped away from her,
and so now it is necessary to come forward to ask for it back.

Female modesty is not some artificial way of "dampening
allure," nor is it, as G. F. Schueler says, a mere distaste for "skimpy
swimming suits." It's much richer than that. Modesty is a reflex,
arising naturally to help a woman protect her hopes and guide
their fulfillment—specifically, this hope for one man. You don't
have to have studied the Buss and Schmitt sex survey to know

that most women would prefer one man who will stick by them, for better or for worse, to a series of men who abandon them. Of course, along with this hope comes a certain vulnerability, because every time a man fails to stick by us, our hopes are, in a sense, dashed. This is where modesty fits in. For modesty armed this special vulnerability—not to oppress women, but with the aim of putting them on an equal footing with men. The delay modesty created not only made it more likely that women could select men who would stick by them, but in turning lust into love, it changed men from uncivilized males who ran after as many sexual partners as they can get to men who really wanted to stick by one woman.

To begin to see modesty's relationship to sexual vulnerability and our secret, highest hopes, we need only consult a 1997 issue of *Cosmopolitan*. Here we find a rather unusual love letter.

> *Below is a generic love letter, with a few key blanks for your man to fill in. Make a hundred copies and give them to him. Ask him to send you one once a week. To make it easier, supply the stamped, self-addressed envelopes. "Dearest _____, I miss you terribly. Your _____ is like oxygen to me. Without it, I would perish. Your beautiful _____ makes me _____ every time I _____. If you were to leave me, I don't know what I'd do. Perhaps I'd _____ in a _____ with a _____. But no suffering could match a life without you, dearest _____. Love always, _____."*

So this is what it has come to, has it? And a hundred copies, too? My, aren't we hopeful. But I thought you didn't care if he loved you, *Cosmo*. Just a year earlier, you were saying, "WHO SAYS YOU CAN'T ENJOY SEX WITHOUT COMMITMENT? Don't Let Yourself Be Brainwashed by Ultra-Conservative Hype—Of *Course* You Should Sleep with Someone Simply for the Thrill of It. Just Like Men Do? Damn Right!"

And yet, in that very same issue of *Cosmo*, a few pages earlier, we found "Lucy" tearfully confessing, "I need constant reassurance from my lover that he really loves and wants me. It means a lot to me that he's willing to do this, even though he must get tired of having to comfort me."

Well perhaps we still do care, after all, but without any way of informing this longing, all we are left with is this desperate hope for the love letter we never got, just so many pitifully meaningless blanks. Maybe this is why we resisted *The Rules*—that book of do's and don'ts which guaranteed its owner it would "get" a man to marry her. Many women bought the book, but just as many were disenchanted and instinctively uncomfortable with it. Some were even angry. I think it reflects well on us that we resisted these rules, even though we were told that they "work"— because it is depressing that it has come to this. We are human beings, after all; we have feelings, and dignity, too. We are not computers who just fill in blanks and follow arbitrary rules. We were meant for something more than that, something higher.

Modesty fills in the blank. It answers not the crude *how* of femininity, but the beautiful *why*.

### THE SIGNIFICANCE OF MODESTY

Havelock Ellis wrote in 1899, "Without modesty, we could not have, nor rightly value at its true worth, that bold and pure candor which is at once the final revelation of love and the seal of its sincerity." Kurt Riezler agreed. "All peoples require a sense of shame in youngsters, especially in young girls," he wrote in 1943, and "shame suits youth and protects the growth of sexual maturity." More importantly, "It plays a role in the selection of the first sexual companion." Was Juliet immodest for loving Romeo? She assures her nurse that she has not "stepped o'er the bounds of modesty," but even if she had, Riezler concludes, "everyone makes allowance to Juliet for the strength of her passion. She may violate the social code as interpreted by nurses; she does not violate the human code. Each of her sweet words is full of modesty."

But just what is "female modesty"? Previous generations would have been surprised to be asked because they took it for granted. Unfortunately, because they took it for granted, this doesn't help us in our investigation. Modesty was gushed over, as in Richard Allestree's 1673 guide, *The Ladies Calling:* "And if we consider Modesty in this sense, we shall find it the most indispensable requisite of a woman; a thing so essential and natural to the sex, that every the least declination from it, is a proportional receding from Womanhood, but the total abandoning it ranks them among Brutes. . . ." This, alas, tells us very little. It doesn't explain why modesty is natural, or why it is essential—it only says that abandoning it would be very frightening. Well, so what? Some things are frightening, but necessary. Like when you have to dress up as something scary on Halloween in order to get candy.

Or listen to Sir Richard Steele, in 1711: "When Modesty ceases to be the chief Ornament of one Sex, and Integrity of the other, Society is upon a wrong Basis." Well, again, why?

And here is Quintus Ennius of Cassandra in the third century B.C.: "Where is she who not long ago was in her right mind, with maidenly modesty?" James Thomson's *Summer,* written around 1730, exclaims, "Check'd, at last, By love's respectful modesty." Huh?

What do all these quotes tell us, other than that these men think female modesty is a good idea? Not much.

One has the same problem with those who attack modesty— usually they never explain why it's a *bad* idea. We know, for instance, that Madame Celine Renooz didn't like it. She considered modesty a projection of masculine shame, and "in reality, only an outrage to [the female] sex"—but it's not clear why.

Before we can decide whether modesty is a good idea or not, we've got to try to uncover this *why.* We do have some clues, and with these clues we may be able to reconstruct the idea.

In essence, a culture that respects a specifically female type of modesty is one that regulates and informs the relation between the sexes in a nuanced—not, significantly, in a legislated—way. Women who dress and act "modestly" conduct themselves in ways that shroud their sexuality in mystery. They live in a way that makes womanliness more a transcendent, implicit quality than a crude, explicit quality. When Peter urged Christian wives to reject the current fashions of the world around them, he didn't tell them to be ugly. Instead he enjoined them to take on a more eternal kind of beauty: "Do not adorn yourself outwardly by plaiting your hair, and by wearing gold ornaments or fine clothing: rather, let your adornment be the inner self with the lasting beauty of a gentle and quiet spirit, which is very precious in God's sight." More recently, the *Sunday Gazette Mail* reports that "women appear to be relying on the power within rather than powerful dressing without." It is a respect for this "power within" that once made it impossible for men to view women merely as sexual objects. Rather, women became something deeper, more elemental: possessors of a deep and wondrous secret that is revealed only to the one who proves himself deserving of her.

The tie between this notion of male obligation and profound

respect for female modesty is no accident, nor was it confined to post-Elizabethan England. German legend tells us the "eternal feminine" gives women the enduring power to spiritualize mankind, while the classic siren leads men to their destruction. These images point to a very real and important truth: what women will and will not permit does have a profound way of influencing the behavior of an entire society. This influence is felt not simply because a woman has traditionally inculcated—or failed to inculcate—the mores in her children and thereby those of the next generation. A woman's sexual modesty puts her, significantly, in a position to be the ultimate worldly arbiter of a man's worth—"Lips that touch liquor shall never touch mine," as the temperance movement's slogan had it. Since respect for her modesty gave her the freedom to withhold affection, so to speak, until a virtuous man came around, men were in turn inspired to become worthy of her. Whether the cause was liquor or something larger, if you strung together enough modest women, they could quite literally change society. This was why, as Stuart Cloete put it in his 1943 *Congo Song,* "The woman was the stabilizing factor . . . world regeneration, when it came—if it came—must come through woman, as life came through her. She was the source."

In a society that respected the power of female modesty, the men were motivated to do what the women wanted. A 1997 issue of *Cosmopolitan* shows us this basic connection very nicely, but this time in inverted form. Its cover is split between two headlines: "ARE YOUR HANG-UPS SABOTAGING YOUR LOVE LIFE?" and "MAKE HIM COMMIT 100%: 25 WAYS TO GET A MAN INTO A ROCK-SOLID RELATIONSHIP."

This is becoming our great modern divide, his commitment problem and her hang-up problem. These two problems have emerged together for a reason. A society which sees her modesty or her "hang-ups" as a problem is necessarily a society which will not be able to get him to commit.

Conversely, a society which respected modesty, or what now goes by "hang-ups," was one in which the men were *obligated.*

### MODESTY AND MALE OBLIGATION

"See, just look at these opening pages," said the librarian in our rare books collection, nodding his head in the direction of the books he had just pulled from a special case. He had been kind enough to show me the first printings of Richard Brathwait's *The English Gentleman* and *The English Gentlewoman*—dated 1630 and 1631, respectively. "See over here?" he said. "A professor came in and was showing her class how sexist Brathwait was. Look at the cover plates—those words around the sketch of the nobleman all

*Frontispiece for* The English Gentleman *by Richard Brathwait, 1630. Courtesy of Chapin Library, Williams College.*

have to do with action, while the noblewoman over there is just
expected to sit and look pretty."

He did seem to have a point. We follow the noblewoman as she
improves herself in "Apparell, Behaviour, Decency, Complement,
Estimation, Fancy, Gentility, and Honour." The nobleman, by contrast, journeys from "Youth, Disposition, Education" to "Vocation,

*Frontispiece for* The English Gentlewoman *by Richard Brathwait,
1631. Courtesy of Chapin Library, Williams College.*

Recreation, Acquaintance, Moderation," until finally leveling off at "Perfection."★ Perfection! Hey, why don't I get perfection?

"Well, maybe the English Gentlewoman," I ventured, "had already *arrived* at perfection?"

The librarian smiled, as if to say "Nice try." We both laughed.

Later, when I was alone with *The English Gentlewoman* and turned from the frontispiece to the first page, I saw a large motto printed in elaborate script: "Mode∫tia, non Forma" (Modesty, not Beauty). It turns out that maybe the frontispiece did not quite tell the whole story. The gentlewoman did get to heaven, after all— but through modesty: "Modesty must be your guide, vertuous thoughts your guard, so shall heaven be your goale." Again and again *The English Gentlewoman* sang the praises of "Bash-full modesty"—in fact, all the other virtues would eventually be described in terms of it. Ideal behavior? "Loving modesty is a Living Beauty." Appearance? "That secret inscreened beauty which best becomes a Woman, Bashfull modesty." "Modesty is the choycest ornament that can adorne you. . . ." Apparel? "Array your selves in comely apparell, with shamefastnesse and modesty." Strength against seduction? "Those, whose spotlesse affections have devoted their best service to goodnesse, and made Modesty the exact mold of all their actions, cannot endure to stoope to such braine-sicke Lures." And just in case the reader is still confused about modesty's importance, *The English Gentlewoman* bids us remember

> *Conceits . . . sweetly tempered without lightnesse; their jests savory, yet without saltnesse; their discourse free without nicenesse; their answers milde without tartnesse; their smile pleasing, mixt with bashfulnesse; their pace gracefull without too much activenesse; their whole posture delightfull with a seemly carelesnesse. These are such mirrors of modesty, patternes of piety, as they would not for a world transgresse the bounds of Civility.*

---

★Translation of the frontispiece, *The English Gentleman: Virtute tute:* "Safely by/with virtue." *Vox laeta, sed anxia lethi:* "A pleasant voice, but distressed by death." *Nitimur in vetitum:* first half of a quotation from Ovid meaning "We strive toward the forbidden." *Ubera et verbera:* "Nourishment and discipline." *Pascimur et patimur:* "We pasture and we survive." *Spes in coelis, pes in terris:* "Hope in heaven, foot on the ground." *Generoso Gemine Gemmo:* "I sprout from a noble bud." *Non arcum semper tendit Apollo:* A quotation from Horace meaning "Apollo does not always draw his bow" (i.e., he sometimes plays his lyre). *Certus amor morum est:* "Love of character is true." *Moderata durant:* "Things done in moderation last." *Hac coelum petitur via:* "By this path heaven is sought."

I tried to imagine what a "pace gracefull without too much activenesse" would look like, and decided that I was definitely not a modest walker. Still, I was intrigued, particularly when I picked up *The English Gentleman* and discovered that the special "Perfection" cultivated by the gentleman—the perfection seemingly denied the gentlewoman—turns out to be perfection in serving *women*. Again and again the book returns to an unequivocal condemnation of deadbeat dads: "If there bee any that provideth not for his owne, and namely for them of his Houshold, he . . . is worse than an Infidell." Indeed, for the man who respected female modesty and "patternes of piety," there was not even a double standard. Thus "the Voluptuous Libertine mis-imployeth time in two respects": not only "in respect of himselfe" but "in respect of those good creatures."

What is the idea behind this link between male obligation and female modesty? If there could be such a thing as a "philosophy of modesty," I think it would be more an argument from internal inspiration than an argument from external authority. It would be similar to John Stuart Mill's distinction between external sanctions of law and internal sanctions of duty, only its appeal would be not merely its utility, but also its rightness and beauty.

The argument from external authority—exemplified by today's sexual harassment codes—treats men, essentially, like dogs. It says to them, *Down, boy, down! Bad dog!* Don't do X, because I *say* so. This argument from external authority is perfectly illustrated, I think, by the T-shirt on the Clothesline Project that says "NO doesn't mean try again in 5 minutes!" This message is outlined in red, like a stop sign. That is perfect, because it is just that—a stop sign. Nothing more.

Modesty, on the other hand, instead of treating men like dogs, invites them to consider an idea. This is the T-shirt that simply asks, in plain blue lettering, "How could you take that which she did not wish to give?" An argument from internal inspiration not only appeals to men as human beings capable of reason, but it appeals to them specifically *as* men, and invites them to consider what the ideal relation between them and women should be. How *could* you? is a perfect way of putting the question because it recognizes that although a man may have the ability to physically overpower a woman, he should not take advantage of her. A Central Park West dentist certainly *could* sexually abuse three women patients while they were under laughing gas—as Dr.

Richard Zinaman was convicted of doing on September 30, 1997—but he should not.

But *why* not, exactly? The 1881 Supreme Court of Michigan ruling in *DeMay* v. *Roberts* shows how what we would consider to be "sexual harassment" cases were once resolved not by talk of sex discrimination but with an understanding of female modesty. A doctor called to attend on a woman in labor brought with him an unmarried young man—who was neither a nurse nor any other sort of "medical associate"—to help out. The plaintiff "consented" to be touched by this young man, but since she was not informed of his "amateur status" her consent was held to be defective: "The defendants were guilty of deceit [and] the wrong thus done entitles the injured party to recover the damages afterwards sustained, from shame and mortification upon discovering the true character of the defendants." Unlike Dr. Zinaman, who sexually abused his women patients while they were under laughing gas, the men in *DeMay* didn't intend anything lewd by touching the woman in labor. But since the sanction for modesty was so strong, it was considered an imposition for any man other than a woman's beloved or a certified doctor to touch her. In 1837, an Englishman named Thomas Saverland brought suit against a kind of premodern Lorena Bobbitt, one Miss Caroline Newton, who had bitten a piece out of his nose when he kissed her without permission. She was acquitted by the judge, who said that's what happens "when a man kisses a woman against her will. . . ."

In 1837, stealing a kiss was serious business. Do these cases go too far? Or have we gone too far today in the opposite direction? Consider the sexual turmoil on our college campuses.

When the Antioch College rules for dating, touching, and kissing were issued, most feminists defended the policy, saying it was necessary to prevent date-rape and other unwanted advances. Then most conservatives weighed in and poked fun at the rules—for instance, George Will wrote about "Sex Amid Semicolons." Others complained that the college was taking the "fun" out of sex. Yet since then, several other colleges have passed similar policies—from the University of Oregon to the University of New Hampshire—and they have found their applications shot up after doing so. Clearly there is a demand for some guidance. But of what kind?

Understanding modesty allows us to step back, both from the conservative smirks and from the feminist heavy-handed regula-

tions. It invites men to consider, What's fun about forcing someone into sex in the first place? A respect for female modesty
would inform the relation between the sexes so that "taking what
you can get" would be an impossible way for a man to approach
a woman, or to approach love generally.

The argument from external authority labels a man as evil if
he date-rapes or sexually harasses a woman. From the standpoint
of modesty, he is behaving abominably, but more crucially, he is
really missing the whole *point*. He hasn't understood what it
means to be a man.

Kierkegaard argues in Volume I of *Either/Or* that the whole
point of seduction is that the woman must give willingly. In Volume II of *Either/Or*, he writes that one truly loves only once, and
that marriage recognizes that fact. If one's spouse is to be one's
only love, then you couldn't understand the erotic unless you
took modesty seriously. Indeed, Havelock Ellis's two-volume
study of sex began with a long section on "The Evolution of
Modesty," because "it is necessary, before any psychology of sex
can be arranged in order, to obtain a clear view of modesty."

Dryden had opinions on date rape too: "Of the general character of women, which is modesty, he has taken a most becoming
care; for his amorous expressions go no farther than virtue may
allow." Today our society makes fun of modesty, and then we are
surprised to find our men behaving abominably. We make fun of
virtue, and then are surprised that men's "amorous expressions"
often go "farther than virtue may allow."

Six months ago while I was warming up in the gym and waiting for my swimming class to start, a 33-year-old woman on the
Stairmaster puffed out this story:

> *You know, men have no respect for women anymore. I can't even get
> guys to wear condoms. They're always whining about it. You know that
> place The Drip? Where you can get set up for dates? Well! I met a
> guy there, went out for three dates with him, and he really turned out
> to be a drip! No, don't laugh, it's not funny! I thought he was nice . . .
> but after three dates when I wouldn't sleep with him, he dumped me,
> just like that! If you ask me, it's because it's way too easy for them.
> Why should they waste time with a girl like me when they can get it
> for free? Do you realize that chances are men can probably find some-
> one to do it with them even without a condom? Do you realize that
> I'm 33 years old? Do you realize that I have just burned 238 calo-
> ries?*

Now *there* is the connection between female modesty and male obligation. How can we expect men to be honorable when a large number of women consistently send them the message that they do not have to be?

"See, that's what some women do," a man says to me, explaining why he has just broken up with his girlfriend, "They try to entangle you in a net of obligation." Now this man is obviously someone who doesn't appreciate the notion of honor or male obligation, but why doesn't he appreciate it? It's interesting that he says *some* women (the bad ones), want men to be obligated to them—meaning in contrast to other women who expect nothing from men. What if all women expected a lot of men? What if all women were faithful and expected the men to be faithful? Then treating a woman well wouldn't be some ensnaring "net," it would be the state of affairs. If you didn't act honorably, you simply couldn't get any women. Sorry, no women for *you*.

With feminism, it often seems as if nothing will get better until we overturn all of society. The beauty of sexual modesty is that by an individual's behavior, things can get a little better now. Flaubert's Félicité didn't have to overthrow the whole patriarchy to inspire Theodore to behave:

*The following week Theodore got her to grant him several rendezvous. They would meet at the bottom of a farm-yard, behind a wall, under a solitary tree. She was not ignorant of life as young ladies are, for the animals had taught her a great deal; but her reason and an instinctive sense of honor prevented her from giving way. The resistance she put up inflamed Theodore's passion to such an extent that in order to satisfy it (or perhaps out of sheer naiveté) he proposed to her. At first she refused to believe him, but he swore that he was serious.*

# Chapter 6

# THE GREAT DECEPTION

> *ANOTHER SCHOOL SEX CASE: A 15-year-old girl*
> *was sexually assaulted at her Queens high school this week,*
> *police said. The victim . . . told cops she was accosted by four*
> *teenage boys about 12:45 P.M. Tuesday in a stairwell at Hill-*
> *crest High School. . . . While two of the boys stood lookout, the*
> *other two sodomized the girl, police said. No suspects had been*
> *arrested as of early this morning, police said. The attack at Hill-*
> *crest occurred less than two weeks after six students were charged*
> *in two sodomy attacks on a girl at Martin Luther King Jr. High*
> *School in Manhattan.*
>
> —DAILY NEWS, OCTOBER 17, 1997

A year earlier, a 1996 headline in *Glamour* ran: "We Sweat. We Swagger. We're as Competitive and Quirky as Men. Will the Media Ever Catch On?" Though it's fashionable to say that women are as physically strong and competitive as men, sexual assault is never equal-opportunity. Sexual assault still goes one way. But today the philosophy that once tamed the conduct of men is thought to be sexist.

By now the attack on modesty is so complete, if you do happen to hear it discussed at all in academic circles, chances are it is treated as a kind of joke—with the sort of bemused detachment we reserve for only our most benighted notions. Ruth Bernard Yeazell's *Fictions of Modesty,* for example, is a fascinating book, an extensive treatment of sexual modesty in literature, but she doesn't consider whether modesty could be anything other than a "fiction." Of the many so-called "fictions of modesty" she outlines, two are "that the lovers' passion was intensified by delay, another . . . that the interval of postponement allowed for female choosing." But what if modesty were not a fiction? What if modesty were real? Remember that woman's prerogative to greet a man on the street first? If she chose to address him, you'll recall, he had to respond in kind, but if she passed him by there was nothing he could do about it. It was stressed repeatedly in etiquette manuals at the time: "It is a mark of high breeding not to speak to a lady in the street, until you perceive that she has noticed you by an inclination of the head." Was that not a genuine prerogative? It is appreciated all the more in its absence. One contributor to Martha J. Langelan's survival manual, *Back Off!* writes that men's assumption that "they have the right to engage us in conversation anytime they please" is one thing that today puts women "in fear." To those who have grown up hearing a constant barrage of crudeness as soon as they step on the street, this earlier understanding which allowed for female choosing seems quite desirable, and real.

Today, of course, we tend to suppose that all of femininity is "fiction." As Andrea Dworkin explains: "The discovery is, of course, that 'man' and 'woman' are fictions, caricatures, cultural constructs . . . demeaning to the female, dead-ended for male and female both."

But for this lesson one doesn't even need to turn to a radical like Dworkin, to the extent that all of popular culture is suffused with this message. A 1996 issue of the fashion magazine *Elle* urges us to "deconstruct the stereotypes of gender," reminding us that "'femininity' is a social construct" and that "men have defined femininity since its inception."

Since men have defined femininity since its inception, there is only one thing left for the liberated woman to do: become masculine, of course. Hence the odd spectacle of a magazine called *Glamour* celebrating the woman who is "sweating" and "swaggering."

Even the most cursory tour of popular culture confirms that as female modesty is derided, with increased frequency are women portrayed as "victims." *Cosmo* urges women to sleep around "just like men do," but just a few pages earlier, a woman confesses that she needs "constant reassurance from my lover that he really loves and wants me." The myth of sameness, instead of helping to cure the insecurity, seems to fuel it.

I often observed this pattern on my college campus. During Women's Pride Week our feminist association passed out "SHAMELESS HUSSY" stickers. Every woman on campus was to affix one to her clothing, proudly announcing she could be as casual about sex as any man. The next day, "Peer Health" urged us on its billboard to "Come on down and see our new oral-sex how-to guides!" In this view, sex is not only no big deal, it's as harmless as

a game show like *The Price Is Right*. *"Come on down!"* Compare
this with the advice a coed would get from her college in 1904:
"I have heard that some young women allow men to touch them,
to hold their hands! My dear girls, never indulge in such frivolous
actions." This was from an address by Northwestern University's
dean of women. In 1904, it was assumed that a young woman had
so many important things to learn, she shouldn't waste time even
holding a boy's hand—she was too dignified for that. Today her
college instructs her on the proper technique for servicing the
boys.

Then, when I picked up my mail at the student union center,
someone bleated in my ear, "Have a safe spring break!" Thrust
into my palm was an official "Williams College E Liberalitate E.
Williams Armigeri Safe Sex Spring Break Thermos," with not
only condoms inside but also something white called "ForPlay
WITHOUT nonoxynol-9." Whatever it was, it was "Water Based,
Watersoluble and Condom Compatible." Well, wasn't that nice.

So what could possibly go wrong, when we were safe and
shameless at last, and all equipped with the newest, most official
oral sex how-to guides? A lot could go wrong. Apparently there
was more to sex than just proper safety and technique, because a
few weeks later, The Clothesline Project sprang up and suddenly,
as it happens, sex was a very big deal. Now the men were told
*"don't touch me again"* and *"I hate you."* The images and words all
pointed to a woman's trust shattered. For a bunch of shameless
hussies, we were pretty upset.

Those heartfelt Clothesline Project T-shirts—*"Why does this
keep happening to me?"* and *"When will this end?"*—bespeak
women who keep falling short, discovering how unlike men we
are. Modesty acknowledged this special vulnerability, and protected it. It made women equal to men *as* women. Encouraged to act
immodestly, a woman exposes her vulnerability and she then
*becomes,* in fact, the weaker sex. A woman can argue that she is
exactly the same as a man, she may deny having any special vulnerability, and act accordingly, but I cannot help noticing that she
usually ends up exhibiting her feminine nature anyway, only this
time in victimhood, not in strength. Why didn't the men at
Williams have a "Clothesline Project?"

Just take a tour of the 1996 headlines—"The Love Calendar"
in *Mademoiselle,* the "Will He Ever Set the Date?" article in *Glamour,* the "Waiting a (Good) Man Out" piece in *Cosmo.* It seemed
like a particularly bad year for thwarted brides. By the end of the

year, one frustrated maid told *New Woman,* "I know he loves me; I love him very much and want to marry him. How can I get him to commit?" Another: "For two years I've been engaged to and living with the most beautiful, loving man. To me, marriage is one of the most important rituals of life, and I feel 100 percent ready for it. Unfortunately, my true love's [friends] have scared him out of wanting to marry. I find myself very depressed that we're not married. I burst into tears easily and usually cry myself to sleep. I'm just dying inside. What should I do?"

Ultimately, though, the question of whether women usually hope for something more than just sex is less philosophical than empirical. The philosophical question is, as always, why?

### AN IDEA AND ITS ENEMIES

Because it was once either entirely taken for granted or entirely dismissed, very little has been written about female modesty. If, however, we take notice of when it has been attacked, we can see why it is a good and necessary thing to reconsider.

Clearly the debate over modesty was raging long before feminism was born. Before the sexual revolution, before ERA, before Margaret Mead learned about sex from Samoan girls, before women even got the vote, there was David Hume. In his *Treatise of Human Nature* (1739), this Scottish philosopher described modesty in terms of its social function: for him, the salient point was that it assured men of the paternity of their children. "But in order to induce the men to impose on themselves this restraint, and undergo chearfully all the fatigues and expenses to which it subjects them, they must believe, that the children are their own, and that their natural instinct is not directed to a wrong object, when they give a loose to love and tenderness."

Hume's contemporary, Rousseau, recognized right away that defending modesty in utilitarian terms alone was just one step away from seeking its extinction. What happens to a notion founded on mere utility when it is someday deemed useless? Obviously, we will do away with the notion altogether. As he wrote indignantly in 1758,

> *Popular prejudices! some cry. Silly errors of childhood! Illusion of laws and education! Modesty is nothing. It is only an invention of the social laws to protect the rights of fathers and husbands, and to maintain some order in families. Why should we blush at needs given to us by*

*Nature? . . . Why, the desires being equal on both sides, should the*
*demonstrations be different? Why should one of the sexes refuse more*
*than the other tendencies which they have in common? Why should*
*man have on this issue different laws from the animals?*

You can tell right away how upset Rousseau was, just from all
the exclamation points. He thought there was a lot at stake in the
debate over modesty. Was he right?

On the surface, it must be admitted that Rousseau's defense of
modesty is quite puzzling. For if he was worried that certain ideas
could lead to modesty's extinction, wouldn't that presuppose a
position similar to Hume's—namely, that modesty is useful, but
not necessarily natural? If modesty were so natural, why would we
need laws to sanction it? And how could ideas threaten it? One
might conceivably explain Rousseau by making a distinction
between suppressing a natural affection and blotting it out entirely. Laws and social pressure certainly can *attempt* to suppress a natural affection, but they cannot prevent this feeling from
manifesting itself in other ways. A culture that attempts to suppress
modesty may appear to succeed, but it cannot prevent the modest
impulse from being redirected—as seems to be happening so
poignantly today in the case of eating disorders.

Whether Rousseau was right remains to be seen. At any rate,
before Rousseau or Hume there was Bernard Mandeville, who
amusingly noted in his *Modest Defence of Publick Stews* that if
woman's modesty is not instinctive it is then built "upon a very
*ticklish* Foundation." Going back still further, Plato, too, seemed to
be ambivalent about modesty. Many have suggested that when he
holds out the prospect of naked exercises for men and women in
the *Republic* he is being ironic, that he is really paying tribute to
the importance of modesty by making it the first sacrifice on the
altar of the perfect city. Yet in the *Charmides* we seem to have a
very straightforward argument for why modesty is not necessarily a virtue. And then there was the Greek philosopher Xenophon,
who in his *Oikomonos* introduced us to the idea that sexual modesty should apply equally to husband and wife. So modesty was a
site of hot contention—Who should be modest? Men? Women?
Equally? Neither? Is it natural? Conventional?—long before our
modern egalitarians drew their swords.

Yet the feminist attack on modesty has been unique in one
important respect. It was not simply, some said, that modesty was
constructed to serve society's interests, as Hume argued, but that

it was constructed *by* men with the explicit intention of enslaving or subordinating women. From the time of Mary Wollstonecraft, whose *1792 Vindication of the Rights of Women* is considered the first feminist work, many have insisted that codes of conduct regulating behavior between women and men—particularly those grounded in a respect for female modesty—infallibly signal sexism and subordination, and should be therefore excised.

Since a woman's modesty made her so evidently different from men, if women were to strive to be the same as men, of course modesty would have to be the first to go. This is why Wollstonecraft entitled Chapter Seven of her *Vindication* "Modesty—Comprehensively Considered, and Not as a Sexual Virtue." She considered modesty in all of its many manifestations—delicacy of mind, moderate estimation of one's talents—except as the kind Rousseau was writing about: sexual virtue for women. This is the only modesty Wollstonecraft refused to take seriously, because it gave men an abiding awareness that women were women: "I am persuaded that in the pursuit of knowledge women would never be insulted by sensible men . . . if they did not by mock modesty remind them that they were women."

Wollstonecraft concluded that sexual modesty was an "unnatural coldness of constitution," and redefined modesty itself such that all traces of sexual virtue were absent: "The reserve I mean has nothing sexual in it." Wollstonecraft's new "reserve" turns out to be more advocacy for her educational program, for women who have "most improved their reason" will automatically "have the most modesty." Wollstonecraft's espousal of education for women is, without question, admirable, but it remains unclear what the content of a "reserve" that has "nothing sexual in it" would be. Wollstonecraft does add at the end of her *Vindication* that "love will teach [women] modesty"—naturally, as it were—which would seem to suggest that she hadn't really given up on a specifically sexual modesty altogether. But one hundred years later, Madame Celine Renooz would seal the lid on the case, calling sexual modesty "an outrage to [the female] sex," really just "masculine shame attributed to woman."

Here we can see how well the critics of modesty understood its logic. It is not merely that female modesty is a guarantor of a very old-fashioned kind of romantic love, one in which he is pursuer and she pursued, he lover and she beloved, he the seeker and she the mysterious and stationary point. That's all so much icing on the cake and, in any case, *is* rather easy to dismiss as socially constructed. Much more significantly, I think, modesty is so threatening to the egalitarians because whenever it emerges, it is *evidence*. It is evidence that woman's experience of love and sex is fundamentally different from man's, and as such it rebukes the androgynous project.

Earlier I argued that modesty is a kind of armor of hope. Perhaps because the attack on this armor was never entirely successful, today's egalitarians have moved on to attacking the hope itself. Have you ever wondered why Andrea Dworkin spills so much ink trying to prove that romantic love is a "mythic celebration of female negation," and why marriage is more properly understood as "legalized rape"? Why should she care so much if women still harbor romantic longings and want to commit themselves to one man for life? I suspect it is because wherever a woman's romantic hopes are allowed to exist, sexual modesty can never be far behind. If she is not made to feel *immediately* ashamed of her romantic hopes, who knows what could happen?

The history of how the intellectuals have misunderstood modesty can be best seen by reading *Refusing to Be a Man,* where John Stoltenberg writes, "The act of prevailing upon another to admit of penetration without full and knowledgeable assent so sets the standard in the repertoire of male-defining behaviors that it is not at all inaccurate to suggest that the ethics of male sexual identity are essentially rapist." But a moment's reflection suggests that Stoltenberg gets it exactly backwards. While the nature of uncivilized male sexual identity may be "essentially rapist," ethics lead men away from such behavior. Catharine MacKinnon says that the threat of being raped is cultural, that if it weren't for our patriarchal institutions, no woman would fear being raped—"To be rapable, a position that is social not biological, defines what a woman is." But men *are* in fact physically stronger than women. It was the cultural respect for women's natural modesty that protected her. Then some intellectuals came along and said that these codes respectful of modesty discriminated. Of course they did. But they also gave women freedom: freedom to walk in the street without having to fear being harassed, stalked, or raped, freedom for a girl to study in school without being sodomized, freedom to be alone with a man and still deserve respectful treatment.

Thus, it is the very codes of conduct which the "antiessentialists" attack—the ones that modesty inspires—that are in fact a woman's protection against rape. Indeed, the primary and most direct consequence of a recovery of modesty's meaning would be an end to a culture that objectifies women and inadvertently encourages the violent acting-out of any deep misogynous impulses. Yet just as it would save many women from harm, so, too, it would confer on women a new version of an old obligation—the obligation to serve as the civilizing force in a culture that seems increasingly uncivilized.

For women may need men—and the laws of men—to protect them against physical threats, but men are equally dependent on women to confirm their masculinity. There is no right or wrong, there can be no position of superiority or inferiority in such an interdependence. As Rousseau put it in the *Emile,* where man and woman differ, "they are not comparable."

### THE CENSORED DEBATE OVER FEMALE DESIRE

*Date: Wed, 24 Jan 1996 09:40:42 EST*
*Subject: Re Dear Professor*

*Dear Wendy, Biologically-based differences between the sexes is an area that I used to follow, but I lost interest in it a number of years ago when rational discourse became impossible. My moment of truth came when I was asked to represent the biological perspective in a faculty seminar with Women's Studies professors who were discussing Anne Fausto-Sterling's book THE GENDER MYTH and was roundly lambasted for suggesting that there were ANY biological differences between males and females.*

Another myth the intellectuals have promulgated is that a culture that respected modesty suppressed female desire. The story told about female desire now goes like this: Once upon a time, before we were all enlightened, everyone thought that women didn't like sex. Now we know that they do, and that's why we're all living happily ever after. Thus, all contemporary discussion about female desire is reduced to a question: do women like sex or don't they? You believe either that a woman's sex drive is exactly identical to a man's, or that women are sexless creatures. William Acton, a mid–nineteenth century medical authority, wrote, "The majority of women (happily for them) are not much troubled with sexual feelings of any kind." Karen Lehrman retorted in 1997, "Clearly, women like sex. They like sex just as much as men like sex. In fact, they have probably always liked sex just as much as men have. But before the sixties, you might not have known this."

The only problem with this debate—other than the obvious comedy of it all (We like sex. No, you don't. Do too!)—is that it is largely a distortion of the real grounds in dispute. With the exception of a few Victorian doctors, the debate over sexual modesty was never really between those who thought women didn't like sex and those who thought they did. It was far more sophisticated and interesting than that. For starters, female desire actually was not discovered in the 1960s. Any cursory acquaintance with ancient Chinese sex manuals or the Torah's commandment of *onah* (the husband's obligation to his wife) will reveal that the ancients developed elaborate systems out of a concern over satisfying female desire. This was important to them because happy marriages were impossible if the women weren't sexually satisfied. Hence, in Judaism, there is the husband's sexual obligation to his wife: before he goes away on a journey, after she returns home from the *mikveh,* and so forth. As Maimonides elaborates:

> 1. The conjugal [women's sexual] rights mentioned in the Torah are obligatory upon each man according to his physical powers and his occupation. How so? For the men who are healthy and live in comfortable and pleasurable circumstances, without having to perform work that would weaken their strength, and only eat and drink and sit idly in their homes, their conjugal schedule is every night; for the laborers, such as tailors, weavers, masons, and the like, their conjugal schedule is twice weekly, if their work is in the same city, and once a week if their work is in another city; for the donkey drivers, their schedule is once a week; for the camel drivers, once in thirty days . . . for the learned, once a week, because the study of Torah weakens their strength; it is the practice of the learned to have conjugal relations each Friday night. 2. A wife may restrict her husband in his business journeys, so that he would not otherwise deprive her of her conjugal rights. Hence he may not set out except with her permission. Similarly, she may prevent him from exchanging an occupation involving a frequent conjugal schedule, for one involving an infrequent one.

From each according to his occupation. If you were someone like Madonna, presumably, you knew to warn the matchmaker against fixing you up with a camel driver. So not only were the sages aware of female desire, but satisfying female desire was considered important enough that a wife could veto a husband's job offer because of it. The whole community would rally around female desire, and take its side against a husband who was going away on too many trips.

Rashi—the author of the most popular commentary on the Bible and Talmud—explains that women have a potentially greater sexual desire than men, but that this desire is not for the merely physical; it is also bound up in a desire that the union be holy. Bernard Mandeville circulated a pamphlet of 1724 which held exactly this view. Women had more sexual desire than men, but, he argued, this was precisely why modesty was important: "to counterbalance this violent natural desire all young women have strong notions of honour carefully inculcated into them from their infancy." The Elizabethan musician Thomas Wythorne agreed, observing that "though they be the weaker vessels yet [women] will overcome two, three or four men in the satisfying of their carnal appetites."

To make explicit what is implicit in the various laws of sexual obligation and restraint, then the reason for modesty is not that women have any less sex drive than men, but that it is of a different kind. To appreciate this distinction, consider the following letter which appeared in *Commentary* in the early 1970s:

> *Leslie H. Farber ["He Said, She Said," March] makes the same error Sigmund Freud and most other psychiatrists have made in presuming to know what women does or does not experience. It is time for man to leave the defining of female existence to woman herself. As a woman who has experienced "undifferentiated lust," I would suggest that if this is not consciously experienced by some women it is due to the excessive repression and denial of sexual feelings brought about by the socialization process. . . . Dr. Farber says: "What she experiences that corresponds to some degree to his undifferentiated lust is an undifferentiated desire to be desired by anyone and everyone." This is typical male talk assuring other men that all women welcome their sexual advances at all times. Actually it becomes very tiresome to have to cope continually with these sexual advances.*

This is a truly fascinating letter because it begins by asserting that a woman's lust is exactly the same, just as "undifferentiated," as a man's, but then the letter ends in a plea for the men to leave women alone, and *not* to assume that they want what men want.

This is a popular position still: the very people who insist men and women are the same then turn around and say women need to be protected from men's advances. So how does one resolve this contradiction? Modesty helps, somewhat.

For men and women may indeed desire in equal quantity, but the *quality* of the desire is different, as this letter so perfectly illustrates. A woman's desire, try as she might to have "undifferentiated lust," is usually going to be wrapped up and informed by things like intelligence, personality, kindness, a certain sense of humor—qualities that are hard to learn about from seeing someone on the street. Though the desire may be equal, what sparks the desire is not the same, and this is what makes a woman walking down the street more likely to be the sought than the seeker, more likely to find persistent advances "very tiresome."

What excites women is much more than the merely visual. This is true of men, of course, as well, but of women even more so. After a new editor gets named to *Playgirl* in 1997, the *New York Post* interviews women on the street to find out "Are pictures of naked men sexy?" Four out of five of the women interviewed respond, emphatically, *No.* Lydia Gobena, 27, from Manhattan explains, "I don't really think the photos in *Playgirl* are sexy. I think that keeping things a mystery is sexier." Tar Puohit, 21, from Cambridge, Massachusetts, agrees: "I don't think what I see in *Playgirl* is sexy because I don't know what's behind the pictures. When it comes to being sexy, I want to consider someone's mind." And 23-year-old Carol Hechmer from Brooklyn: "I think that *Playgirl* is too blatant. That old-time stuff where it's so naughty you have to be intelligent to understand what's going on—that's sexy."

So a woman may feel intense sexual desire for her boyfriend or husband—perhaps as Rashi, Mandeville, and Wythorne suggest, she may even feel more than he does for her—but when she is flipping through a *Playgirl* magazine or walking home from work she is unlikely to feel lust for every man she sees. This is what makes respect for her modesty so important. For without it, she can be harassed, stalked, or raped—and today, unhappily, she often is.

Here is another example of the different quality of female eroticism, this time from a 1997 issue of *Marie Claire*. Jayne Napier, 30, tells the interviewer that she hasn't had sex for 14 months: "I date a lot and meet men who initially interest me. I go out with them thinking there might be potential. But having sex isn't going to help me decide if this may be a person I can have a future with. Some of my male friends tell me I'm being too choosy. I say there is no such thing. When they ask me when I last got laid, I tell them I haven't met anyone worth sleeping with." Does this mean this woman has no desire or is "sexually repressed"? Not at all. Much of what is attractive to her, though, is meeting someone she "can have a future with." In this light, the old saying "a woman is more particular" did not mean that women were sexless creatures, but rather, that part of what was sexy was this context of emotional intimacy. But more significantly, "A woman is more particular" was a signal to men not to impose themselves on women on the street. As Rousseau put it: "The desires are equal! What does that mean? Are there on both sides the same ability to satisfy them?"

So far, we have toured only why modesty may be necessary and beneficial: it helps women protect their romantic hopes, it is well suited to the special quality of female desire, and male respect for it gives women freedom from harassment and rape. Yet all these accounts of the necessity of modesty merely circle around a much more fundamental question: Is it natural?

# Chapter 7

## CAN MODESTY BE NATURAL?

> *"Rule Forty-two. All persons more than a mile high to leave the court."*
>
> *Everybody looked at Alice.*
>
> *"I'm not a mile high," said Alice.*
>
> *"You are," said the King.*
>
> *"Nearly two miles high," added the Queen.*
>
> *"Well, I shan't go, at any rate," said Alice; "besides, that's not a regular rule; you invented it just now."*
>
> *"It's the oldest rule in the book," said the King.*
>
> *"Then it ought to be Number One," said Alice.*
>
> *The King turned pale, and shut his note-book hastily.*
>
> —FROM ALICE'S ADVENTURES IN WONDERLAND

Is modesty the oldest rule in the book, or did we just invent it just now? Rousseau thought modesty was natural: "With regard to the modesty of the [female] sex in particular, what gentler arm could this same Nature have given to the one destined to defend herself?"

At first it seems that the very existence of an immodest society should be sufficient to prove Rousseau wrong. If modesty were so natural, then there would be nothing to discuss, and no immodesty to criticize. Everyone would simply be naturally modest, right?

Not necessarily. I think you can observe how modesty is natural even—perhaps especially—in immodest societies. Here are my proofs:

### 1. THE HOWARD STERN PROOF

The great political theorist Leo Strauss thought that in democratic societies, people interested in questions of virtue couldn't make their cases explicitly. Sometimes I wonder if Howard Stern isn't really a conservative in disguise. More than anyone else in America, Howard reveals the stubborn existence of female modesty even among those who deny its natural claim. And often quite poignantly. Like a kind of "Where's Waldo?" shtick, the underlying theme of each of Howard's shows is actually "Where's Modesty?"

He invites strippers and porn stars on his show, they sit down in their revealing clothing and their easy nothing-fazes-me manner, and then the game begins. Can I touch your *this,* and can I touch your *that?* And then the inevitable command to come over, *C'mon!* Just take off your top. What, *no? Why the hell not?*

A very good question.

For these women who make a profession out of "being comfortable with their bodies," as it turns out, always have their limits. They "just met" him. What he's asking is just "too gross." Or simply: "No way! Not in front of *everyone!*" Howard is an expert at calling their bluff, at making the unsquirmable squirm. *I'm cool,* these earnest porn stars announce upon entering his studio. Everything in their manner and dress expresses a kind of teasing hopefulness: See, Howard, I can be *just* as cavalier about sex as you—really! Yeah, right. Each walks off with a perpetual cringe. Many also have "working names." If the strippers on his show are perfectly comfortable with what they are doing, then why do so many of them go by fake names? One explains that it's "because if someone on the street calls you by your working name, you know not to pay attention." Why would such a split between your life ("the real" you) and work be necessary, if they weren't ashamed of what they do? How many ear, nose, and throat doctors have "working names"?

Even though I admire his project greatly and suspect he is a closet Straussian, I would never go on Howard's show because I understand how this particular game is rigged. Howard always wins, always makes a fool out of each and every one of his woman guests, because men always win the game of vulgarity. It is no accident that most sexual-harassment lawsuits go one way. As Stendhal put it, there is everything to gain by a woman "above the vulgar level" having reserved manners, since "the game isn't equal."

Consider this 1997 *New York Times* report: "The witness acknowledged telling two coarse sexual jokes at the conference but insisted that she had told them only to friends and never in the presence of Sergeant Major McKinney. Mr. Gittins persuaded the presiding officer, Lieut. Col. Robert Jarvis, to instruct the woman to acknowledge the content of the jokes. She had resisted doing so, saying it would embarrass her to repeat them in front of strangers."

Women can try to be as vulgar as men, but they almost always end up chickening out. They are the ones who usually end up filing the lawsuits because they are the ones who end up feeling injured. And they are right to feel injured, because they are invariably the object of the vulgar joke. What complicates matters is that men don't really win at the game of vulgarity, either. They may be better at playing it than women, as Stendhal says, but where does it lead them?

Andrea, 28, tells me, "I've often wondered why, when I see men crowded helplessly around the pornographic magazine section, I never feel hostility toward them—although I am told that is the appropriate emotion—but, rather, just *sorry* for them." The problem with the game of obscenity is that it is essentially a lonely game. And perhaps this is why the man doesn't really win, in the end, because it's pitiful for a man to admit that he hasn't grown up, that he cannot relate to a woman in any more interesting way. So vulgarity is a man's game, one that the man seems to win, but in the long run one might say women and men both end up the poorer by playing it. Women, I think, are trying to play the wrong game. We try to be as vulgar as possible, because we have been told that this is the proof of our "liberation," and invariably we wind up feeling excluded. Well, we are excluded—that is the point.

As Rousseau predicted in his *Emile,* if we should seek to raise our daughters like men, "The men will gladly consent to it! The more women want to resemble them, the less women will govern them, and then men will truly be the masters." Could Rousseau have been right in saying that when the differences between the sexes are appreciated, each sex needs the other, and when women pretend to be men, men tend to need them less?

Demi Moore can go around all she wants saying, as she does in the 1997 film *G.I. Jane,* "Suck my dick," but the fact remains, she doesn't have one. Why are women today taking all their cues from what the men do, trying to play all their games—even to the ridiculous point of pretending we have the anatomy which we do not, in fact, have? I thought feminism was supposed to be against penis envy.

If vulgarity is a game that begins by excluding women, but ultimately excludes men from themselves, modesty is the game both can play. It begins as a woman's game—one, interestingly, where she appears to lose, "to be missing out"—but really she invites a man to relate to her in a way that is both uniquely human and ultimately more erotic. So modesty may superficially seem to be just a woman's game because it is one that she must begin, but in playing it she invites men to relate to her in a different way, a way that ultimately means that the men win, too, because they are no longer cut off from adult masculinity.

To me, then, one proof that modesty is natural is the way you can observe women instinctively trying to pull men away from crudeness as soon as they love them. A 1997 *Cosmo* introduces us to "Sherry," 30, who is very upset that her live-in beau "comes to the dinner table dressed only in his underwear." She is successful at work, an assistant book editor in New York City, but feels defeated when faced with underwear at the dinner table. "When I complain, he says, 'Oh, come on. It's just us, and it's comfortable.'" Since this is a serious situation, *Cosmo* calls in etiquette expert Nancy Tuckerman, who was Jacqueline Kennedy Onassis's social secretary in the White House. "Men are simply not as bothered by bad manners as women are," she observes, "But manners hold a relationship together. . . . They're about being considerate. Forget them, and you get into trouble."

A year earlier, *Mademoiselle* took up a related question. Advice columnist Blanche Vernon, frustrated with the number of letters she'd been getting on what-to-do-when-my-boyfriend-starts-burping, wrote, "I used to think the why-don't-men-ask-for-directions question was the defining issue of the gender wars. Wrong. Body noises is the subject that truly polarizes us." If it's occasional, no problem, *Mademoiselle* advises, but "if he's purposely provoking you, try this: Without even mentioning the rude noises, suddenly lose interest in sex . . . pull out a fat mystery novel." A sex strike for better manners? Isn't that a little extreme? Not if it's important, which it evidently seems to be. To the woman, it isn't just manners but the dignity of the whole relationship that's at stake.

Howard Stern is the first to admit how sad it is when women trade in their pedestal in order to become the butt of men's jokes. As he put it in a 1997 interview: "If a guy embarrasses you, get rid of him! No woman should put up with a guy who acts like I do on radio."

### 2. THE WINDY DAY PROOF

Female modesty is everywhere on a windy day. Mike Royko wrote the best thing on this subject in 1986:

*While walking across a windy downtown plaza, I saw a pretty young woman and immediately felt sorry for her. She appeared to be suffering from a physical disability. She walked hunched forward and tilted to one side. Both of her arms were thrust straight down and held rigidly against her right thigh. As she crossed the plaza, I thought how sad it was that she had to go through life dragging herself around that way. She entered the glass-walled lobby of the building and suddenly began walking normally. For a moment, I couldn't understand why she had been walking so grotesquely. Then, another woman on the plaza gave me the answer. This one wasn't hunched over as severely as the other one had been. But she leaned to her right side and her hand tightly clutched her skirt. Of course. She was wearing a slit dress. Both had been wearing slit dresses. But because the plaza was windy, they were preventing their dresses from flapping open in the breeze.*

After that episode, Royko made an effort to observe women who wear slit dresses, and noticed that "when the wind blows, almost all of them are overwhelmed by modesty and take measures to prevent their thighs from being overexposed." Some hunch over, others "use the big-purse-or-attaché-case trick, holding it in front of them like a leather fig leaf."

Royko couldn't understand why people "spend money to buy garments that are clearly designed to display their thighs," then scurry around like Quasimodo, the hunchback of Notre Dame, to cover them up. So he conducted interviews. He asked women why they bought slit skirts, if not to display their thighs. They replied, "It's the fashion." It was indeed. *Esquire, Time, Newsweek, The New York Times,* and *Women's Wear Daily* were all reporting on slit skirts and "The Lusty Woman." But on the streets, there were only embarrassed women.

### 3. THE "DON'T-SAY-IT-THAT-WAY" PROOF

In Julia Alvarez's novel *How the Garcia Girls Lost Their Accents,* Yolanda doesn't end up sleeping with Rudy.

She sees "his body beautifully sculpted by light and shadows. I did yearn for him, but I yearned for so much more along with that body, which I must have sensed Rudy would never give me. . . . I was tearful and pleading: I wanted to feel we were serious about each other before we made love." Rudy doesn't believe in serious, and they have many struggles in his dorm room, where they would lie

*side by side, cuddling and kissing, Rudy's hand exploring down my*
*blouse. But if he wandered any lower, I'd pull away. "No," I'd say,*
*"don't." "Why not?" he'd challenge, ironically or seductively or exas-*
*peratedly, depending on how much he'd imbibed, smoked, dropped. My*
*own answers varied, depending on my current hang-ups, that's what*
*Rudy called my refusals, hang-ups. Mostly I was afraid I'd get preg-*
*nant. "From getting felt up?" Rudy said with sarcasm. "Ay, Rudy,"*
*I'd plead, "don't say it that way." "What do you mean, don't say it*
*that way? A spade's a spade. This isn't a goddam poetry class."*

It isn't just her fear of pregnancy that is at issue here, for even
five years later, after she is on the Pill and has had several lovers,
Yolanda still throws Rudy out when he shows up on her doorstep
and opens with "you look like you've gotten past all your hang-
ups." He talks the wrong way, and it offends her "that he didn't
want to do anything but screw me, get that over with."

I often think of the don't-say-it-that-way question, because of
the things I hear from men.

"But how can you not like the wham-bam-thank-you-ma'am
song? Every teenager likes that song." Or, "Still? But I thought
since you dated someone for a while you would have gotten
over your hang-ups by now." Or the seduction-by-blackmail:
"Listen to me. I've been keeping track of the times you've said
no and if you say it one more time I'm going to get really
angry." And my favorite: "You know something? You would
make a really good porn star! No, wait—don't be mad—I meant
that as a *compliment*."

Guys, you're not supposed to *say* this stuff to women. Why do
the men of my generation not know this most basic thing? My
guess is that it's because they have no understanding of female
modesty, because they've been raised to believe that women are
exactly like men in every possible way. They don't mean to be
crude or insulting; they just don't understand that women are different from them.

**4. THE YOUNG GIRL PROOF**

Young girls are embarrassed about everything. Even after 30 years
of consciousness raising, nonsexist upbringing, and confidence
building, they're still embarrassed about every single possible
thing they could think of to be embarrassed about. *Young and
Modern* magazine has a special "Hall of Shame" section so readers

can register their mortification on a regular basis. In 1998 there were a lot of bra-stuffing tales of horror, like this one:

> *I'm really flat, so I stuff my bra with tissues. One day I was outside the house reading when my brother and his friend walked by on their way to go swimming. I was totally into my book, so I didn't realize they'd come up behind me till they lifted my chair and threw it—and me—into the pool. Pieces of tissue immediately started coming out of my bra! When the guys figured out where they were coming from, they completely cracked up. Now whenever my bro's friend sees me he says, "My nose is runny. Do you have a tissue?"*

Even those girls who pretend not to be embarrassed and opt for a more exhibitionist route usually end up more shamefaced:

> *A couple of my friends and I were driving to a concert one night. When one of them dared me to moon a car at the next stoplight, I said, "Sure!" I figured I wouldn't know the people, so it wouldn't be a big deal. When we stopped, I opened the window, pulled down my pants, and stuck my butt out. I was laughing so hard I didn't notice that the car beside us was full of guys from my school—including my crush! After I saw them all laughing, I wanted to die! Believe me, my mooning days are over.*

Boys get embarrassed, but never to this degree—in the way that it becomes an omnipresent, overriding concern, in the way that special magazines are created just to provide an outlet for all the permutations of embarrassing moments. Boys also seem to have no qualms whatsoever about mooning their crushes. Indeed, it is usually their crushes they select for the privilege.

The fact is, there are simply not enough magazines out there to soak up all the embarrassment that spontaneously burns girls up at a certain age. "Dear *Help!,*" yet another blushing girl writes to the editor of *American Girl* in 1996: "Whenever I get embarrassed my face gets real hot. When it happens in school, someone always says, 'Hey! Your face is so red!' That makes me even redder.—*Embarrassed*"

*American Girl* replies: "When you're embarrassed, your nerves send extra blood into the tiny blood vessels in your skin. Doctors call this *vasodilatation* (VA-zo-di-LA-tay-shun). The rest of us call it a blush. Blushing is a reflex . . . it's natural. As you get older, you won't be embarrassed as easily and will probably blush less. For now, when you feel a blush spreading, think of something cold, like ice water."

Exactly. It's natural. If modesty were not natural, but inculcated into women, then the older and more cultured a woman got, the more modest we could expect her to be. But instead, the opposite seems to be true. Girls seem to become instinctively modest around boys as soon as they hit puberty, and our culture teaches them that this is a problem. In simpler cultures where modesty is never systematically worn down, the young women are even more embarrassed. Or as Anatole France observed, "We know likewise that peasant women are far more loth than town-bred women to expose themselves to a doctor, even when it is a matter of life and death."

But if it happens to porn stars on the Howard Stern show, to our most sophisticated women on windy days, to Latina girls trying to lose their accents, and to all other girls desperate to stop the unending tide of blushes, maybe all this embarrassment is sticking to us for a reason. Maybe there's a reason why "My Most Embarrassing Moment" is still the most common school assignment; maybe it's the most common human problem.

A young woman once explained to me why she was embarrassed around a man she no longer liked. As she endearingly put it: "I saw Paul the other day, you know the guy I used to have a crush on, and I was so mad because I blushed and *he didn't even deserve a blush!*"

He didn't deserve a blush, but she couldn't help it. When I hear something like that, it assures me that female modesty is natural.

Of course, even if we didn't have any of these proofs, we would know that female modesty is not just some nineteenth-century construct. The twin themes of modesty—of sexual vulnerability, and of what-is-about-to-be-revealed being more exciting than what is seen—are as old as humanity itself. Before Antonio Canova's *Venus Italica* (1812), there was the ancient *Venus Pudica* (Venus of Modesty), and the *Venus de Medici*. Stories about paragons of female modesty—and the men they inspired—date back to the Bible. Before Samuel Richardson's *Pamela* or Charlotte Bronte's *Villette,* there was Xenophon's depiction of the "faithful wife of Susa," Dante and Beatrice, Penelope and Odysseus, Andromache and Hector, Jacob and Rachel, and of course, Isaac and Rebekah.

There are the laws of family purity in Judaism and the "sacrament of love" in Christianity—the mystery of woman Paul says is

Venus Italica *by Antonio Canova, 1812 (Palazzo Pitti, Florence, Italy). Courtesy of Archivi Alinari.*

symbolized by the "veil." The Koran details what parts of the body must be covered, and "in Sanskrit," according to sociologist Kurt Riezler, "the word for shame means the reserve and defense that in the game of love is appropriate to the female part even in the eyes of the libidinous male." Modesty seems to be universal, cross-cultural, and very old.

Even Simone de Beauvoir thought modesty was natural. Though Beauvoir is considered one of our most radical feminists, advocating as she does in *The Second Sex* that women should liberate themselves from the roles of wife and mother, she believed that modesty was one of the few feminine traits that really did have a biological basis, one that protected women. "There will always be certain differences between man and woman; her eroticism, and therefore her sexual world, have a special form of their own and therefore cannot fail to engender a sensuality, a sensitivity, of a special nature." Modesty's natural basis, according to Beauvoir, was not the risk of pregnancy (for the contraception she advocated would do away with that), but more a specifically feminine vulnerability that is inherent in the sex act itself: "Her modesty is in part a superficial acquirement, but it also has deep roots. . . . One of the reasons why modesty paralyzes young men much less than women [is] because of their aggressive role, they are less exposed to being gazed at; and if they are, then they have little fear of being judged, for it is not inert qualities that their mistress demands of them: their complexes will rather depend upon their amatory power and their skill in giving pleasure." Therefore it is most preferable, wrote de Beauvoir, that "the young girl slowly learns to overcome her modesty, to know her partner." Beauvoir predicted that in a society that trivializes this need, sex will be violent and young women will be left without recourse.

But if modesty is indeed natural, then how could it be a virtue? Kant thought that since modesty flows from the natural circumstances of women, and is not the result of any rational struggle, it couldn't qualify as moral: "The girl is not so much virtuous as she has the capacity to make men virtuous. Although it may seem paradoxical, women are the greatest means of [producing] chastity in men, because an otherwise fickle person is made through nothing more chaste than through his love of a girl."

But the very fact that a young woman has the "capacity" to make men virtuous by acting *in accordance* with the ways of modesty seems to suggest that she still has a choice in the matter. Though the instinct may be natural, one still has to decide how to cultivate it—and the fact that in our society a modestly dressed woman is the exception seems to make this point only clearer. In Kantian terms, then, a woman who struggles with her culture and opts for modesty would, in fact, seem to be acting virtuously. The woman clutching her slit skirt on a windy day is neither moral nor immoral because she can't seem to help herself in bending to modesty's demands. But the woman who gets up in the morning and decides not to wear slit skirts? The woman who manifests in her dress that she wants to invite men to relate to her in a different way? Well, she just might be virtuous.

## WOMEN WHO CAN'T TAKE A COMPLIMENT

Up to this point my investigation has been limited to sexual modesty, but now I want to briefly take up the other kind of modesty, the sort we associate with humility, because it offers a useful comparison. In her engaging and much-discussed book, *You Just Don't Understand,* Deborah Tannen reviews the many sex differences in conversational styles, one being that women are, for the most part, much less boastful than men. We meet Charles and Margaret, husband and wife who are both successful lawyers. In public, Charles repeatedly mentions "cases he has won, and important people he knows," even to the point of dropping names of people he has only met once or twice. Yet "for her part, Margaret tries to hide her success. She deliberately avoids letting on if she knows important people whose names arise in the conversation, and she never alludes to her many accomplishments."

Tannen furnishes numerous other examples—of boys who describe themselves as "perfect" and girls who won't say anything good about themselves other than that they want most "to help people." One of the great strengths of *You Just Don't Understand* is that Tannen usually does not judge these male and female conversational styles; a male tendency for "report talk" is not better than a woman's desire for "rapport talk"—only different. However, the case of boasting is an exception. Here Tannen does take the male method of self-presentation to be the "correct" one, and in her section "Never Boast or Brag" explores why women don't behave as boastfully as they should, that is to say, why they're not more like men. She concludes that "women's feelings that they should not boast come from explicit training as well as peer pressure in childhood." She wishes, therefore, "to recommend that women learn to display their accomplishments in public, to ensure that they receive the respect they have earned."

But what if the female response were a perfectly acceptable, even valuable, one? Is it really so desirable that women ape men's behavior?

Psychologists are frequently puzzled when women fail to measure up to male standards of bragging in public. Another related feminine tendency which annoys them is the way women recoil from praise, or "can't take a compliment." I read in my Psychology 101 textbook that one study exhumed the following sex difference in reactions to reward: a man's motivation tends to increase with positive feedback, while a woman's motivation, it turns out, drops when she is given positive feedback. "Why should men and women regard praise in different ways?" My textbook's answer, not unlike Deborah Tannen's, is "the difference in the ways males and females are socialized. Females are more often trained to be dependent, while males are socialized to be independent and achievement oriented."

If this question were on the exam, I wouldn't pass it. The "right" answer isn't consistent with my own experience or with what I have heard from women who report they "can't take a compliment." For instance, Karen, 24, tells me:

> By now I've learned to say thank you, rather than cringe, but when I was younger everyone got mad at me for not being able to take a compliment. People get very mad at you when you can't take a compliment. It's a very important thing to know how to do. Now I know how to do it, but I still feel the same way as when I was younger. When someone praises me a little bit I feel happy, but if someone praises me a lot, what I think—no, more like what I feel—it's like a kind of sticky-sweet storm or something. I don't know why. You know how you're inside a carwash when the scary blue pompoms are swishing? It's like that only I forgot to close the windows, and so I'm being washed, too. I feel soaped and goopy, and it's like a bell goes off, it's too much, it's too much, get it away!

If you ever talk to a woman who "can't take a compliment," and press her on it, you will invariably find that she can't explain her reaction in any other terms but visceral ones. "I don't know why." Or sometimes: "It's just how I feel." Women are usually embarrassed by this kind of bashfulness, because they recognize that it doesn't endear them to others—"People get very mad at you when you can't take a compliment"—but often they remain incapable of controlling it. They always report a strong, instinctive reaction. Of course, it is certainly possible, as my psychology textbook holds, that what seems to be an instinctive reaction is really just the product of years of carefully socialized dependency-training. But today women are more often socialized to become *inde*pendent. So given that this recoiling from praise response persists, even in an era where women are socialized *against* dependence, isn't it possible that there is something more than mere "socialized dependence" going on?

A fascinating 1993 study in the journal *Sex Roles* records some unexpected findings on why "females present themselves more modestly than males in achievement situations." After interviewing 600 college students during the course of two studies, psychologists found that in public, when forced to "disclose," women would underpredict their first semester grade point averages, due to "concerns about the others' feelings," while in private, the women's estimations of their achievement were no less than the men's.

The implications of these findings are profound: women may be modest in public not because they have low self-esteem, or actually think they are doing poorly, but for some other reason entirely. Specifically, their evidence suggests "that girls and women may provide lower estimates of their abilities than boys and men because of a gender difference in self-presentation, not necessarily because of a gender difference in self-confidence." As the authors conclude,

> *This is consistent with Gould and Slone's (1982) findings that females gave more self-derogating attributions about their failures in a public than a private setting, and Berg, Stephen, and Dodson's (1981) findings that females gave less self-enhancing attributions about their successes in public than in private. These findings raise the possibility that what appears to be a lack of self-confidence among girls and women may, at least in some instances, be a desire to present themselves modestly.*

Is feminine recoiling from praise, then, necessarily bad? When I think of my motivation to write this very book, I have a different explanation as to the purpose of this kind of bashfulness. It was precisely when I got negative feedback about this topic that I became convinced it was worth investigating. I didn't understand why, I sensed some force operating beyond my control, but the more smirks I received, the more I was told I was crazy for being interested in this, the more I knew that I must write it and that I *would* write it. And so here we see, in miniature, how female modesty—in this case manifested as an inverse relationship between feedback and motivation—might have an important social purpose. The man who is praised may think "Yes, yes! More, more!" but the woman who is praised may be conveying to the world by her bashfulness, *I have my own compass, thank you. I have my own sense of what is good and what is right, and it's not always what everyone else says it is.* In the light of her natural modesty, a woman's different, independent reaction can be seen not as some problem to be "fixed," but as an important force directing us, perhaps, to what is really important.

The most modest woman is then, in a sense, the most naturally impertinent one.

## THE CONCEIT OF MODESTY

In Vladimir Voinovich's comic novel *2020,* a famous writer named Sim Simych tells a reporter, "Your life's too easy, you've gone soft, you don't understand that you have to fight for your freedom and sacrifice yourselves." "How should we fight for it?" asks the reporter politely. "By renouncing everything you don't need," he replies sternly. "All anyone should have is what he absolutely needs. Take me, for example. I am a world famous writer, but I live modestly. I only have one house, two cottages, a bathhouse, a stable, and a small church." "Tell me, is the lake yours?" the reporter asks. "Yes, I also have one small modest lake."

Speaking about his elaborate retouching of his 1930s and 1940s paintings, Willem de Kooning said, "I was so modest then that I was vain." In Philippians 4:5, we are enjoined: "Let your modesty be known to all men."

These statements may not be as contradictory as they seem. Golda Meir was on to something when she said, "Don't be so humble. You're not that great." There are, to be sure, degrees of falseness, but all kinds of modesty are in some sense "false." In the case of moderate estimation of one's abilities, there is no way of verifying if someone *really* thinks he's not so great, or if he's merely trying to portray himself as modest. As for the sexual virtue, while seeming to be a delicate announcement of innocence, it is really quite brash in its message.

"Pfffffft!" sexual modesty says to the world, "I think *I'm* worth waiting for, and worth concealing. So not you, not you, not you, and not *you* either."

This is certainly not modest. As one 27-year-old Orthodox woman put it to me, with a toss of her long black hair, "there is a saying that goes *Ein b'not yisrael hefker.* It means that the daughters of Israel are not available for public use." She was taking obvious, almost haughty, satisfaction in the fact that she wasn't sleeping around with just *anyone*. And when Julia Alvarez's Yolanda wouldn't sleep with Rudy because he was always complaining about her hang-ups, she was saying that she had too much dignity to give herself to such a jerk.

So one of modesty's paradoxes, then, is that it is usually a reflection of self-worth, of having such a high opinion of yourself that you don't need to boast or put your body on display for all to see. A modestly dressed woman is one who is too important for "public use." On the other hand, it is bragging and exhibitionism which we instinctively associate with insecurity. As Norman Lamm points out: "You meet a person who is always bragging, always talking about his own achievements, boasting of his attractiveness or intelligence or talent or wealth, and you know intuitively that you have just met a person who despises himself."

In this light, it makes sense that so many studies should find early sexual intercourse for girls to be correlated with low self-esteem, and waiting until you're older to be a sign of self-worth. This is why, when people ask me, Isn't it immodest to write about modesty? I always answer, yes, of course it is. But I think girls today could stand to think more of themselves.

When in 1990 the *Orlando Sentinel Tribune* reported a new rule that required bathers to keep their breasts and backsides covered, several supporting the decision talked about the importance of "having pride in yourself." Faith Perkins, 65, said that "although she's no prude, seeing young girls walking on Sarasota beaches with their backsides bared is disgusting. 'It doesn't have anything to do with morals. It just turns my stomach. I have an 8-year-old granddaughter, and we're trying to teach her to be modest.'" Janice Shields, 44, of Orlando agreed: "People have to have some pride in themselves. The morals need to be lifted a little higher." Sexual modesty is often associated with pride, which is interesting because one usually assumes that pride is the opposite of modesty. Perhaps there is a difference between the pride that counts as one of the deadly sins (the outer, boastful variety that is concerned with what others think, often called vanity) and the pride that comes from inner sense of dignity—modest pride?

If someone's modesty seems particularly false, it's probably because they are so conceited that they're afraid no one will be able to stand them unless they constantly self-flagellate. But the extreme case helps us understand the general principle. All modesty may be a conceit, in that it is invariably a reflection of one's self-worth, but just because it's a conceit doesn't mean that it isn't natural, or that it isn't a way of manifesting our uniquely human dignity. For even someone whose modesty seems noxiously false is still demonstrating by it a concern for the opinion of others. Think of Uriah Heep. Could there ever be a rabbit equivalent of Uriah Heep? Uriah Heep may be disgusting, with his sweaty palms and intolerable unctuousness, but he is *our* Uriah Heep. He's one of us because he is disgusting in a uniquely human way. And as for sexual modesty, why shouldn't we be particular? Our capacity to discriminate is what built civilization. Should it really come as such a surprise that when we began to tolerate everything, our society became less civilized?

So just because modesty is a conceit doesn't mean it can't also be natural or uniquely human. Or, to put it differently, just because modesty is false doesn't mean it isn't true.

In fact, some of the most surprising people think modesty is true.

### THE COMMON SENSE OF MODESTY

In my senior year in college, Mary Daly arrived to give a speech on campus. It was a very big event for our college, because she's such a famous author—of *The Church and the Second Sex, Pure Lust, Gyn/Ecology*—and one of feminism's leading lights. Chapin Hall, our largest auditorium, was packed.

I approached her after her speech, and I was surprised that we got along so nicely. I told her about our coed bathrooms, and she said, "Privacy's very important; I wouldn't want that."

I couldn't believe it. I would have thought that someone like Mary Daly would be against modesty, because that's "sexist"— what I was hearing from the feminists in my classes. But here was feminism's most radical, most official paladin, and she was all in favor of modesty. Who knew? She even signed my copy of her book *Wickedary,* and in the kindest, most encouraging way possible: She wrote, "Courage to a proud prude! Stay Crazy (Sane)!— Mary." Inside the book I learned that the virtue of pride is derived from prude, which once meant "a wise or good woman."

I was very proud of my signed *Wickedary* and showed it to all my friends. One of them told me that she only signed it because she didn't know that I was *"an extreme right-winger."* Had she known that I was an *extreme right-winger,* she "wouldn't have touched [my] *Wickedary* with a ten-foot pole!"

Maybe so, but that only makes her endorsement of modesty

even more interesting. When she didn't know that I was an "extreme right-winger"—that is, when she didn't hear anything other than, isn't this strange, what's going on?—she was on my side. When she heard nothing but the idea itself, she was in favor of modesty.

Modesty, therefore, is common sense. Everyone needs to have privacy.

And secrets, too.

## SECRETS AND MODESTY

"Dear *Help!,*" writes nervous "Blabbermouth Elly" to *American Girl* magazine in 1996: "I'm bad at keeping secrets. Every time someone tells me a secret, I blurt it out. I'm afraid my friends won't like me if I keep telling their secrets." When the stuffed creature named Talking Elmo hit the shelves of American toy stores, the first thing he said when you squeezed his bright red furry stomach—before "*Play* with me!" and before even "Elmo *love* you!"—was: "Tell Elmo a *secret!*" Little children instinctively understand the importance of secrets. As soon as they like you they want to tell you a secret, and it's always a very serious matter. Girls giggle when they share secrets, but it would be a mistake to assume that's because they make light of them. They giggle so much precisely to cover up how important their secrets are. If they can't keep a friend's secret, like "Blabbermouth Elly," they immediately feel bad about it and recognize it as a moral failing.

Having secrets seems to be a way of asserting one's essential dignity, one's importance in the world. And sharing secrets is a way of recognizing the dignity of someone else—of ratifying trust, confirming the importance of a friendship. Even if it's just you and Talking Elmo, since you shared a secret, your stuffed toy becomes *ipso facto* important.

Even before a child is capable of whispering a secret, he is always capable of playing Peekaboo. It is the most basic human game. Before "I think, therefore I am," there is something else: "I hide, therefore I am." Because I can withhold myself, this proves I exist. This is why Peekaboo is so delightful to a baby—because it involves the discovery that there is a self to withhold.

If the baby is a girl, she will probably grow up to devour Frances Hodgson Burnett's classic *The Secret Garden,* where lost, orphaned Mary Lennox finds her true self in a walled garden, and *The Velvet Room,* by Zipher Snyder, where another lost girl finds solace in a secret room. Then there are Louise Fitzhugh's classics, *The Long Secret* and *Harriet the Spy*. Boys have secrets too, but they're not as obsessed with them. And when they are obsessed, it's usually with knowing the secrets of girls. On the cover of the magazine *XXX Exposure,* we find the screaming headline: "TOTALLY SHAMELESS GIRLS SPILL ALL THEIR EXPLICIT SECRETS!" You never see a gay male pornographic magazine with the headline "TOTALLY SHAMELESS BOYS SPILL ALL THEIR EXPLICIT SECRETS!" Why? It is a girl's discovery of self which is intimately entwined with her discovery of secrets: of how, by withholding from some, she creates trust with others. Since the woman in pornography has no self, no individuality, since she is instead an object, an empty repository of fantasies, she can have no secrets.

When you're young, other people's secrets never seem as interesting or important as your own. Even well into adulthood, "inside jokes" are usually the best jokes of all. Yet there's really no objective standard to measure whether someone else's secrets are any more interesting than yours. You prefer yours only because you see them from the inside, and they announce your importance, whereas other people's secrets do not, and may even actively exclude you.

As you grow up it begins to dawn on you that nobody really cares about your secrets because people have more important things to worry about. That's kind of a letdown, but life goes on—for most people, anyway. There is, however, one important exception to the nobody-cares-about-your-secrets rule. When you love someone you want to protect their secrets, and guarding them becomes just as important to you as your own secrets, if not more so. You usually don't want to burden them with your secrets, but you want to protect theirs. Unfortunately, sometimes it happens that you think you can trust someone with a secret, because you love him, not realizing that after you tell him this secret, he will proceed to repeat it to his friends—perhaps even 12 of his friends. That's always a surprise, like pressing the bright furry red stomach of your Talking Elmo and learning you got the sinister Elmo Who Talks Too Much. ("Tell Elmo a secret, and Elmo will tell it to *everyone.* Heh-heh-heh . . .")

But there is no way of knowing beforehand whether you can trust someone with a secret, just as there is no way of knowing beforehand that love will fade. All you can do is gather yourself up, laugh, and think—Well, at least I didn't tell him any of my *really important* secrets. This may be childish, but so is the capacity to trust another person, and if you want to hold out the hope that someday you will meet someone you can trust completely, I think you have to insist—stubbornly and childishly—on your right to keep some things private.

Of course, if you do know beforehand that you're the sort of person who can't keep anyone else's secrets, it means there's something really wrong with you. In a 1997 issue of *New York* magazine, for example, there is a Personals ad in which a man advertises for a companion and specifies, between "nonsmoker" and "must love the sun," that he will not abide any "previous baggage." When someone announces that he is incapable of sharing another's secrets, actually finds this important enough to advertise right on page 91—*"No Previous Baggage"*—it means that he is incapable of love. It means, I can only treat a woman as a means to my gratification—I could never consider her an individual, an end in herself, someone who comes with dignity and secrets (a.k.a. "baggage").

Take that stanza in William Blake's "Love's Secret," for instance: "I told my love, I told my love, / I told her all my heart, / Trembling, cold, in ghastly fears. / Ah! She did depart!" This is apparently a common problem, then. But when your love flees from your secrets, it probably wasn't really you he loved. Or maybe you just told too much, too soon, and you exceeded his secrets quota. Better luck next time.

Rule number 60 of George Washington's *Rules of Civility & Decent Behavior in Company and Conversation* pleads, "Be not immodest in urging your Friends to Discover a Secret."

So what is the connection between secrets and modesty? Between the child obsessed with keeping secrets and the childish adult incapable of keeping any, there is an ideal to be found. The proper balance seems to have something to do with modesty. The beauty of sexual modesty is that it protects your secrets for the man who truly loves you. Having sex with anyone and telling your secrets to everyone have a lot in common. It is no accident that sexual promiscuity is associated with our tell-all let-it-all-hang-out talk show culture. Everything is public because there is no longer any private realm. Our dignity is in our secrets. If nothing is secret, nothing is sacred.

In a way, then, this peculiar human armor of modesty protects us against the illusion that we could ever be truly known by strangers. Erwin Straus points out that our shame arises naturally because, unlike other animals, only humans have a private and a public sphere. Our shame, indeed, is what makes privacy possible.

You may think you see me, the modestly dressed woman announces, but you do not see the real me. The real me is only for my beloved to see. Therefore, whatever you may say or think about me doesn't really matter. The woman who complains about sexual harassment or "elevator eyes" is not a frail, weak woman, nor is she the invention of a few radical feminists. She is, rather, a woman exposed and expressing a very real fear: that the one who is judging her is not the one who loves her, not the one who knows the "real" her. Hence, he is *presuming*. A respect for modesty would prevent men from leering, from presuming to judge women whom they have not earned the trust of.

## A POSITIVE CONTENT TO WOMANHOOD

"Just because you're a woman doesn't mean you can't be a doctor or a lawyer." Girls of my generation grew up on this expression. *"Just because you're a woman."* It was a motto like mother's milk to us, and now it is the philosophy behind Take Our Daughters to Work Day. *"Just because you're a woman."* In other words, being a woman is a kind of handicap that with hard work, one can overcome. Some are born deformed; others are born women, but be brave. I'm sure you'll make the best of it.

Yet now that we are free to be anything, doctors and lawyers, now that we've seen that women can be rational, and that men can cry, what we most want to know, and what we are not permitted to ask, is what does it mean to be a woman in the first place? Not in terms of what it won't prevent us from doing, mind you—we are not unaware of our bountiful options—but what is meaning*ful* about being a woman? Rosie the Riveter was riveting only because she didn't usually rivet, and now that so many Rosies do, we most long to know what makes us unique again.

Two different women said to me, nervously, before graduation: What's wrong with me? I want to have children. One had landed a job with an investment banking firm; the other was *supposed* to land a job with an investment banking firm because that's what her father wanted, but the scouts who came to campus complained she wasn't aggressive enough. *What's wrong with me? I want to have children. . . .*

Once at my college's main pharmacy, I passed a collection of New Age candles. Two other women were browsing and making their selections: There was a "Banishing" Candle, and then one to bring "Male Forces." The woman near me grabbed the second-to-last "Male Forces" candle, and so I decided to try that one since it was so popular. I greedily swiped the last one, and learned that it contained patchouli, benzoin, pine, cedar, and juniper. It even came with a special incantation:

> *Male Forces, that I need, come to me with all speed . . .*
> *Father Sky and Master Sun, as I light this candle, great god come . . .*
> *Herne the Hunter, hear my plea, gods of Earth, Fire, Air & Sea . . .*
> *Manitu, native father, on you I call, words go out to bring them all . . .*
> *In perfect trust, send to me what is just . . .*
> *Harming none and helping all is how it shall be . . .*
> *This I make true 3x3x3 . . .*

When I arrived home I lit this tall yellow candle and recited this poem, only to look down and notice that, darn it, I'm still female. Only, a female who reeked of juniper and patchouli. The spell didn't work. But then I saw I had neglected to read the disclaimer on the candle wrapping: "Remember, you get as much energy out of your workings as you put into them." In other words, if the spell didn't work, it's your own fault.

I think of all the other women who lit this candle hoping it would make them men and blaming themselves for the fact that they're still women, and it depresses me. In 1998, a *New York Press* female columnist writes that she "didn't resent these guys when they dumped me so much as want to *be* them." Her girlfriend Ruby, though, gives her hope: "Ruby made me feel like for the first time in my life, I had a chance of becoming what I'd always wanted to be: a guy."

A young woman today has basically two options open to her: to pretend she's a man, or to be feminine in a desperate, victim-like way. There's Rene Denfield; she's a boxer, her book jacket announces. There's Camille Paglia; she's very tough and even has a taste for gay male pornography! "Take your blows like men," she advises young women in *Vamps and Tramps.* Then there are the women whose femininity is expressed by sleeping with a lot of men and then lamenting how much they resent men. Whether a young woman should opt for man or victim, the message sent by our culture is clear: it's not a good thing to be female.

A high school girl explains to a *New York* magazine reporter why she is sleeping with so many guys, even though she doesn't really want to: "You have to make them think you're one of the guys. For a girl to get accepted, she has to be down and dirty. They have to see you not give a shit, not be a priss—be like a man, basically. To be a cool girl you kind of have to stab girlkind in the back." Meanwhile, on the floor, among the fashion magazines, the reporter notices an article about girls who cut themselves because of depression. "Yeah, I did that," the girl admits sadly, "I don't know why. . . . One day I just got so upset and I wanted to cut myself."

For the past forty years, all talk about sex has coalesced around two basic positions: either men are evil and should become more like women—the position often called "gynocentric"—or women are the bad ones and need to become more like men, the position first taken by the sexual revolutionists and later adopted by many antifeminists. After surveying the landscape of these experiments— from the misogyny of the sexual revolution, to the gynocentric response, and now back to misogyny again—one might be forgiven for wondering if we should stop switching roles and making ourselves miserable. Maybe we're fine the way we are.

The sexual revolution seems to have failed mostly because it ignored the differences between the sexes—specifically, the importance of female modesty. When it failed, when women began to discover that they were uniquely compromised by a sexual free-for-all, there was an attempt to restore order. Women's liberation may have been a valiant attempt to restore that order, but it, too, failed because it was reluctant to consider the importance of natural modesty, and held that all differences we observed were the result of oppression. Hence all their ways to restore order, such as through sexual harassment legislation, have been like trying to put a Band-Aid over an amputated limb.

The current antifeminist consensus recognizes that these feminist legislations have not worked, but never offers any positive vision of how the sexes can relate. And so we are caught up in a vicious circle, because today's antifeminists seem to want to return to the free-love heyday that caused many of these problems in the first place. The only thing standing in their way, it seems, is AIDS, and so we are at an impasse. But why do we have to spend all of world history repeating the same mistakes when we can learn from them?

Modesty is our way out. For women who are tired of being told they must be either men or victims, modesty offers a new choice. Its rich, but often ignored, cultural legacy offers women a positive content to womanhood. This is how a return to modesty could end the war between the sexes. Many young women today don't think their lives should be spoiled by their parents' mistakes, and we would want nothing more than to return, if we could, to the days before all of these experiments. Not only do we think there are differences between the sexes, but we think these differences can have a beautiful meaning—a meaning that isn't some irrelevant fact about us but one that can inform and guide our lives. That's why we're swooning over nineteenth-century dramas and clothing.

We want our dignity back, our "feminine mystique" back, and, along with it, the notion of male honor. Our mothers tell us we shouldn't want to give up all the hard-won "gains" they have bequeathed to us, and we think, what gains? Sexual harassment, date rape, stalking, eating disorders, all these dreary hook-ups? Or perhaps it's the great gain of divorce you had in mind? We look to a different, more romantic, generation for our role models.

## MODESTY AND BEAUTY

When my grandparents were dating, whenever my grandpa would attempt to hold my grandma's hand at the movies, she always ran away to the bathroom. During one film she could disappear to the bathroom five or six times.

I'm like a 3-year-old with this story. Whenever I get discouraged I ask them to tell it to me again: "Tell me the story about how grandpa tried to hold your hand and you kept getting up and going to the bathroom." I already know the story. In fact, by asking for it I've pretty much told it myself, but I need to hear it told with my grandpa's chuckle. "Your grandmother! She was always escaping to the bathroom!"

A sweet story, you say. Well, thank you. But before you pat me on the head, may I tell you the ending of it? My grandparents have a wonderful marriage. Not the kind of marriage one sometimes sees with elderly couples—you know, where the wife becomes a kind of policeman, barking out how many prunes her husband can have, while her sullen spouse sulks bitterly—but still a romantic marriage. From the way my grandma glows when she speaks his name and the way he speaks to her, always very tenderly, you can see that they are still very much in love after sixty years together.

I keep returning to this story, to this image of my grandma at 19, running up the aisle of a darkened movie theater, alarmed and excited. The more I reflect on this minor, silly story, the more I come to think that maybe it isn't so minor, and maybe it isn't so silly, either. Maybe it's even essential. Maybe the story of this great love between my grandparents comes down to the story of my grandmother's modesty.

Would they have stuck together through hard times if they had lived together for years before? There is obviously no way of knowing, but from what we know of couples who live together, it seems unlikely.

Another amazing thing about my grandma is that she is *always* beautiful. I don't mean subjective beauty, as in, she-is-beautiful-because-she's-my-grandmother, but *objectively* beautiful. If you weren't related to her I can guarantee that you would be jealous of her. No matter what she is doing, no matter what time of day, with makeup or without, she always has a glow surrounding her, kind of radiating outward and enveloping everyone within a ten-foot radius.

Once when I attempted to explain to someone how beautiful my grandmother was—we were having a class discussion about cosmetic surgery and superficiality—my interlocutor listened patiently, then said quickly, "Yes, yes, I know what you mean, *inner* beauty's important, too." But I wasn't talking about *inner* beauty. I was talking about objective outer beauty, the kind of outer glow which I think must come from knowing what is important. When people have too much plastic surgery they tend to lose their beauty, as if God were punishing them for losing sight of what real beauty is. But sometimes this may be the husband's fault:

> *Art dealer Alec Wildenstein's estranged wife says she went under the knife for numerous face lifts in a desperate bid to look younger and keep her billionaire husband from straying. "I did it for him," Jocelyne Wildenstein, 52, told the Post. . . . "He wanted me to have a younger appearance," the copper-haired mother of two insisted sadly. Alec was busted in September after he allegedly pulled a licensed gun on his wife and her two body guards when Jocelyne surprised her naked hubby in their bedroom with a 19-year-old blonde.*

My grandma has a golden necklace to go with her golden glow, a necklace made up of ten golden circles. Each circle has the first name of one of her grandchildren, and on the back, his or her birthday. We all love this necklace the best of all her necklaces, and when we were little would clamber all over her to see "where am

I on the necklace?" "is this me over here?" "which cousin am I next to?" and "let me see if you got my birthday right." We all fit together because my grandma was there to connect all of us.

In her world there are words that still mean things, people to depend on and steady you, real things beyond yourself to long for. She doesn't need antidepressants to "set the floor" under her, because she had my grandfather, whom she could always depend on.

Why are none of my grandmother's friends anorexic? Why are even the plumpest of them contented? Joan Jacobs Brumberg recently undertook a very interesting study of girls' diaries in *The Body Project*, and made the discovery that girls are much more self-conscious about their appearance today than they were a hundred years ago. In the 1890s, she found, a girl scribbled the following New Year's resolution, typical for a young woman at that time: "Resolved," she wrote, "to think before speaking. To work seriously. To be self-restrained in conversations and actions. Not to let my thoughts wander. To be dignified. Interest myself more in others." In the 1990s, a typical diary reads: "I will try to make myself better in any way I possibly can. . . . I will lose weight, get new lenses, already got new haircut, good makeup, new clothes and accessories."

But these pressures—to be perfect and thin and have no laugh lines, all while balancing a career and a perfectly orgasmic sex life without any hang-ups—were not bequeathed to us by the patriarchy. It was our eagerness to abandon those codes of conduct which informed our lives and grounded us, the ones that pointed at what is truly important. Who told women that they couldn't be round, that they had to cut themselves off from their bodies? Who told women that even if they wanted to stay home with their children, they shouldn't be allowed to? It wasn't the patriarchy. If you flip open to any page of *The Second Sex* or *The Feminine Mystique,* you are bound to find more misogyny than in the writings of Aristotle and Norman Mailer combined—sexist as they might have been, at least these men never called women "parasites." Simone de Beauvoir: "What is extremely demoralizing for the woman who aims at self-sufficiency is the existence of other women . . . who live as parasites." Ann Ferguson in *Blood at the Root:* "Since housewifery and prostitution have the same structure, it is hypocritical to outlaw one and not the other."

Kierkegaard wrote that when "the eternal element in love becomes an object of derision, the temporal element alone is left," but his distinction could just as easily apply to womanhood. Today the debate over beauty is divided between feminists who say that women are objectified by the male gaze, and their conservative critics who insist that there is no such thing as a beauty myth. Modesty allows us, once again, to step back. There is a beauty myth—to the extent that we have lost sight of what is truly beautiful in women—but the origin of this beauty myth is our attack on the idea of eternal beauty in women. After all, the goals of the 1890s girl, wishing to be "dignified" and "restrained," one could say—and many did—are sexist goals. As John Stoltenberg has written: "Her charity, her mercy, her grace (not for nothing have men personified all those abstractions as female in legend and art!) are in fact the emblems of female subordination to rapist ethics." This is now accepted dogma. But if charity, mercy, and grace are all deleted, what remains of womanhood?

We said that it was sexist to suggest womanhood meant something more than just breasts and lipstick, and now we are left wondering why we are stuck with just breasts and lipstick. The temporal feminine has replaced the eternal feminine. The expectation that we be good is gone, but filling the void is the pressure to be good in bed. Womanhood today is so crude largely because of the attack on female modesty.

I hope I have a grandchildren-necklace someday. But it's very hard to separate the kind of person my grandmother is from the kind of person my grandfather is.

# Chapter 8

# MALE CHARACTER

*March 18, 1997*

*Dear Wendy,*

*Of course I remember you, and I do have some ideas on modesty. It really is inexorably entwined with dignity, and I think applies to both sexes. Probably both necessary for the survival of any society in a palatable form, where people accept one's need for privacy and yet the importance, also, of mutual intimacy that's supportive, not reciprocally dependent. Without modesty, social lives are pretty rugged, tending to be characterized by mutual slyness, or bullying and crass ruthlessness, in reducing the experience to an unrewarding competition. Keeping "rules" of consideration and grace, wrapped in a "modesty" approach, prevents us from punishing each other, as we are all capable of doing under the pressure of social competitiveness, where caring, unless it is genuine, can disappear in a flash. Sending respectful signals to each other is also what helps us recognize others who can genuinely maintain consideration of another's needs and feelings. Well, you asked!*

—A MALE FRIEND FROM MILWAUKEE

An ad for British Sterling reads, "Once in a while a man comes along who isn't afraid to be a gentleman." What can it mean to be "afraid to be a gentleman"? After years of attacking gentlemanly behavior—of Jill Johnston, for example, warning us of the evils loosed upon the world by "the age of shrivelry" in *Lesbian Nation; The Feminist Solution*—men are literally afraid to be nice to women. Every man has a story about the time he opened a door for a woman, and she slammed it on his hand, and every woman a story about a door slammed in her face. Mark my words: if you pose the simple question "should men open doors for women?" to a random male passerby, nine times out of ten he will chant in eerie Orwellian fashion, "*People* should open doors for *people!*"

Since there can no longer be any talk of the proper relation that ought to exist between the sexes—for that would be "imposing values"—all we can do is furiously sue for sexual harassment, hold rallies against date rape, and write articles about why there is nothing much we can do about stalking. Since we can no longer preempt these kinds of problems with commonly enforced codes of conduct, we can only seek punishment once an actual crime has occurred. But there is a significant difference between the nuanced, more supple codes of conduct which sought to prevent rapes, by inspiring men with respect for female modesty, and heavy-handed regulations that attempt to substitute for such respect by warning of the perils of depriving women of equal opportunity. The latter view, instead of encouraging respect for women, seems to have made them weaker. Instead of informing the relation between the sexes, demystifying codes of conduct as "sexist" and equating marriage with rape has poisoned it.

Yet our popular culture—our fashion and entertainment industries—is, slowly but surely, breaking through this layer of accepted dogma, and increasingly portraying women frustrated by our state of affairs totally devoid of codes of conduct. One *Seinfeld* episode has Elaine overflowing with bags of groceries, while pal Jerry won't lift a finger. She's huffing and puffing with the bags up to the apartment, and he pretends to be completely oblivious to the fact she's carrying anything until, finally, they arrive through the door and he delivers the punch line in a tone one would use for a servant: "You can just set them over there— thanks." In a different episode, Jerry grabs the first-class seat on a plane, while Elaine is stuck in coach. And in another, Elaine has a sore neck because she had to lift a bike herself.

But, one might retort, so what? So men no longer carry packages and open doors for women. It's more than that. Should the Titanic disaster happen today, reveals a 1998 *Glamour* poll, a majority of women say that it would be sexist for a man to give up his lifeboat seat for a woman. A woman's life should not be spared before a man's, say 66%. Around the same time, a Manhattan beautician claimed that she had spotted serial killer Andrew Cunanan— the man who eventually murdered fashion icon Versace—earlier in the year, but because the cops had flirted with her and behaved unchivalrously, the serial killer got away. Her account was later confirmed by police records. "They should be a little old fashioned and use their feet and run back with me," she lamented, "It was only a couple of streets." But by the time the cops had finished teasing her about her French accent, the suspect had vanished.

A society that has lost its respect for female modesty is not just one which no longer teaches men to be protective of women, it is a society which treats its women as a kind of joke.

Some women in the 90s, recognizing that we were better off when the men were taught how to relate to us, are advocating that women now "demand chivalry of men." But, unfortunately, as we are learning, demanding chivalry doesn't seem to work. Coty's "Longing" perfume advertises with the slogan, "Make a Man Remember." But you can't *make* a man remember. You can certainly want him to, but you can't make him. Part of what made modesty beautiful was that it was not scheming, but good in itself. As Ruth Bernard Yeazell eloquently notes, the main reason Richardson's fictional heroine Pamela succeeds in turning her would-be seducer into a husband is because she is not calculating: "B's conversion suggests that men's designs on women may be subverted and transformed when they come to believe that women themselves are undesigning."

Marx, Georg Lukács was reported to have quipped, couldn't explain death or unrequited love, and just as no one has the right to be loved back, women do not have a right to make men remember them, nor a "right to be courted." In order to court women men must, in some sense, need to court women. Do people imagine men courted women in the past because they simply found it more fun than casual sex? No, it was because women's modesty required it. Moreover, in order to seek a pledge of marriage, one must live in a society where the law says that the pledge is really a pledge.

I cannot make the man sitting across from me treat me with courtesy or court me. The men are ultimately the ones who will have to decide what it means to be a man. So, then, is it more manly for a man to be boorish around a woman or to be gentle? Somehow boorishness has come to be associated with manliness, when in fact it is just boyishness.

Part of the problem is that we said it was sexist for a man to be gentle around a woman. For instance, a checklist from the West-chester Coalition of Family Violence agencies includes "an over-protective manner" as evidence you might be abused. In this light, the more boorish and less protective, the closer a man is to the liberated ideal.

Yet conservatives are just as much to blame for the current state of affairs as the radical egalitarians. They too have encouraged boorishness, but for an altogether different reason: they have looked upon being rough to women with a fond boys-will-be-boys attitude. Too many egalitarians equate male gentleness or protectiveness with subordination, while too many conservatives equate it with effeminacy. Both sides are wrong. A man should be gentle around a woman. That's part of what it means to be a man.

We need to flip everything around again and associate manhood with knowing how to behave, not misbehave, around women.

## MALE SEXUAL MODESTY

I think people are afraid to talk about female modesty because they fear it will be related to some sexual double standard. But in fact, female modesty is related not to a philandering male, but to male modesty. As far back as the Bible, Noah curses his son Ham for staring at him drunk and exposed (Genesis 9:21–27). Then God reiterates the importance of modesty for men in Exodus 20:23: "Do not ascend My altar by steps, that your nakedness may not be exposed upon it." Later in Exodus (28:42–43), the importance of men covering up will be stressed once more, and even the exact length of linen breeches is detailed.

Among Orthodox Jews, both husband and wife must refrain from touching one another for a period during each month: the laws are not called *taharat Haishah,* "woman's purity," but *taharat haMishpachah,* "family purity." Additionally, both male and female are prohibited from being alone or in *"yihud"* with one another unless they are married. And remember those seventeenth-century Brathwait guides that stressed the importance of female modesty? They also included the injunction, "the Voluptuous Libertine misimployeth time in two respects": not only "in respect of himselfe" but "in respect of those good creatures." The Spur Posse is not a nineteenth-century phenomenon, it is worth recalling, but a thoroughly modern one. It is today's male who is thought manly by "scoring." In a different time he proved his manhood by being honorable. Success with women used to mean being faithful to one of them.

Closer to recent times, the White Cross–White Shield campaign that began in 1874 to promote chastity before marriage and fidelity within marriage urged a single standard of purity, binding on men and women equally. And any tour of Coney Island photos of the turn of the century shows that the men wore covered-up swimming outfits too—a bare chest was very rare.

What exactly is male sexual modesty, then? Scholar Anthony Fletcher notes, "Full manhood was unattainable without the process of courtship, marriage and household formation, but young men knew that these things implied the abandonment, or at least control, of their drinking, whoring and gorging." Thomas Ricketts, for example, "discovered in bed with a married woman at Farnham in Berkshire in 1637, found himself greeted by 'a spice mortar, a platter and a candlestick ringing and making a noise' and an attempt to put him in the stocks."

So male modesty, like female modesty, seems to involve moderating one's sexual activity and generally reserving it for one's beloved (who is expected to be one's spouse). But male modesty also seems to be strongly tied to the notion of honor and obligation. What is male honor, then? For starters, it seems to have a lot to do with men not talking with others about their women, or anyone else's woman, for that matter. You can still observe a concern for it today. If someone is "a jerk," it is usually because he talks about women in a consistently crude way. Indeed, talking about women in a vulgar way is such a sign of bad character that the very first rule of Frances Benton's "Men's Manners" chapter warns men against it:

> 1. *Talking About Women. A well-mannered man does not talk about his conquests. He does not, in fact, say anything about a woman which would give others a questionable opinion of her integrity or morals. Most men automatically accord this courtesy to their wives or sweethearts, but they may be less respectful about a woman whose relationship with them is more casual. Locker-room bull sessions about women are poor manners.*

This concern about the debasement of women seems to go beyond concern for the woman's reputation, and has more to do with the character of the one doing the talking. Among some men, this particular understanding of male honor is still kept alive today. "I have a general rule when a guy brags to me about a woman or discusses some intimate detail with me," says Chad, 45: "if he's talking, he's probably not doing." What does that mean, I asked—can't men ask for advice, the way women do?

"No, general advice is fine, but if a man gets extremely specific, something's up." See *YM* magazine in 1998: "Q: Why do guys tell other guys they've gone further with you than they really have? A: Some lie 'cause they want to sound cool and impress other guys. But most of us can tell when a dude is talking trash. And most of us think it's pathetic."

A Don Juan reputation, therefore, often seems to be a correction for sexual insecurity. But of what kind? Male fear of inadequacy is very different from female fear of rape. Male and female sexual modesty may be equally important, but they will be different just as the sexes are different. To appreciate how they are related, one cannot ignore this difference. For example, male sexual modesty does not seem to inspire women the way that female sexual modesty has the power to inspire men. Female modesty can trigger male sexual modesty, but it doesn't seem to work the other way around. A young woman not having sex is quite often a woman waiting for someone interesting to come along, whereas a guy not having sex is perceived (perhaps unfairly) as just a guy who is not having sex. She often can, but won't, whereas he often would, but doesn't have the opportunity. If all girls suddenly announced they would not sleep with boys until they quit the gangs and gave them engagement rings, society could very well change overnight, but if the boys made a similar announcement about the girls, everybody would probably burst out laughing.

Havelock Ellis compares male and female modesty this way: "The woman who, under some circumstances and at some times, is extreme in her reticences, under other circumstances or at other times, may be extreme in her abandonment. Not that her modesty is an artificial garment, which she throws off or on at will. It is organic, but like the snail's shell, it sometimes forms an impenetrable covering, and sometimes glides off almost altogether. A man's modesty is more rigid, with little tendency to deviate toward either extreme. Thus it is, that, when uninstructed, a man is apt to be impatient with a woman's reticences, and yet shocked at her abandonments."

### MALE HONOR

Like modesty, which once made every woman a lady, male honor was what made every male a man. A man of honor was someone who respected female modesty—that is, every female's modesty, whether she was rich or poor, from the country or the inner city.

"Honor, in the chivalric code, could not be contracted into," as Anthony Fletcher puts it, it could not be bought. It was fought for instead, often at the cost of one's life. A wonderful study by Cecilia Morgan in the *Canadian Historical Review* nicely captures what male honor once meant:

*An insult to a woman's chastity was deemed a socially acceptable reason for issuing a challenge. Such was the case in the fatal shooting of the first attorney-general of Upper Canada, John White, by John Small, the clerk of the Executive Council, on 3 January 1800. The affair was precipitated by comments that White had made about the chastity of Small's wife, Elizabeth. Angered by Elizabeth Small's snubbing of his wife, Marrianne, White told his friend David Smith, the surveyor general, that not only had he slept with Elizabeth Small but he had ended their relationship from fear of "injury to his Health from the Variety and frequency of her Amours with others." . . . Her reputation for sexual continence having been impugned, it was now Elizabeth Small's turn to be snubbed. Once Small became aware of the reasons behind this behavior, he confronted White and, after asking him if he was responsible, challenged him to a duel. The two men met in the back of the government buildings at the foot of Berkeley Street on 3 January 1800. White had stated that he would not aim at Small, since he did not want to hurt him. Both pistols, however, went off simultaneously, leaving White mortally wounded. He died thirty-six hours later and, in a grand gesture common to many unsuccessful duelists, forgave all involved. . . . The notion of honour that both combatants fought to maintain encompassed more than just the need to uphold certain norms of sexual behavior—honour also meant male financial responsibilities and obligations for family members.*

"God forbid," as Fielding wrote to Richardson after reading *Clarissa*, "God forbid that the man who reads this with dry eyes should be alone with my daughter when she hath no assistance within call." A man who did not respect female modesty wasn't more manly—he was less of a man. A man who had intercourse with a woman without being absolutely sure of her consent (what now goes by "date rape") wasn't displaying his masculinity, only his immaturity. He was announcing, in effect, that he didn't understand what it meant to be a man.

What other things do we mean today when we say someone "doesn't know what it means to be a man"?

After the Supreme Court found that alimony rewards had to be gender blind in 1979, it became unconstitutional to assume that a woman needed financial support after a divorce. Since then, reported a 1997 *Wall Street Journal,* the number of women court-ordered to pay alimony to their husbands has skyrocketed. "A man of character wouldn't take it," said one of these women, Grace Ainslie, who is now 62. "A man of character . . . he'd get a job."

What does it mean to be a "man of character"? Does it just have to do with paying, or is it something more profound? Consider the difference between the following reflections. Both are men, both write on male sexual propriety. The only difference is between the times they lived in. Here is Roland Barthes in 1978:

> *Gossip reduces the other to he/she, and this reduction is intolerable to me. For me the other is neither* he *nor* she; *the other has only a name of his own, and her own name. The third-person pronoun is a wicked pronoun: it is the pronoun of the non-person, it absents, it annuls. When I realize that common discourse takes possession of my other and restores that other to me in the bloodless form of a universal substitute, applied to all the things which are not here, it is as if I saw my other dead, reduced, shelved in an urn upon the wall of the great mausoleum of language. For me, the other cannot be a* referent: *you are never anything but you, I do not want the Other to speak of you.*

And here is "Edward Lee," about 20 years later in a 1997 *Marie Claire* article: "You shouldn't spend the next day together after you've had sex. That's the time to call your best friend and say, 'Guess what happened last night?'"

In 1978, one's lover would be protected from the cold outside world. Maybe not at pain of death, as in 1800, but there was still a sense that part of the meaning of being someone's lover was to protect and be protected. Twenty years later, not only is the lover's claim totally ignored, but the only reason for having a lover seems to be to impress this outside world. There are no private claims. Everything is debased and ruined to serve the appetite of the public.

Next, consider the complaint of this woman, whose husband has become a kind of "Grammar Cop" in public:

> *One day, over brunch with old friends, he did it again. "Honey, it's 'my sister and me,' not 'my sister and I,'" he said, buttering his bread. I blew up. "How can you embarrass me like that?" I hissed as our guests peered into their soup bowls. "Do I ever make you look ridiculous?*

*God, I even laugh at that same dumb joke you tell every time we go*
*to a party!" Red-faced, he mumbled an apology. Finally, I thought, he's*
*got it.*

What is the connection between (1) the man who will support
his ex-spouse, even when no longer required to by law, (2) the
man who does not gossip about his love life, and (3) the husband
who does not correct his wife in public? In all three cases there is
a rejection of the conventional—whether embodied by some
reverse alimony law, the curious giggling of one's friends, or the
laws of grammar—and a fidelity to a different and higher authority. Perhaps a man of honor, then, is he who guards the private and
the high against the public and the low.

## THE DEMISE OF MALE COURTESY

A fiftyish lady who worked at our college's pharmacy once greeted me, excitedly, with the following story: "My mother called me
yesterday and said that when she was taking the streetcar in Boston,
a young man actually got up and gave her his seat!" Within a certain circle of women, incidents of chivalry are now traded like
sightings of aliens or solar eclipses. There are also incidents of
thwarted chivalry to be traded, which are sometimes even better.
Ed, 71, a retired doctor: "I used to stand up when a woman came
in the room because I feel uncomfortable sitting down, it's so
impolite, but now if I do they laugh and give me looks that say
'Hell, I'm stronger than you anyway, old man, so who you standing
up for?' Now I stand up just for elderly women. But in the old days
we stood up for both, the older women and the younger women."

Tony, 55, a businessman: "I was out with my wife and one
other woman and when I got the other woman's coat for her and
reached to help her with it, she practically ripped the coat out of
my hands, said 'Nobody has ever done that for me!' and stomped
off and waited, fuming, by the door."

Peter, 36, a lawyer: "On the bus sometimes, when I don't want
to give up my seat for a woman and I feel guilty about it, I think
to myself, well, this is the nineties, she won't want me to give up
my seat, anyway. It's strange that this is what is going through my
head, because I know that I'm not getting up because I don't
want to and I'm feeling lazy, but still that's how I excuse myself."

Older men tell tales of thwarted chivalry, but the younger ones
typically don't even try. In my freshman year in college, I accept-

ed an invitation to dinner with a guy on campus I thought I had a lot in common with. We sat down and the first thing he blurted out was, "My two favorite words are dreamboat and fornicate." I wasn't sure how to respond. He continued his announcement, "Yeah, the woman who is meant for me will walk right up to me and say 'hey, dreamboat, wanna fornicate?'" Silence. Long pause. "Well, uh, thanks for sharing," I laughed nervously, "I think I might have to go soon."

When I think of the men who have told me about their "babeometers," or why I should sleep with them because love is just a nineteenth-century construct, I notice they are very earnest about what they say. There is no malice or intent to "harass" me. I'm not hurt; usually I'm just trying hard not to burst out laughing. The truth is that most young men today haven't a clue how to behave around women, and it's largely not their fault. They're not evil, they're ignorant. They may be nice, intelligent, and funny, but no one has bothered to sit them down and tell them how to behave, about what to say and what to do. About the fact that, for starters, a girl is not going to overcome her "hang-ups" if you call them "hang-ups."

The need is not for nonsexist upbringing, but for precisely a good dose of *sexist* upbringing: how to relate *as* a man *to* a woman. Today we want to pretend there are no differences between the sexes, and so when they first emerge we give our little boys Ritalin to reduce their drive, and our little girls Prozac to reduce their sensitivity. We try to cure them of what is distinctive instead of cherishing these differences and directing them towards each other in a meaningful way. We can never succeed in curing men and women of being men and women, however, and so these differences emerge anyway—only when they do, they emerge in their crudest, most untutored form, such as swearing, stalking, and raping. And then we are shocked, and conclude that men must be evil. But how can men open doors for us again, when we slam them on their fingers? Any return to male courtesy must begin with a change in women.

One night around midnight in my sophomore year, there was a knock outside my door. I was reading in bed, not exactly dressed to answer the door, but my stereo was playing softly, so there was no use pretending I wasn't in. "Who is it?" "Open up, c'mon!" a male voice demanded. I recognized the voice: it was the guy from down the hall. "I can't, I'm not dressed." "Well, put something on then, I'll wait! I want to ask you a question." Then, "Don't be

rude!" If you thought that perhaps *he* was rude to arrive uninvit-
ed and demand entry, perhaps you didn't realize that there are no
rules any longer to regulate gentleman callers. Indeed, to suggest
that there ought to be is supposedly "sexist" and "infantalizing" of
women. But is it?

Take one of those "emblems of subordination," hat tipping. In
retrospect, maybe hat tipping wasn't such a crazy way of greeting
a woman, after all. If you read the instruction manuals for the etiquette of hat lifting, it is clear that a man lifted his hat as a way of
recognizing a woman's presence *without* staring at her. Indeed, a
proper hat lifter wouldn't even steal a glance at a woman out of
the corner of his eye. As Emily Post elaborated in 1923, "In lifting his hat, a gentleman merely lifts it slightly off his forehead and
replaces it; he does not smile nor bow, nor even look at the object
of his courtesy. No gentleman ever subjects a lady to his scrutiny
or his apparent observation." Hat tipping, then, wasn't subordinating; it was, precisely, a guard against subordination—or "lookism,"
if you prefer. Consider these rules from a 1956 etiquette book:

> Walking with a Woman: *a) In general, a man walks on the curb side
> of the street. . . . In walking with two women, a man should keep to
> the curb side to avoid turning his back on one while talking to the
> other. b) A man always opens a door for a woman, and holds it for her
> to go through. In the case of a revolving door, he starts it off with a
> push, and then lets her precede him. c) A man carries packages or suit-
> cases for a woman. . . .* Rising for a Woman: *a) A man rises when
> a woman comes into a room, and remains standing until she sits down
> or leaves, except at a large party where people are coming and going all
> the time. b) A man rises when a woman comes to the table (or half-
> rises, at least, in a crowded restaurant), and remains standing till she
> sits down or asks him to sit down. c) A man also rises when a woman
> leaves the table. . . . d) A man rises to speak to a woman or to be intro-
> duced to her. . . .* Courtesies to Women Strangers. *This takes a lit-
> tle observation on your part, and it's hard to draw up fast rules about
> it. If a woman drops her glove in the street, you'd certainly pick it up.
> . . . It is not particularly charming, incidentally, to race a woman, young
> or old, for a vacant seat. Tip your hat when you're thanked, and take
> care to keep the whole thing impersonal so that it doesn't look as if
> you have ulterior motives.*

One can certainly criticize these rules as sexist, and many have.
Today, forbidden behavior includes candlelit dinners ("prostitu-

tion," according to University of Colorado professor Alison Jagger), opening a door for a woman (sends a clear message that "women are incapable," says philosopher Marilyn Frye), and gestures such as moving furniture and giving up one's seat (part of a whole continuum of "protection rackets" that brainwash women into thinking they need men, points out Nancy Henley). John Kasson sums up the intellectual's case against chivalry succinctly: "The entire ritual structuring of urban life, although performed in the name of honoring women, assumed and encouraged their subservience to men." This is now conventional wisdom, and we now act (or rather, fail to act) accordingly. But were we right? Did urban rituals of courtesy really only ratify the subservience of women?

The simple fact is that a man who observed all of the above rules was a man who treated a woman with respect, a man who was incapable of being boorish. He was too busy doing nice things to be boorish. This is why I doubt that if men are taught to relate courteously to women, women would be suddenly thrown out of all the professions, as some contend. Maybe, on the contrary, it would be much easier for the sexes to work together. Perhaps we wouldn't have to waste so much time with sexual harassment lawsuits. In the old view, if you weren't considerate to women, you weren't really a man. Or as G. W. Docine's 1852 manual put it, *Manners Maketh Man*. Today the men are nonsexist, but are the women happier because of it? We don't have Kasson's rituals "performed in the name of honoring women," but we do have sexual harassment, rape, and stalking. We have, essentially, raised a society of men who do not know how to relate to women *as* men.

The idea that male courtesy is oppressive is so imbedded in our culture now that even a mainstream manners guide for girls, incredibly, contains a section criticizing manners for boys as—you guessed it—sexist. The guide doesn't recommend door opening for women or serving women first at a restaurant because "these traditions don't make much sense now that we all know men and women are equal."

So girls should learn to be polite, but not the boys, because that's sexist and unequal. Of course, when in the absence of any rules these same boys sodomize girls on the playground, everyone is shocked and wonders why our boys can't be more civilized.

To the elite, even thinking that you might *be* a man is not per-missible, akin to being a Nazi. Bram Dijkstra warns us, "The genocidal mentality was a product of ideas that continue to govern our sense of self. The monster of Nazism still roams among us—for the fictions of gender dualism that permitted it to gain power still darken our lives." And John Stoltenberg has written, "The idea of the male sex is like the idea of an Aryan race," since "the Nazis believed that from the blond hair and blue eyes occurring naturally in the human species, they could construe the existence of a separate race—a distinct category of human beings that was unambiguously rooted in the natural order of things . . . but there simply is no Aryan race. There is only the idea of it—and the consequences of trying to make it seem real. The male sex is very like that."

With this in mind, it is no wonder Stoltenberg must conclude in *Refusing to Be a Man* that even our physical differences are culturally determined. Sure, there are some individuals who happen to have been born with "enough elongated tissue around your urethra so you can pee standing up," but it is better to understand that "we are born into a physiological continuum." Females, needless to say, are just "individuals who happen to be born non-penised." (Still a pretty sexist way of looking at it, if you stop and think about it—why isn't he one who is nonvaginaed?) At any rate, Stoltenberg concludes that "male sexual identity is the conviction or belief, held by most people born with penises, that they are male and not female." Thus, he prefers that we have sex "genital tubercle to genital tubercle."

Meanwhile in the women's magazines, we can read about how, when, and with whom to fake orgasm, and about whether we should risk taking testosterone supplements. Though testosterone supplements can cause women a sixfold increase in risk of breast cancer, plus higher cholesterol levels that compromise heart health, not to mention voice changes and beardlike growth, doctors are still prescribing it for "females with flagging libido." It's the new "therapy for their own sexual healing," reported *The Wall Street Journal* in 1997. In 1998, women were even encouraged to take the anti-impotence drug Viagra.

So the women are refusing to be women and the men refusing to be men. Has all this faking made relations between the sexes any better? It doesn't seem to have.

In circles outside the elite poststructuralist academy and the ranks of various extremists, most young women long for a courteous man. When despite all his nonsexist schooling, a man does dare to open a door for a woman, he is snapped up right away. *The New*

*York Times* describes one such marriage in 1997, between Lisa Chookasezian, the editorial manager of the American branch of News Limited and Times Papers, and a fireman, Noel Maitland:

> *On their first date, she says he behaved like a knight who had time-traveled to the 90s. "He was so gentlemanly," she said. "He took off my coat for me. When I stood up to go to the ladies' room, he stood up, too. He even buttered my bread for me—he still does. I was in total shock. I thought, 'I kind of like this.'" As they continued to date, Mr. Maitland became more chivalrous. "He leaves little notes for me everywhere," the bride said. "One time, he left a note in my room that said, 'There's 13 notes in here. Find them.' I'd pick up a bottle of hair spray and there'd be a note. There was under my pillow— 'Lisa is the prettiest little napper in New York City.'"*

Ultimately, it seems that only men can teach other men how to behave around women, but those men have to be inspired by women in the first place, inspired enough to think the women are worth being courteous to. Perhaps this is the reason sexual harassment legislation has been, in large part, a failure: it essentially involves women telling men how to behave. Women can't tell men how to behave—they either inspire, or fail to inspire. Today we inspire them by slamming doors on their fingers, pushing them away when they help us with our coats, and then, when they learn their lesson and begin to treat us with equal-opportunity boorishness, we change our minds and seek to enforce by fiat the respect which was once grounded in custom. But it's rather hard to get the heavy arm of the law to regulate such delicate matters, particularly when the law is not grounded in any cherished idea, but only meant to mediate and correct for differentials of "power." The government could never court-order a man to write "Lisa is the prettiest little napper in New York City."

What the courts can do, and are continuing to do, however, is make male courtesy illegal. Take the demise of "Ladies' Night." In *Koire* v. *Metro Car Wash* (1985), a judge found that reduced prices to women at certain bars and car washes on specified days of the week violated California's Unruh Act, which prohibits discrimination based on sex and other classifications. Women patronizing the defendant's businesses were harmed "because the discount practices reinforced harmful sexual stereotypes and in effect hindered men and women from seeing each other as equals." One might naively think that the women attending ladies' nights at bars *wanted* to be treated like "ladies" or wanted the car wash discounts.

Judge Daniel R. Moeser explained in a similar ruling in Dane County Court, Wisconsin: "The Court finds harm in the practice of ladies' night discounts in that it promotes the stereotypes that (1) men are the financial providers and that women, because of their inferior economic status, need special discounts." It is the role of the Court to "avoid perpetuating dangerous stereotyping and sexual discrimination." In *Pennsylvania Liquor Control Board* v. *Dobrinoff* (1984), the Commonwealth Court of Pennsylvania found that temporarily exempting women patrons from even bar *cover* charges violated the Pennsylvania Human Relations Act. A few years later the Woodside Delicatessen in Maryland tried to circumvent an impending crackdown on ladies' nights by instituting a "Skirt and Gown Night," but to no avail, for in *Peppin* v. *Woodside Delicatessen* (1986), the Maryland Court of Appeals bravely rooted out "Skirt and Gown Night," too, finding that it was intended to function as a ladies' night—with shocking numbers of subversive free drinks infiltrating the delicatessen and thrusting themselves into the palms of innocent women.

The most interesting thing about this most enlightened trend is that in almost every case the judges making the decisions and the plaintiffs bringing the suits turn out to be men. Thus has it now become standard practice for men to cloak themselves in the language of equal opportunity to distract from the self-serving nature of their real complaint. Yet which is truly more paternalistic—the business that opts to treat well its female customers, who, after all, choose to come through its doors; or the male judges who intervene and say women are too stupid to recognize that they really don't want to be treated well?

Surely the egalitarians never intended to take away freedoms women already enjoyed. But once an idea is in common currency, it doesn't matter whether the consequences were intended or not; the idea drifts into the culture in ways no one anticipated, and the damage must be assessed. The ban against respectful treatment inevitably migrates to other areas in the culture. Under the guise of fretting over "subordinating" women, too many spineless men are in reality trying to escape from their obligations—and ever more often, succeeding. The same philosophy that seeks to ban ladies' nights can also be used, conveniently, to defend deadbeat dads. In fact one anti-ladies' nights opinion contains exactly this language, warning us against "sexual stereotyping . . . where women are considered dependent, weak, and in need of financial support—otherwise known as 'romantic paternalism (the pedestal-turned-into-cage problem).'"

As the history of no-fault divorce laws and gender-blind alimony rewards demonstrates, the courts have adopted all too eagerly this cowardly pedestal-turned-into-cage excuse, with devastating effect to the institution of marriage. It's when your ex waxes equal opportunity that you know you're in trouble. "What do you mean I'm late on my child support? Surely you don't believe in romantic paternalism, poopsie-pie?" The mother left with four kids to raise when her husband runs off may find it a dubious honor to be liberated from "romantic paternalism." She does not want to be told that hoping Dad will face up to his responsibilities means she is suffering from some kind of delusion.

These laws and court orders that outlaw chivalry have not been liberating for women. They have taken away everything from our freedom to choose to go into a bar and be treated well, to the freedom to opt to stay home and raise children instead of being forced into the work force.

At one point in our history, we did allow the law to reflect basic differences between the sexes. In *Tigner* v. *Texas,* a 1940 Supreme Court case, the Court found that "the Constitution does not require situations which are different in fact ... to be treated in law as though they were the same." This principle actually originally applied to antitrust laws, but the notion of allowing the law to reflect "differences in fact" was extended to sexual differences as well. In *Goesaert* v. *Cleary* (1948) the Court upheld a Michigan statute that forbade females to act as bartenders unless she "be the wife or daughter of the male owner." As Justice Frankfurter explained in the opinion of the Court, "The fact that women may now ... indulge in vices that men have long practiced, does not preclude the States from drawing a sharp line between the sexes."

If that's what the people, through their representatives, decided, it wasn't the business of the Court to say otherwise: "The Constitution does not require legislatures to reflect sociological insight, or shifting social standards, any more than it requires them to keep abreast of the latest scientific developments." The concern here—how quaint it seems now—was that barmaids would be treated crudely. That is why the statute didn't apply to the daughter or wife of a male owner, because it was assumed that no one would dare take liberties with them. As Justice Frankfurter elaborated: "Michigan evidently believes that the oversight assured

through ownership of a bar by a barmaid's husband or father min-
imizes hazards that may confront a barmaid without such protecting oversight."

Today, of course, with the advent of affirmative action and the
Court's stretching of the Equal Protection clause, the law is not
only no longer permitted to manifest "differences in fact," but
must actively work to redress these differences. Thanks to our unisex constitutionalism, now a company in which female workers
are not "properly represented"—in comparison to the proportion
they exist in the surrounding population—does not simply reflect
the different choices, interests, or abilities of men and women,
respectively. Rather, it is a lawsuit waiting to happen. Underrep-
resentation, even in firefighting units, is always evidence of discrimination, and requires a quota to be redressed. If women aren't
as interested in sports, it must be a violation of Title IX. What is
sought is no longer equality, but sameness. Indeed, the federal
Education Department's Office of Civil Rights is so vigilant in its
pursuit of androgyny that its investigators actually demanded to
know why at Johns Hopkins the women's basketballs were smaller than the men's. The answer is that women's basketballs are
designed to accommodate smaller hands.

At one point the law reflected differences between the sexes,
then there was a period of brief neutrality, and now the law seeks
to wipe out any differences that manifest themselves. Now that
the relations between the sexes have become less a matter of custom and more a subject of litigation, are the women better off? In
1948, women were not allowed in places where they might be
treated poorly, and in the 1990s, thanks to all the ladies' night
opinions, it's seen as suspect to allow women into places where
they might be treated well.

So what to do? What is the fate of the twin ideals of modesty
and honor? Have the intellectuals and the courts spoiled relations
between the sexes irreparably? Was that wedding between Lisa
and Noel really a eulogy for an old and soon-to-be-forgotten
regime? Will it soon become illegal even to leave little romantic
notes? Is there no more manhood and womanhood, only *Zerris-
senheit,* torn-to-pieces-hood?

Not at all. In fact there is much to look forward to, for the
romantic woman and the courteous young man are—often to
their parents' horror—starting to make a huge comeback.

## Part Three

THE

RETURN

Chapter 9

# AGAINST THE CURING OF WOMANHOOD

> *When I meet women who are over 55 who have just fallen in love and are miserable, I always ask, "Are you on hormone replacement therapy?"*
>
> —GLORIA STEINEM, 1998

Some of the nicest young women I know are on Prozac— or, rather, the women I know on Prozac were once the nicest women I knew. Now, not all women have, or should have, the same kind of sensitivity, and I have nothing against the woman who is, so to speak, naturally tough. But it worries me that sensitivity in women is now seen as pathological. It's effectively a concession to misogyny. Consider the following description of a man's ex-girlfriends:

> *My ex-girlfriends? Well, let's see . . . she was a nut, and then she was a nut, and then her . . . let's see . . . yes, she was a nut, and then . . . yeah, she was a nut, too, come to think of it! It's strange that I've such bad luck, to date so many nuts. Anyway, then there was what's-her-name, who was evil. She left me. God, that really sucked! She was really evil! And then there was another nut . . .*

What makes a man perceive a woman as "a nut"? And can *all* women be nuts? A silly question. Clearly all women can't be nuts. What does it mean, then, when a society judges that a considerable number of its women are, in fact, nuts? Could it tell us something about how we view womanhood? What Edward Sandford Martin said in 1899 about girls bears repeating: "There is nothing the matter with girls . . . They are a good invention of the kind, and the kind is indispensable and has never been beaten. If you don't think so, there is something the matter with *you*. When a race or a nation doesn't think so, it is an infallible symptom that there is something amiss with that nation. There isn't any surer test of the progress of any people in civilization than its appreciation of girls."

It seems that something is gravely amiss with our civilization.

## FIXING THE LIVING WOMAN

In a 1995 issue of *American Woman,* Lynn O'Shaughnessy asks, "Is Prozac the Prescription for Happiness?" The answer turns out to be yes. "Since Prozac came on the market in 1988," she finds, "more than 17 million people have turned to the antidepressant to chase away the blues. Over six million Americans are now taking the drug, mostly women between the ages of 20 and 50. . . . Some say this little green-and-cream colored pill not only chases away the blues, but PMS, anxiety and overeating too."

Why are so many women on Prozac today?

Peter Kramer's fascinating 1993 book *Listening to Prozac* contains a few clues. Kramer begins with a useful tour of Donald Klein's research on "rejection-sensitivity," a type of "hidden mood disorder." Klein began his research with antidepressants in the late 1950s and eventually rose to become the director of research at the New York Psychiatric Institute. Along the way Klein uncovered "hysteroid dysphoria," which described those who were not depressed but had a "marked fear of rejection" and a "desperate emotional state." Later, Klein would rename those with a "pathological vulnerability to loss" as suffering from "rejection-sensitive dysphoria" or "overreactive dysphoria."

Klein's innovation was finding that MAOIs—monoamine-oxidase-inhibiting drugs—acted to "set a floor beneath patients . . . prevented the bottom from falling out." Klein's discovery in technical jargon was this: "A crucial consequence of putting these patients on MAOI inhibitors is that they do not become dysphoric upon loss of admiration." Dysphoric means unhappy, so if you "do not become dysphoric upon loss of admiration," that means that if your beloved should turn to you one day and say, "I never loved you. I was really just infatuated with you," you would bounce back: "That's cool! No problem."

You can already see the difficulty, which is that it seems very strange *not* to become dysphoric upon loss of admiration. Since Donald Klein's ideal woman is so unnatural, it is perhaps not surprising that he found so many real women to be ill.

For Donald Klein's "hysteroid dysphorics" turn out to be "usually females" who "may feel hopelessly bereft when a love affair terminates." Also "their emotionality markedly affects their judgment." Plus "they are fickle, emotionally labile, irresponsible, shallow, love-intoxicated, giddy, and short-sighted. They tend to be egocentric, narcissistic, exhibitionistic, vain, and clothes-crazy. They are seductive, manipulative, exploitative, sexually provocative, and think emotionally and illogically." To top it off, "In their sexual relations they are possessive, grasping, demanding, romantic, and foreplay centered," and "when frustrated or disappointed, they become reproachful, tearful, abusive and vindictive."

As Kramer aptly notes, "Klein's [description] may sound less like a neutral syndromal description than a misogynist's picture of womankind."

Kramer does seem troubled by the way that sensitivity in women is seen as a problem for Klein, and yet he seems to have few qualms about prescribing Prozac to cure just the "problem" Klein described: "If you can 'set a floor' under emotionally brittle patients—consistently spare them the terrible pain and disorganization that follow losses—without putting their health and safety at risk, then the concept of rejection-sensitivity becomes useful in practical terms."

Enter Gail, one of Kramer's early success stories. On Prozac, "her sensitivity to social slights had diminished." Then there is another woman who on Prozac "compensated for emotional shakiness with extraordinary social skill." And "if Lucy," another of his patients, "can be spared the pain that rejection causes her, she will not need to behave in a dependent or self-injurious way." Among college students, there are all those "'easy blushers,' keenly aware of their appearance in social interchanges" who may need fixing. Later we meet a patient whose "hunger for approval frightened men off." Thankfully, "Prozac allowed her to date a variety of men calmly." This is cited as one of Kramer's successful case studies, but maybe it shouldn't be. Maybe a woman shouldn't be dating calmly—maybe it should be dizzying and tailspinning and all the rest. Maybe the floor should drop.

"Having seen Prozac in action," Kramer writes, "I now look for signs of rejection-sensitivity in any patient with marked social difficulties." He prescribes Prozac for "Sonia," who is not depressed, indeed, "not even sad," but does have an unacceptably "ethereal temperament." And let us not forget "Sally" who suffers from "entrenched timidity" from early childhood, and though "social introversion, when well established in adult life, is a difficult trait to change," Dr. Kramer prescribed Prozac for Sally with an eye to making a "more profound difference." Soon Sally "even asked men to dance, and she dated a number of them." By the time a year had passed, "she was dating two men steadily, without worrying how things would turn out." This is an achievement?

According to a pamphlet I discovered on *Preventing Teen Dating Violence,* "Thinking girls are too sensitive, overly emotional or irrational" is one of the first "signs that someone may be a batterer or a rapist." In effect, by drugging these women, we have accepted the rapist's view of womanhood. Our culture is continually frustrated with women the way they are, and seeks to loosen them up. Or as Kramer puts it with greater delicacy: "Prozac does not just brighten mood; it allows a woman with the traits we now consider 'overly feminine,' in the sense of passivity and a tendency to histrionics, to opt, if she is a good responder, for a spunkier persona."

But in a culture which is as hostile to femininity as ours, where sensitivity is taken as dangerous evidence of having "a tendency to histrionics," a woman cannot, significantly, just "opt" for a more jaded, "spunkier" persona. She is *put* on Prozac. She has her new spunky persona assigned to her—by a medical professional, an expert, who tells her *there is something wrong with her the way she is.* She is a "chronic overreactive dysphoric." She is a "hysteroid dysphoric." She suffers from "rejection-sensitive dysphoria." These labels are very different from the ones you see at department stores when you're trying on a new hat. Spunky hats flatter women the way they are, whereas spunky Prozac insults them the way they are.

In a brilliant 1997 Op-Ed article in *The New York Times,* Jenny McPhee tells of a conversation she overheard in a restaurant: A woman was confessing to her friend how embarrassed she was to be excited for her wedding day. As Ms. McPhee remarks, these days "Women are deeply ashamed of themselves for being women." In a 1998 issue of *Self* magazine, in fact, you can find advice columnist Helena Rosenberg soothing women who persist in wanting to get married at all: "Stand tall. Admitting that you'd like to get married does not signal an affliction, merely a defensible life goal. Take that brown paper bag off your head." A *defensible life goal?* One may be forgiven for thinking she is referring to roaming around Uganda, not to starting a family.

I am fortunate to live in a very liberated age. These days a girl can become a doctor, a lawyer, enlist in the military, join a basketball team, expect to pursue a career, to be able to drop her children off at day care, and have as many abortions as she wishes. Her sexual options are no longer restricted: both the premarital and the extramarital affair are now open to her. In short, a girl can do whatever she wants to do, become anything she wants to be— with one crucial exception. Prozac teaches us that there is only one thing nowadays that a girl is not allowed to grow up to be, and that, strange as it may seem, is a woman.

## FAKING THE FATAL WOMAN

Here is Nicholas Christopher describing the appeal of the *femme fatale:*

> *As vivid and exciting as the femme fatale can be in film noir, her antithesis, the nurturing, supposedly redeeming woman is usually unrelievedly pallid and passive—to the point of repulsing us, as well as the hero. She is most often the girl back home, or the faithful, long-suffering wife. . . . Antiseptic, static, sexually repressed, socially rather dull, she lives with her parents and works as a schoolteacher; she wants to marry and have kids and never leave her hometown.*

The *femme fatale,* or "disastrous woman," is no boring long-suffering wife. Rather, she inflicts suffering. She is not repressed; she is tough and strong. You don't have to read Camille Paglia's *Vamps and Tramps* or hear Margaret Atwood say "Equality . . . means equally bad as well as equally good" to know that today a fatal woman is *the* thing to be. What is less well known, however, is when and how, exactly, one goes about becoming her. How does one transform from this boring "supposedly redeeming woman" who is "pallid," "sexually repressed," and "wants to marry and have kids" to today's more socially acceptable woman-as-sexual-predator?

An interesting thing about the favorable account of the "active" female sexual predator is that it typically trivializes some other woman's suffering along the way. When we say that someone is a "long-suffering" wife in contrast to the hip lady who gets the wife's husband, we do not mean that she is *really* suffering; we mean that she's a drag. When Simone de Beauvoir called the Marquis de Sade a "great moralist" because he taught us "all the insipidity and boredom of virtue," she didn't just stop there. She added that "actually, whipping a few girls . . . is rather a petty feat." In order to equate sexual violence with sexiness, we must first harden ourselves against the objects of the violence.

A similar process takes place in the mind of the individual girl who internalizes these messages and attempts to fashion herself after the fatal woman. Peter Kramer puts his finger on the internal transformation when he asks, of his rejection-sensitive women, "Why should all emotionally vulnerable women become *femme fatales?*" In a society with no sanction for male honor, it is no longer acceptable to say that a man has caused or in any way contributed to a woman's suffering. That's only the way pathetic women talk, according to our culture. A woman soon learns that all blame for suffering lies within herself, for being too "sensitive." She resents this sensitivity of hers, then trivializes it, and finally she acts in such a way as to constantly negate it. Sade's view of woman—always ready to be degraded—is internalized, then celebrated as the hallmark of a woman's true liberation.

When on two successive weekends in November 1997, the State University of New York at New Paltz held taxpayer-funded conferences on women's sexuality called "Revolting Behavior," and enlisted young women to take part in various sado-masochistic rituals, some were confused as to why treating women as sexual objects was liberating for them. When, during "Women's Pride Week," my college's Feminist Association passed out "SHAMELESS HUSSY" stickers, many were also greatly perplexed.

But to be fair, there is a philosophy behind all this vamping and tramping that was not entirely misguided and did have a certain logic: By adopting the words that misogynist males once used to put women down, we would be freed of the pain such words caused us. By embracing the vocabulary of female-hatred, we would be released from its sting and would ultimately render those words meaningless. At last we could "reclaim" our identities as women. Thus in 1998, Elizabeth Wurtzl writes a book entitled *Bitch,* following the summer 1997 hit tune by Meredith Brooks, "Bitch." As the singer explains in a 1998 issue of *Glamour:* "We're taking back a word that has always had a negative connotation."

Unfortunately, though, what we are learning is that a female misogynist is just as bad as a male misogynist. Either women are unique individuals, ends in themselves, or they are just a group of sexual objects and predators, nothing more. It's the same view, one as old as the fifth-century poet Palladas: "Women are as bitter as bile; there are nevertheless two circumstances where they are pleasant: in bed and when they are dead."

There is an old misogynist Latin saying which translates something like "when a woman is openly bad, then at least she is honest." How different is this from Naomi Wolf's mantra, "we are all bad girls"? A truly misogynist culture like our own loves to encourage the so-called fatal woman or "bitch," because she confirms its suspicion that all women are really evil, and if we were honest, we would admit it. What it cannot bear is a real, *living* woman—someone with hopes, dreams, secrets, and all of that other schmaltzy stuff which Dr. Klein & Misogyny, Inc. take as evidence of being "emotionally labile."

And so it tries to cure her. That's what people are saying to me, essentially, when they tell me that I'm too "intense" and how "I will have many men" if only I will "loosen up." *What?* they are saying, You *care?* How embarrassing for you. You're emotionally vulnerable? There's still one of you *left?* Well, forget your rules—just become a *femme fatale.* Put on a shorter skirt, a tighter shirt, and put yourself on the block. That's what we do. See how many men you will attract. But what if I don't want to be a *femme fatale?* What if all the *femme fatales* I know are depressed and depressing, and I don't want to be like them? If it's hard for you to be indifferent about sex, just try harder. Take Prozac. But what if what I want to be is exactly the opposite, namely, a living woman? Sorry—that is the one thing you are not permitted to be.

Camille Paglia may be right in saying that the *femme fatale* has existed throughout history, but I think she tells only one half of the story. Do most women really want to be fatal women, or do they want to be just the opposite, namely, living women? With the sexual revolution, this shadow woman became propped up as a model that was impossible for most of us to match.

A typical specimen of our times is writer Marya Hornbacher, who whittled herself down to 52 pounds to rid herself of "an excess of general intensity." Scattered throughout her book, *Wasted: A Memoir of Anorexia and Bulimia,* are stories of humiliating casual sex, along with these self-criticisms: "Too much fantasy." "Too intense and entirely too much." "Too emotional, too passionate." "Intense." "I was tired of being too much, too intense . . ." "Beneath the skin I wore . . . was something horrible, something soft and weak . . . and tearful and needy." "Chaotic, needy softness." "The self I'd had, once upon a time, was too much. Now there was no self at all." "If I had been a different sort of person . . . less intense . . ." Even when she is at a somewhat normal weight, Marya still laments that "I have not become a noticeably less intense person." She takes it as a personal failing that, even on Prozac, she has been unable to cure herself of her intensity.

I hear this all the time from women my age, this business of being too intense. "People say I'm too . . . *intense.*" Head bowed, ashamed. A quick glance over the shoulder. Will anyone witness, how intense? Will they be perhaps arrested? These are the women who end up on Prozac. They see their very natures as the problem, and like Marya Hornbacher, they find nowhere to run from themselves. But women are, generally speaking, intense creatures. This is not necessarily bad. Passion comes in handy in the search for romantic love; it is also well suited to motherhood and to the religious life. But in a cynical culture that trivializes everything transcendent, a woman's passionate nature will be directed against herself. As Marya puts it, with her innocent precision: "I felt like yearning was specific to me, and the guilt that it brought was mine alone."

So she tried to "escape the flesh and, by association, the realm of emotions," but she succeeded only in sustaining permanent damage to her internal organs. She contracts infections weekly and can never have children.

But why? Maybe it is normal for a young woman to be "intense," and being cavalier is what is strange. Maybe wanting to forge bonds with others is normal, and it's cutting ourselves off from enduring attachments that is perverse. Maybe *not* having "rejection sensitivity" is what is sick, and *in*vulnerability to loss the real pathology. If being blasé about sex were natural, why would so many women have to be on Prozac in order to carry out what their culture expects of them?

Incidentally, if you're not sensitive to rejection, doesn't that also mean you're indifferent to love?

# Chapter 10

# MODESTY AND THE EROTIC

*Samuel G. Freedman's article "Yeshivish at Yale" (March 24) evoked vivid memories of helping my daughter move into her U.C.L.A. dorm in her freshman year. At one point, after visiting the restroom and observing a huge pair of hairy male feet in the next stall, I wanted to carry all her boxes and clothes back to the car, my conservative Catholicism clashing head on with this blatant display of unisex facilities. However, the more I considered the situation, the more I became convinced that such proximity would probably dispel any mystique—just as sharing a bathroom at home with her brothers held little attraction. In the end, my instincts proved correct.*

—Margaret D. Taormina, Glendale,
California, 1998

Seemingly every year, another study announces that married women are more orgasmic than single women. At first I wonder, Do I really need to know this detail? But then I read on and I am transfixed. Married women generally feel safer, which our scientists report is a precondition for being able to relax. A University of Chicago survey of 3,432 Americans ages 18 through 59 found that monogamous married couples reported the highest sexual satisfaction, while singles and marrieds who have multiple partners registered the lowest. Mark Clements Research polled more than 1,000 Americans and found that 67% of married couples said they were "happy with their sex life," as against 45% of singles. After surveying 100,000 women, *Redbook* magazine found that the most strongly religious women were "more responsive sexually" than all other women.

Everyone, including the scientists themselves, is always surprised when these studies are released, because we have been taught that the married are oppressed, the religious are boring squares, and the swinging singles are the ones having all the fun.

But maybe that's only because we misunderstand sexual modesty. Let us set beside these mysterious studies Balzac's quip that "the most virtuous women have in them something which is never chaste," and we have an even thornier problem. If a return to modesty can save a generation of women from the ravages of a culture that affords us precious little respect or protection, then how can it also be that modesty seems, at times, more exciting?

When during my freshman year in college I came across John Kasson's *Amusing the Million: Coney Island at the Turn of the Century*, I was floored by it. Charmed by the quaint pictures and how civilized everyone looked, I was quite surprised to learn that they were actually being *bad*. It turns out that unchaperoned young men and women used to flock to Coney Island in order to perch on amusement rides which contrived to *seat them close together*, and often they would even *get engaged to be married* there.

What world was this, where getting engaged could sound like a dirty thing, and where people could misbehave in jackets, ties, hats, dresses, and parasols? Not just the upper classes, either, but everyone. What world was this, where men would send to friends excited postcards reporting that they saw "Little Egypt" dance the Hootchy-Kootchy? Where the naughtiness of violating sexual propriety involved wrapping your arms around your boyfriend's neck in the dark? The "Cannon Coaster" ride advertised, "Will She Throw Her Arms Around Your Neck and Yell? Well, I Guess, Yes!"

It may be true, as Naomi Wolf writes, that now "we are all bad girls," but this is precisely why being "bad" is no longer transgressive for my generation. Now that Sade's world has invaded our classrooms, our movies, and our streets, he's no longer so shocking. *We*, after all, started our sex education in elementary school, and analyzed Nabokov's *Lolita* and William S. Burroughs's *Naked Lunch* in our literature classes. Most unmarried people we know are living with someone, and many married people we know have had an affair—or several. We've grown weary of reading in our women's magazines how "affairs can support a marriage." Adultery is now immensely boring. But actually being *faithful* to one's beloved? Imagine that. Reading—and enjoying—Samuel Richardson's *Pamela*? Now that's something new, something radical. Modesty is now what is sexy—and maybe it always was.

Certainly sexual modesty may damp down superficial allure, the kind of allure that inspires a one-night stand. But the kind of allure that lasts—that is what modesty protects and inspires. This is why there is no contradiction in the following *Los Angeles Times* account of a girl who dresses modestly but also wants to be attractive to boys:

> *Black nylon stockings and patent-leather shoes peeking out from beneath Ajla Nuhbegovic's tunic clash flirtatiously with her head scarf and neck-to-ankle garb. Between licks of a dripping ice-cream cone, the enshrouded 12-year-old says she has every intention of wearing lipstick, eye makeup and jewelry when she's old enough. She shrugs off what some might see as an incongruous melding of religious modesty and a young girl's interest in being attractive to boys.*

Modesty damps down crudeness, it doesn't dampen down *Eros*. In fact, it is more likely to enkindle it.

"The number of dates you have before sex may predict the longevity of a relationship," says Reza Jarra, 26, a surgery resident, in a 1997 issue of *Marie Claire.* "If you have sex on the first or second date, you're embarking on a short-lived, physical, passionate relationship. If you wait, there's more to fall back on." But why, if you wait, is there more? And of what, exactly?

Consider the great disappointment of the nudists. "The largest association of nudists, the American Association of Nude Recreation, has doubled its membership within the past 12 years, to 50,000," Jennifer S. Lee writes in a 1997 *Wall Street Journal* article. "Nude is natural. The philosophy is body acceptance," gushes Leonite Moore, the president of AANR.

And yet, though more of us may be going nude, increasing numbers of us are disappointed. Maxine Paetro, for instance, who took off on a nude cruise, reported these unexpected findings in a 1996 issue of *New Woman:* "Breasts point up, down, sideways . . . I see tummies with scars, folds of fat, creases, wrinkles . . . I've never seen this many naked people ever, and I'm not in the slightest aroused by the sight." Even a man who assumed there was nothing he would rather see than a girl taking off her top on the beach was so disillusioned when it actually happened that he was moved to pour his heart out to *Mademoiselle*. At first, when "Allison" peeled off her top, the author's "jaw dropped. My pulse raced. My eyes rested where I knew they shouldn't." He said, "Damn, Allison." Allison shrugged. "I just got back from France," she explained. "You don't mind, do you?" Then she added, "It's not illegal."

It was true: In New York State, where the author and "Allison" were sunbathing, it was ruled in 1992 that toplessness must be equal-opportunity, that women as well as men could go without shirts in public. But then after a few minutes of shock, our author noticed that he really didn't care anymore. Neither did the other men: "The male response, though, was eerily tame . . . the guys sitting nearby kept their eyes well-socketed." Why? "Here's what I think the real reason was: By taking off her top—a simple gesture any man would make without thinking—my friend had broken the spell, neutralized the taboo."

A recent complainant to "Dear Abby" recounts a similar broken spell:

> Dear Abby,
> I let myself be talked into a visit [to a nudist club] and not once during the entire weekend did I see any reaction to the nudity of others. No one seemed interested in the bodies of others at all. . . . You begin to realize nude is just that—nude. Nothing is left to the imagination at all. And without imagination, there's no interest in even looking. I understood this, but my husband seemed terribly disappointed.
> —STILL LAUGHING IN FLORIDA

In contrast, in Malaysia when a man and a women are shown alone in a room—dressed—for more than three seconds, it implies that they have had intercourse. It must be interesting to be alone with someone in Malaysia.

A good example of the playfulness modesty encourages is the existence of the "modesty piece," often worn with a tucker and covering the "pit of the bosom" in mid-eighteenth-century women's dress. If the concern were mere prudery, then dresses of the period would have been simply high-cut. Instead, women wore gowns with a low *décolletage* and then inserted a modesty piece. But low *décolletage* and a modesty piece would seem to cancel each other out—unless, perhaps, the modesty piece was removed later in the evening? The imagination is certainly compelled. Did they play games to see who could last the longest with her modesty piece in place? No, that couldn't be. Nobody had any fun until the 1960s—or so we have been told, anyway.

In a 1997 issue of *Vogue*, Hadani Ditmars describes the wives in Iran who arrive at the embassy in long black *chadors,* then emerge inside "unveiled and surprisingly chic." Underneath it all is usually "something sexy and trendy." A popular Tehrani couturier confides to her, "My theory is that after the Revolution, women's taste in fashion became wilder and sexier. . . . When you're forced to cover up publicly, what you wear in private becomes more revealing."

Someone who is almost naked in front of strangers, on the other hand, has little left to reveal to her lover. One finds the same pattern among Orthodox Jews. "Despite an ascetic life and modest outerwear," finds a 1998 *New York Times* report: "it is not uncommon for Orthodox women to enjoy sexy undergarments. Across the heart of Orthodox Brooklyn, there are at least four well-known shops selling the kind of racy lingerie found at Lavender Lace. Their owners say business is brisk."

By the end of my freshman college year, I had accumulated a small pile of turn-of-the-century beach photographs of women in covered-up bathing suits. I noticed that whether the women were upper class or farmer's daughters, whether they were frolicking on Coney Island or in Sea Girt, New Jersey, they always wore the same mischievous expression. I hovered over these photographs and wondered at them. Why was the look on their faces more wicked than any to be found at your standard I'm-comfortable-with-my-body nude beach? What *was* this sexual drama we gave up?

In my sophomore year the first glimmerings of an answer began to dawn on me. I was eating in one of our dining halls—a cafeteria with a very high ceiling and beautiful, wide windows—and I plopped my tray down at the most innocuous-looking table, where a bunch of young men and women were chattering away. It soon became clear to me from their conversation that I had alighted near the Williams Wrestling Team.

"Oh?" I queried them, trying to make polite conversation, "so we have men's and women's wrestling teams? That's nice." Well, I was told, there's really just one team, called the Williams Wrestling Team.

"You're kidding me," I said. Nope, they weren't.

"Wait a minute. I'm sorry, do you mean to tell me . . ." I paused to gather my thoughts. "You're trying to tell me that men and women on this campus *wrestle* one another . . . for sport?"

"Oh, don't worry," one girl reassured me, with a toss of her dark brown mane, "It's *nothing sexual.*" Everyone at the table nodded earnestly, and kept filling up on tacos and orange soda.

I almost choked on my Diet Coke. *"Nothing sexual?* Are you guys serious? You're rolling around on the floor, gripping each

*MODEST AND MISCHIEVOUS: New Jersey Salt Water Day for Farmers, 1897. Courtesy of the Museum of the City of New York, The Byron Collection.*

*NUDE AND BORED: Founding meeting of United Free Beaches of Florida, 1982. Photo by Al Bailey, courtesy of The Naturist Society.*

other God knows where, *pinning* each other down, and it's *nothing sexual?"* They were obviously pulling some kind of prank on me.

"Of course not!" One young man put down his taco for a moment, indignant. "We're all very mature about it." I still couldn't believe them.

"I know you're pulling my leg. We don't really have coed wrestling here, right? Maybe you heard I didn't like the coed bathrooms, and so now you're pretending we have coed wrestling too, like in the *Republic* or something. Well, very clever. I almost fell for it."

Finally one young woman burst out, exasperated, "Why do you keep *asking* us if we're kidding?! Does *everything* have to be sexual for you?"

That comment made me drop the topic, made me think that I was in the wrong. Somehow, for assuming that there was anything sexual about a nice young man and a nice young woman just rolling around together on the floor and pinning each other down for sport, I was made to feel that *I* had the dirty mind. Here they were just trying to get some good clean exercise, and I had to go and spoil it with my leer, make it into something perverted.

And that's when it hit me: Maybe my mind really *was* dirtier than theirs. By some ironic collection of turns of fate—whether it was my escaping from sex education or my sexual inexperience—everything was much more fraught for me than it was to their jaded eyes. They had had all the sex education and all the experience, and yet in a weird way they were much more innocent than I. For all their experience, they were, in some fundamental way, prudes, because they were blind to the power of sex. They were "mature," which is to say, emotionally detached, but that meant they were essentially clinical about things that to me would seem extremely intriguing and occupy my imagination for hours. I was lucky I didn't find any guy at that table attractive, or I might not have been able to concentrate on my economics problem set that evening.

Incidentally, I still didn't really believe we had a coed wrestling team until two years later when I read about it in our school newspaper, the *Williams Record:* "Increasing in Number, Women Stake Out Turf on the Williams Wrestling Team," ran the headline one fall day in 1996. I peered in amazement at the report and learned that this was no prank. "All four women said that they have been impressed by the relaxed manner in which the team has accepted them. 'They were mature about it,' [commented one woman wrestler], 'they never asked us "Why are you guys doing this?" and several were helpful and taught us things.'"

I was intrigued by our coed wrestlers, and after I heard about them started to collect data on other coed phenomena on campus. A female freshman shared with me the final paper she had written for her sociology class. She had been studying the effect of the coed bathroom on gender roles in many freshman "entries." (Freshman dormitories at Williams are divided into "entries," or several floors making up a family-like unit.) Of one entry, she reported:

> One evening a couple [of] women were singing loudly in the bathroom, at about one in the morning. Several men from downstairs wanted to sleep and asked them to "shut up." The two sang for a couple [of] more minutes and then stopped. One woman went in the shower; the other was in the bathroom dressed. In came the guys with a bucket of water and they dumped it on the clothed woman and went back downstairs. They came up again shortly thereafter and dumped another bucket of water on the girl who had just gotten out of the shower and had only a towel on.

As my informant sadly concluded in her study: "This incident divided the men and women of the entry, just as their Junior Adviser had made the division between women and men when it came to streaking." Streaking? Yes:

> In one anecdote submitted by a male, he tells a story of going absolutely nude through his dorm. Accompanied by another man, who totally agreed, he justifies his reasons for exposing himself to both men and women without any qualms: "Now let me try to tell you why I do things like this. First and foremost, this is not sexual for me at all. . . . I just feel totally free in the nude. It is the greatest thing in the world. . . . Being nude totally rules. The sense of liberation is incredible. . . . I feel that nudity also makes us closer than we already are as an entry. I mean, totally nude, there is really absolutely nothing to hide behind. It would also help to increase self-confidence, poise, and self-esteem.

There it is again: "This is not sexual for me at all." I recently read a wonderful book by Rabbi Manis Friedman, which recounts an incident that reminded me of my coed wrestlers, streakers, and bathers, for whom nothing is sexual: "Not long ago, a group of teenagers asked me how to keep kosher while on a canoe trip. *Kosher* usually refers to what food is permissible under Jewish law, and that's of course what they meant. Should they take trail mix or dehydrated omelets? But more broadly, as everybody knows, kosher means something's okay to do."

> *"Who's going on this trip?" I asked them.*
> *"Four boys and four girls."*
> *"I can't help you," I said. "It's already not kosher."*
> *"What do you mean?"*
> *"Four boys and four girls going off into the wilderness on a canoe trip is not kosher!"*
> *These good, clean-cut kids were offended. "We've been doing this for years, we grew up together, we went to kindergarten together. Every year we go on this canoe trip and we don't misbehave. In fact, sometimes we even share sleeping bags."*
> *"In that case, you don't need to see a rabbi," I told them. "You need to see a shrink. You're in big trouble!"*

"When teenagers easily dismiss the sexual side of a male/female relationship, and claim to be 'just friends,'" Friedman continues, "it's not a virtue or an accomplishment; it's a sad loss. And what we have lost is our ability to be naturally sexual."

In a 1998 issue of *Mademoiselle*, in fact, a woman writes in for guidance about just this problem: "Now that we live together, I never want to have sex with my boyfriend. We're still affectionate. Is this typical, or is there something wrong with me?" It seems to be typical; in *Elle* magazine, a woman about to be married writes in with the same unmistakable difficulty:

> HELP! *I'm a healthy twenty-nine-year-old and I haven't had the urge for months. . . . Now I just go through the motions for my fiancé's sake. I never fake it—I'd feel like I was lying if I did. . . . It's not that my fiancé isn't attractive to me anymore. I think he's absolutely adorable—he's sexy and hot, and I still crave being intimate with him. I love him body and soul. We've been together for four years and we're planning a wedding this year. I try to be romantic and fan the flames as much as possible. What am I doing wrong? I've always been sexually active and thought I was pretty good. . . . I don't want to fall into a rut before I'm even married!—*Oh Where Oh Where Has My Libido Gone?

*Elle*'s advice columnist E. Jean is disappointed in this woman and reprimands her: "I want to tell you the one and only fact I know about sex: *A young lady who isn't taking a whack at fabulous sex is an idiot.*"

Far be it from me to disagree with an expert, but flagging libido lady's problem doesn't seem to be failure to "take a whack," but rather, that she no longer has anything to look forward to. If anything, she seems to have been "whacking" too much. The advice modesty would offer makes much better sense: instead of trying harder and harder, and getting diminishing returns, she should *stop* having sex with her fiancé—until their wedding night. That would give them something to look forward to.

As Mae West put it, "Censorship made me." Transgressing what is impermissible, or what was once impermissible, makes things much more interesting. In 1910, a woman found guilty of dancing the turkey trot could be sentenced to 50 days in prison or $25. This happened to quite a few Paterson, New Jersey, women, apparently, who had violated the anti-turkey trotting sign. And in 1916, the Illinois Senate Vice Committee would hold hearings on the dangers of dance halls. As one sign at a popular nightclub at the turn of the century read: "Do not wiggle the shoulders. Do not shake the hips. Do not twist the body. Do not flounce the elbows. Do not pump the arms. Do not hop—glide instead. Avoid low, fantastic and acrobatic dips."

In Frank Capra's *It Happened One Night* (1934), when Clark Gable and Claudette Colbert are trying to hitchhike, Gable makes fifteen different furious thumb gestures and fails, while she merely lifts her long skirt and a car immediately stops. And then there is the plot of the movie, which hinges on whether the bed sheet—a.k.a. "the walls of Jericho"—separating their respective sleeping areas will come tumbling down. (The wall eventually does, after Gable and Colbert are married). The power was in the breach of all these rules and walls. Because the culture sanctioned modesty, when you wanted to have fun, you knew *exactly* what to do. You just flipped the "don'ts" into "do's": when dancing, be sure to wiggle the shoulders, shake the hips, twist the body, flounce the elbows, indulge in low, fantastic and acrobatic dips . . . and, of course, eventually tear down the wall of Jericho.

But what happens when there is no longer a wall to tear down?

Without modesty, we are lost—not excited by anything much, and not knowing what the problem is. With each new book, you can see our culture frantically searching for what it has lost. *The*

*Kiss* is published and the culture wonders, Is incest sexy? Is that what we're missing? *The End of Alice* is published and the culture ponders, Is pedophilia sexy? Is that why we're not satisfied? Should we be having sex with little kids? We are trying everything now, everything is permitted, and yet we're still not having fun. *Marie Claire*'s October 1995 issue features a pull-out "Low-Libido Checklist," the better to figure out what's wrong with you, and in the following year, "I Wish I Liked Sex More" is the lead article by Susan Jacoby in *Complete Woman* magazine. But maybe we're not having fun *because* everything is permitted. Maybe without modesty, we forget what is erotic.

Once when a man was kissing me, he said in my ear reassuringly, "See, if we had sex now, it would be out of Attraction and Affection." I immediately recoiled in disgust. "Attraction and Affection?" I asked. "Yes," he said. Yuck, I thought. I found myself wondering—how could he be so . . . priggish? There seems to be something vaguely prissy in casual sex that I hadn't expected to find there.

"But I don't want just Attraction and Affection," I pointed out. "I want something More Than That."

"Like what?" he asked, amused.

I was rather embarrassed to have to explain to my date so explicitly what I had hoped would be implicit. So I said somewhat ironically, "Well, you know . . . uh, passion, true love, etcetera . . . "

"But don't you think that could just be *vanity?*" he asked me, in a soft, patient voice. "You want someone to be in love with you out of *vanity.*" Then he added, "Besides, the kind of love you're talking about—that's very nineteenth century. That's not the Jewish view."★

I certainly felt enlightened, but I also didn't feel like kissing him anymore. Then he informed me that maybe I just needed to

---

★I did some research, and this isn't true. Love actually dates from before the nineteenth century. Not only can you find stories of people who loved each other in the Bible and in Ovid's poetry, but you can find stories of love in many non-Western cultures as well. There were tales of romances combining chivalry with love in China, for instance, even in the Early Han Periods (c. 300–120 B.C.). If you're like me and you've been hearing your whole life that love-is-a-Western-nineteenth-century-construct-so-just-get-over-it, you might find James J.Y. Liu's survey of *The Chinese Knight Errant* to be enormously encouraging, as well as interesting (Chicago: University of Chicago Press, 1967). Of particular interest with respect to modesty is *A Tale of Chivalrous Love (Hsia-yi Feng-yueh Chuan),* a story of the romance between T'ieh Chung-yü and Shui Ping-hsin, whose personal name means "Ice Heart"—ice here signifying purity, not coldness.

learn how to masturbate, to get over my hang-ups. "In Judaism, the girls are allowed to, you know."★

"But the whole point is that I want someone *other* than myself."

"Yes, but that's why you're supposed to *fantasize,*" he explained.

So I shot back, "But fantasizing is for people who have given *up* on the fulfillment of their hopes in real life, and I haven't given up on *my* . . ."

To which he retorted; "No, you can fantasize about things you still hope for. You can fantasize about a job, and hope you'll get it later."

That stumped me, because I realized he was right, and I fell silent. And in my silence, it occurred to me how ridiculous this conversation was.

We're on a date together, presumably to find out if we should seek each other, and we're arguing about whether I wouldn't be better off if I just sought myself. This is annoying, uninspiring— and so *prudish.*

This is when I first started to develop my theory that, contrary to conventional wisdom, modesty is very different from prudery.

### MODESTY VS. PRUDERY

"She must have been abused by her father.""Maybe she had a Bad Experience, poor thing."

Conventional wisdom has it that the woman who returns to modesty is hiding, running away from sex. This is because today modesty is often confused with prudery. But it is not prudery. Indeed, promiscuity is really much closer to prudery. Whether she decides to have scores of men or none, promiscuous and prudish women in some sense embrace the same flippant world view, which one might call the *nothing-fazes-me* world view. As types, they represent two sides of the same unerotic coin, which flips over arrogantly and announces to the world when it lands: "*Ha!*— I cannot be moved." Modesty is prudery's true opposite, because it admits that one *can* be moved and issues a specific invitation for one man to try.

---

★This also isn't true. According to Ramban's commentary on *Niddah* 13a, despite a woman's being exempt from the duty of procreation, masturbation is still considered a sin. See Rabbi Ellison's *The Modest Way,* trans. Raphael Blumberg (Jerusalem: Ahva Press, 1992), p. 48.

Promiscuity and prudery are both a kind of antagonistic indifference, a running away from the meaning of one place in the world, whereas modesty is fundamentally about knowing, protecting that knowledge, and directing it to something higher, beyond just two. Something more than just man and wife. "Therefore shall a man leave his father and his mother and cleave to his wife and they shall become one flesh."

A 1995 issue of *Mademoiselle* dishes out this unexpected "sex secret":

> *THINK YOU KNOW WHAT HE WANTS IN BED? Surprise! . . . Gary, the toy designer, says he's unsure how to tell his girlfriend that he's less than aroused by her lingerie. "Sometimes Gwen will surprise me with a see-through negligee because she thinks that's what I want to see her in . . . but I think I get more excited by seeing her in an oversize T-shirt."*

We thought that with the sexual revolution we could reverse the Fall, forget what we know, but that knowledge keeps coming back to haunt us. Adults may enthusiastically pass out condoms and teach us not to be embarrassed, but those on the receiving end find that without embarrassment, we simply don't have as much fun. Thus the sixties failed not just on moral grounds, as conservatives say, but much more significantly, on its own terms. The legacy of the sixties was simply not an erotic legacy. Those who came after it found either sexual violence or at best a series of stale hook-ups. We now have a nunnery in every bedroom.

Take Katie Roiphe's accounts of her sexual experience. You would expect someone who is against "fifties propriety" to have a lot of dirty stories to tell, but usually her stories are just plain sad or, in a way, simon-pure. Like this one:

> *When I was young, sex seemed to many of us like traveling: you could see the insides of different apartments, eat breakfast in coffee shops in other neighborhoods, and generally see the way other people lived their lives—and then slip back into your own. It was an experiment, an escape, a way of playing at being something you were not.*

Well, I liked to see the insides of different apartments too when I was younger, but that's why I baby-sat. So who is the real innocent here, I wonder? The cool girl who has sex by way of a how-do-you-do, or someone who is more careful?

When I think back, for instance, to how many kisses I gave boys in the fifth grade, I see that it didn't matter to me because I didn't feel anything. It was just like playing checkers. But once I started actually to feel something, I instinctively pulled back. I didn't pull back because the patriarchy told me to pull back, or because I was abused in some way and had been rendered incapable of feeling. Quite the contrary.

I'm going to tell you a story which illustrates my point, though I'd much prefer not to tell it. I think a misunderstanding of this pulling back is at the heart of our misunderstanding of modesty, so I'm afraid I have to tell.

Typically enough, my loss of innocence took place when I was away from home, at camp. Only I wanted most to go to *debate* camp, believe it or not, in order to collect lots of articles for that next season's debating topic. So my loss of innocence took place at Northwestern debate camp, the summer after my freshman year in high school.

One evening, I suddenly found myself one floor above the room in which I usually slept. This room, as it happens, was the bedroom of my instructor. I don't recall exactly the circumstances under which I had alighted there. I only remember that during the previous five weeks it had been very important that I convert my instructor to my free-market sympathies, and that I saw my journey up to his bedroom as a kind of culmination of my efforts. Subconsciously, of course, I was infatuated with him, but I wasn't aware of it at the time. Crucial to any loss of innocence story, of course, is that you don't realize the significance of what it is you are doing, and that was certainly true in this case. All I was conscious of was that he was a nice fellow, and that even though he was 10 years my senior, he still didn't understand why the Federal Reserve Board aggravates the business cycle. Since I liked him, I was obviously very concerned about this deficiency, and in my teenage know-it-allness hoped I would be able to show him the light before the session's end.

"And really, by the time the FRB can correct for a dip, it's just too *late* and it only ends up making things *worse!*" He was very pleased to find me sitting on his bed, making one last effort to convince him that the federal government mustn't intervene. He nodded patiently, even argued with me in proper sporting fashion, and meanwhile I noticed he had gotten up and locked the door, and also pulled down his window shade. Well, that was cer-

tainly interesting, I remember thinking—was there really something so shameful in a discussion of Milton Friedman?

"Excuse me," he said suddenly, interrupting my rant, "do you
have a boyfriend?"

"Sure, I've had lots of boyfriends," I responded cheerfully and
proudly.

"No, what I mean is, have you actually *done* anything with
them?"

*"What?!"*

I was very offended by this insinuation that I hadn't done anything important with my boyfriends. I hadn't, of course, but how
did he know? Was it that obvious? One of my biggest concerns
growing up was that I would be a weirdo because I didn't take sex
education, when all of my friends did, and that, as my teachers
said, I "wouldn't know what to do" as a result. And now my worst
fear was coming true. I was, in fact, a recognized weirdo.

"I can't believe you're even *asking* me this," I said diffidently, in
my most arch, sophisticated voice, "I've done *tons* of stuff with my
boyfriends." He didn't seem convinced.

"Yeah, like with who?"

"Well, for example . . ." I'm ashamed, in retrospect, with how
quickly a lie flew up to my lips, but what can you do? . . . "with my
friend Amy's older brother. We did *everything* together. And Amy
doesn't even *know* about it!" And neither did Amy's older brother.

"Well, what exactly did you do? Did you do . . . *this?*" Then he
made an obscene gesture not appropriate for a family readership.
Suffice it to say I recoiled in horror. "Of course not! *Gro*—wait—
yes, I mean, yes, of course we did *that*. Sure we did that—and a
lot more, too. Really," by now my voice sounded hurt, "I'm *telling*
you I've done everything with *everyone*. Why won't you believe
me?" Then, "I don't appreciate that you don't believe me."

"I believe you," he said earnestly. Then, "c'mere for a second,"
beckoning to me.

"*What?* No, thank you—I'm not coming over *there*." That's
when he started to laugh. What was so funny? Should I be offended, or should I laugh with him? Was he laughing at me?

It was hard to tell. He got up, sat next to me on his bed.

"Oh. Well, anyway," I chirped, "I've really enjoyed having you
as my debate counselor. We had some fun arguments."

"Yes, well, thank you. I've enjoyed being your debate counselor."

At this point he started to stroke my hair, and I felt such a queer feeling overtake me. I suddenly felt very unsteady and dizzy, and the more he stroked my hair, the queerer I felt. There was definitely a positive correlation. *This can't happen!* was what I immediately thought. Now, I would later learn that this feeling is the reason you're supposed to *continue*, but I didn't know that then. I instinctively pulled back. I had to, because I felt as if I were turning into a liquid version of myself, and as far as I was concerned, if this didn't stop very soon, when my parents arrived to pick me up they would have a puddle for a daughter.

"Wait a minute!" I suddenly sat upright—"I think I have to go downstairs now."

"Well, goodnight." He looked very serious.

And I rearranged my clothing, put my hair back up in a ponytail, and sort of stumbled downstairs, sober but drunk. Then I took a long, guilty shower.

Why, you may ask, was my shower guilty, when he had only touched my hair? Well, that was exactly why—because from so little I had felt so much. Though someone touching my neck could make me feel weak in the knees, this was to most people around me "no big deal."

So what was I going to do about it? The problem is that today, for young women, there is no longer any social sanction for this natural pulling back. This pulling back, which is the result not of prudery—or *pace* Freud, frigidity, sexual repugnance, or some concealment of genital deficiency—but on the contrary, of intense sexual feeling, of a kind of awe and wonder of where it all will lead, is in our society seen as a problem to be "fixed." Even in societies where there was more of a social sanction for modesty, there was always this crucial misunderstanding. Take Stendhal, for instance, who in my opinion comes the closest to the root of modesty's puzzle when he asks himself why the most sensitive women—let us call them the "high responders"—are always the ones who end up being the most sexually reticent.

Stendhal concludes that it's such a shame the high responders are drawn to modesty, because these are the women who are the most fun to have sex with—the very ones who are, in effect, "made for love." And here you thought such talk could only be found in the world of the trashy romance novel, but no, Stendhal wrote that, too: "An excess of modesty and its severity discourage sensitive and timid women from loving, just the ones who are made for giving and feeling the delicacies of love." Then a sour footnote notes the existence of women "the most made for love" who opt, out of "lack of spirit," for the "prosaic sanguine temperament" instead.

Although I am generally inclined to the view that the imagination knows no sex, and that the purpose of writing is to appeal to the universal human, here is one of those cases where I can really see the point of those who say sex does matter. I may not believe in such categories as "women's writing" or "men's writing," but I do think being a man, or being a woman, may color your view of something. And in this case, I think the fact that Stendhal is a man may be relevant, and has led him to misunderstand female modesty. For his quarrel with female modesty, as a man, seems to be: it's not fair that the high responders should be the modest ones, because then the sensualists are hoarding their sensuality. His logic, from an economic point of view, is certainly impeccable: if the high responders would give up their silly modesty and be more promiscuous, then society could maximize their sensuality, and more men could enjoy them.

But though Stendhal's conclusion may be perfectly logical, I think it is nonetheless the wrong conclusion to reach about modesty. What seems to have escaped him is that it is no accident the sensualists end up hiding behind modesty, because it is modesty which protects their sensuality—for the right man, that is. If the sensualists tried to overcome their natural modesty and to become more promiscuous, as Stendhal suggests, then their experiences would have less meaning for them, much of what excites them would be diminished, one man would serve more or less as well as any other—in other words, they would no longer *be* sensualists.

But at least in Stendhal's time, though modesty might have been misunderstood, there was social support for it.

Today, not only is there no social sanction for pulling back at the onset of sexual awakening, but the young woman who dares to is immediately descended upon from all sides, from the magazines she reads to her dearest friends—all who are glad to explain to her that in this golden era of choices and opportunities, waiting for a little more than the norm is the one choice not open to her. *Cosmo* sums up this woman's plight perfectly, in typical *Cosmo* deadpan: "Let's face it. . . . In this age of instant gratification, there's something a little perverse about people who refuse to satisfy their deepest needs."

*Something a little perverse.* If Richard von Krafft-Ebing were alive today, instead of fetishism, sadism, and masochism, his *Psy-*

*chopathia Sexualis* would have to focus mainly on modesty, since it's the woman who waits who is now treated as a freak.

A young woman tells Sally Cline: "Being a virgin definitely wasn't smart. . . . The girls who stayed clannish got it worst. They were told they were prick teasers or piss-offs, or the boys called them abnormal, or prudes, or said they'd turn into lezzies." It's as if wanting to wait for more is taken to be some kind of cultural crime. Indeed, when in the 1998 movie *Wild Things,* a guidance counselor asks an auditorium filled with high school students, "What is a sex crime?" a smart aleck in the front offers, "Not gettn' any!" Everyone giggles since the lesson was supposed to be about rape. Yet instead of expressing frustration, the teacher laughs too—with the sort of knowing smirk that admits the smart aleck gave the true answer.

To be sure, this view is not a new one, but has a long legacy in the annals of misogyny. "Green-sickness," after all, used to be known as the virgin's disease. In 1554, John Lange published his advice that copulation was the best cure for it (presumably, one imagines, with a clip-'n-save coupon in the back, good for a referral to *him*). This was still the minority view, though, the theory being trotted out to insult a virgin one was angry at, as in: "Out you green-sickness carrion! out, you baggage! You tallow-face!" as Capulet says to his daughter Juliet when she dares to choose the man she loves. In the old days you believed that someone's virginity was sick when you hated her. This kind of reductionism wasn't original with Freud. It just used to be recognized as an act of aggression. But after the sexual revolution, this view of virginity—putrid, disease-ridden, and threatening to the social order—went from a fringe misogynous insult to the prevailing sensibility. As a 1998 issue of *Cosmo* reminds us, "few men want a wide-eyed virgin who has no clue what she's doing."

The result has been that in this post–sexual revolution era, a young woman may freely cohabit, but she may not choose to wait. If she does, there must be something wrong with her.

So, without a social sanction for this natural pulling back, what is a young woman to do if she wants to be true to what she feels? She must get up every day and essentially live a lie. In manner, dress, and speech, she must engage in a strategy of deception so that no one will find out that she isn't doing what she is supposed to be doing. That is what I did, and I became expert at it. I even fooled myself on occasion.

## DEVELOPING A REPUTATION

When I returned from debate camp, I immediately told my friends and family about my debate counselor, but without giving details. I didn't intend to lie, but when they drew the conclusions, I didn't exactly bend over backwards to correct them. Everyone was very proud of me. I sensed somehow that I had done extremely well. The tale of my tryst with my debate counselor was soon passed from student to student.

When you're young, you learn to cling eagerly to anything that will give you the appearance of being normal. And having sexual experience, I understood right away, was normal. Indeed, the more extensive the experience, the more normal one was. So thanks to my tall tale from debate camp, in this respect at least, I "passed" as normal. I think if they had known the details, or rather the nondetails, everyone would have been less impressed. Even my best friend and debate partner Sara never suspected what didn't happen at debate camp. We shared everything, but even when I was safely ensconced in her room, and we were laughing and deciding who we liked, I never, ever got up the nerve to confess to her what I hadn't done. One just doesn't talk about this kind of thing nowadays. If in a different age a young woman had to be ashamed of sexual experience, today she is ashamed of her sexual inexperience.

Apparently, I'm not the only one who did this. In a fascinating book by Lillian B. Rubin called *Erotic Wars,* I was delighted to find someone just like me. Hannah, a 15-year-old from suburban Chicago, told Rubin: "I haven't found someone I feel comfortable with, so I haven't felt the need to have sex yet. I don't see the point in rushing anything; I'm young; I have time. But only my very best friend knows the truth. The other kids don't know because I lie and say I'm doing things I'm not. As long as you say what they want to hear, nobody bothers you. It's when you're different that they don't like it."

I don't know how Hannah has ended up, but for me my debate coach story didn't last very long. Soon the questions started to emerge. My good (which is to say, bad) reputation started to crumble. If I was really the bad girl I pretended to be, then why did I rarely go out? People were always asking me this. Why did I never attend any of the big parties? Why only the prom and homecoming?

In time, the questions became louder and more insistent, poking millions of holes in my carefully cultivated sophisticated reputation.

Why did no one ever see me with my mysterious older boyfriend? Well, because we were, uh, having secret trysts all the time.

I eventually had to develop a more comprehensive strategy. Around the middle of my sophomore year in high school, I discovered the popularity that was to be had if one wore extremely tight shirts and sweaters. I noticed that if I wore something that was tight and low-cut—particularly if I often bent over to pick something up—nobody would ask me *any* questions. They would just smile knowingly, and I would wink knowingly back. And that did it. That was really all it took. So if no one saw me going out after school, they saw me looking provocative during school, and that was enough to gain approval.

Ultimately, I soon discovered that people don't actually have to see you doing dirty things. As long as you can plant the idea in their heads that when you are out of view, you're doing something wicked, you'll do just fine. So when you do eventually appear in public, try never, *ever* to be seen with a man fewer than 15 years your senior. That was my strategy in college, and it worked like a charm too. Remember, you're much too sexually sophisticated for boys your own age. For if you are linked with anyone your own age, people might start thinking you're just any normal girl, as opposed to an extremely sophisticated one, and before you know it they will have outed you as a good girl and then your bad reputation will be *ruined*.

Never has one girl done so little with so many older men.

At the same time, while I was presenting myself in this way in public, in private I found myself making up all of these ridiculous rules. Suddenly, I decided, I would always leave the bedroom door open, I wouldn't see R-rated movies, I would always call men "Mister," and so on. People would ask me why I was making these rules for myself and, frankly, I hadn't a clue. I think I sensed there was something I needed to protect—namely, my virginity—even though in public I knew it was something to be ashamed of, so privately I experienced more freedom in living within some limits, even if they had to be self-imposed.

Finally, after years of pretending to be she, I eventually discovered that our much slobbered-over bad girl isn't even as sexy as I once thought. This was a sour surprise. Because, like Naomi Wolf in *Promiscuities,* I had assumed that becoming "bad" and in touch with my "shadow slut" would yield a new era of erotic promise for women generally. Suppression was only for prudes, for women who didn't "own" their sexuality.

In *Newsweek* I read about a girl who declares, "Yeah, I'm a slut! My body belongs to me. I sleep with who I want . . . I'm not your property!" Yet it reminds me of how I was with boys before the onset of any sexual feeling, all so much sixth-grade sex play. She seems to be very enthusiastic about proving that she is cool, but there is nothing *erotic* here.

At age 21, I finally decided to end my adolescent deception. I was tired of hearing that I would "have many men" if only I would "loosen up." If what you want is so different from what people around you say you should, at a certain point you must give up all hope of pleasing them. After all, if I really loosened up, I could become a prostitute, but do I really want that kind of popularity? That's when I decided that I would wear only clothes I was comfortable with and would try to avoid men who preferred to see "if we're compatible." I know right away that probably we're not going to be compatible.

But it was reading Kathryn Harrison's book, *The Kiss,* that made me want to go public. After reading her revelation that she had had sex with her father, I realized how upside down things have become. Here she was sleeping with her father, for God's sake, with few qualms whatsoever, and here *I* was, ashamed of my sexual inexperience, devoting all my energy to keeping up appearances and worrying that someone would find out what I hadn't done.

It's high time sexual modesty came out of the closet. Not only can you not get AIDS from it, not only is it morally right, but as we have seen in the previous two chapters, modesty is really much more exciting than promiscuity. Without any obstacles in the way of desire, what is there to desire? Did you know, by the way, that Mary Wollstonecraft was opposed to sexual modesty precisely because she thought it was too dirty? In her *Vindication* she called it a "lascivious" philosophy of "refined licentiousness," one that "inflame[d]" children's "imaginations" and "prolong[ed] . . . ardor" in adults.

We thought we could have everything and everyone, and really we came up with nothing. "If it feels good, do it," was the motto of the sixties, and after we did it, we found it no longer felt good. We thought that giving up extra-erotic considerations would liberate the erotic, but in fact it spoiled it entirely. The proverb "woo, wed and bed her," often found in English dramas and ballads in 1500–1800, was changed to just "bed her," and this change turned out not to be sexy, as we expected, just depressing.

Indeed, the feminist Sally Cline now refers to the sexual revolution, in retrospect, as the "Genital Appropriation Era":

*What the Genital Appropriation Era actually permitted was more access to women's bodies by more men; what it actually achieved was not a great deal of liberation for women but a great deal of legitimacy for male promiscuity; what it actually passed on to women was the male fragmentation of emotion from body, and the easily internalized schism between genital sex and responsible loving.*

Hence, as Valarie Frankel reports in a 1996 *Mademoiselle* article, women are now holding back on intercourse on precisely erotic grounds. We meet "Heather," who is 24: "I said I wasn't ready for a commitment, but really, I just knew that the holding back was more exciting for me. It was like, 'The suspense is killing me; I hope it lasts.'" Andrea, 27, who "was raised Catholic" and therefore "held off on intercourse for as long as I could" finds that "there's something special about holding off—once you have intercourse, the mystery is gone. Restraint is exciting." The article also includes helpful tips to get your boyfriend interested in not having sex, such as "It's not that you'll NEVER have intercourse," and "He'll have a more responsive partner."

The women interviewed, as well as the sex researchers, agree that the sexual revolution was man-centered, and that women lost out. Dr. Robert Francoeur, Ph.D., author of *The Scent of Eros,* explains, "In the old system, men proved their manhood. In the new system, women are saying, 'To heck with the old rules. What about me?'"

Of course, in rejecting the "old rules" of the sexual revolution, and returning to rules that are more centered on women's emotional needs, today's young women are returning to even older rules—often, those very rules of modesty their own mothers once called sexist.

But the return to modesty among today's young women represents more than just a rebellion against their mothers' rules. It is a rejection of something more fundamental, of a philosophy which dates from before the sexual revolution. "Virtue," Simone de Beauvoir wrote in 1951 apropos of defending Sade, "chimerical and imaginary, encloses us in a world of appearances; whereas vice's intimate link with the flesh guarantees its genuineness . . . if virtue arouses no sensation, it is because it has no real basis." The persistence of sexual modesty challenges and ultimately refutes this equation of the libertine with the erotic, because those who are returning to virtue are doing so for precisely sensual reasons. They are often totally secular, but have found vice boring and insipid. Beauvoir said that Sade showed that "no aphrodisiac is so potent as the defiance of Good," and now history has proved her and Sade wrong.

Modesty is the proof that morality is sexy.

It may even be the proof of God, because it means that we have been designed in such a way that when we humans act like animals, without any restraint and without any rules, we just don't have as much fun.

# Chapter 11

# PINING FOR INTERFERENCE

*I'll never forget the night during my sophomore year, when my
college girlfriend closed her eyes, wiggled out of her panties and
prepared to abandon her virginity. I was 20 at the time; she was
barely 18. Her father had just dropped us off at the hotel,
knowing full well what was about to transpire. . . . The night
before the big event he sat me down in their den. I prepared
myself for an angry tirade. Instead, he spoke with the voice of a
pensive diplomat. 'I'm glad she chose you,' he said. . . .
Although Karen's mother and father blessed our union, Mother Nature didn't. The next day, the Midwest was hit with an
unusually ferocious snowstorm. . . . [But] later that afternoon,
her father came downstairs, holding his blue wool cap in one
hand and a set of expensive gleaming silver car keys in the
other. Prepared to trust me with his only daughter, but not with
his brand-new Volvo, he shook the very foundation of parental
propriety by offering to drive us to the hotel.*

—"My Girlfriend's Father—What a
Man!" by Eric Tisdale, *Glamour*, June 1998

This boyfriend may have thrilled to Karen's "world's most
open-minded father," but what about Karen herself? The
author—who is no longer Karen's boyfriend but her friend, he
informs us—writes that they now look back on that night and
"laugh." But when they were alone in the hotel room, our author
records, Karen started screaming.

One of the T-shirts strung along my college's "Clothesline Project" read: "Sometimes I don't WANT you to MIND YOUR OWN
BUSINESS." I identify the most with this one, because what I'm
always wondering is, Where *is* everybody?

I particularly think of everybody when I reflect on my experiences with men. If I found myself suddenly and spontaneously
making up all these strange rules, such as separate rooms, open

door, no R-rated movies, always call men "Mister," it was only because I was constantly aware of this ever-present void, of the fact that there would be no everybody for me.

Yet in retrospect, why wasn't there an everybody? Maybe you've never asked yourself this question, and you're perfectly content with the fact that our culture drops off condoms and then runs away. But I'm not. Most people today either attack you or fall totally silent. No one offers advice anymore, so instead we have lawsuits and date-rape charges, after the fact. The more I think about it, the stranger the absence of everybody seems. We just wordlessly toss our girls to the wind, and when the wind blows them home, we are surprised to find that they are anorexic or have cut or burned various parts of their body. Everyone acts as though this is perfectly normal.

But it isn't normal, is it? Finding yourself in your debate counselor's bedroom at 1:00 A.M. is most definitely abnormal. This man could have raped me. He didn't, though. I was lucky that he was moral. To me the strangest thing, however, is that I distinctly remember his co-counselor seeing me slip into his room, and he didn't do a thing about it. He just laughed and waved at me. But there was a rule about not creeping up to your male counselor's bedroom at 1:00 A.M. We have so few rules these days, and even when we do, no one seems to enforce them. Why is no one enforcing our rules? Don't they care about us at all?

At one of our high school dances, I remember seeing a crouched football player under the stack of lunch tables that had been cleared away to make a dance floor. I called out to him as I made my way to the girls' bathroom. He didn't respond. I sank down to his level. "Oh my God he's bleeding! Somebody come here, quick." There was a razor blade on his knee and his right arm was slashed up.

"Oh, he always does that," someone said. "Don't pay any attention to him," someone else said. But he was bleeding all over the place. How could everyone pretend everything was normal? I ended up yanking off his shirt and wrapping it around his arm. I remember his eyes coming to a focus from the pressure, his looking down quizzically at his spotted shirt and saying softly, indignantly, "Hey, you're ruining my white shirt!" Sometimes you think you're saving someone's life, and in fact you're just ruining their white shirt. It's a fine line, but which side do you err on? Today adults err on the side of not intervening at all, and so we are in the ridiculous situation where college women have to emblazon on T-shirts, in big black lettering, "Sometimes I don't WANT you to MIND YOUR OWN BUSINESS."

I often find myself lecturing adults about why they should be lecturing me, which is a strange position to be in. I'm always pining for someone to young-lady me. As in, young lady, what are you doing? Where are you going? But no one ever young-lady's me, so I have to young-lady myself.

A 1956 etiquette book warned: "A woman arriving at a hotel without any luggage invariably arouses the suspicions of the house detective. By all means, carry a small bag, even if it's just an overnight visit. This advice is from chapter 17, entitled "As Others See Us." If there are any others who see us today, we wouldn't know it.

I have secretly hoped, when someone has kissed me in public, that a police officer will interfere quaintly, and say, "I'm sorry, we don't do that around here." But no one ever does, and it just feels weird to me, not necessarily being kissed in front of onlookers, but being kissed in front of onlookers who walk right by. So I then have to muster my own moral indignation, and my voice rings false and small: "um, people can *see,* people are *looking.*" But of course it's in my imagination, because people aren't looking. The truth is that people couldn't care less.

The irony, of course, is that if somebody did interfere, I'd probably end up doing—and not doing—exactly what I wanted anyway. And yet still I think it's very important for these things to be *said.* For what's the point of kissing someone in public if it's no longer even an indiscretion? What's the point of being singled out for a kiss, when anyone can kiss anyone at any time? It's just not as interesting.

"TORI'S SURE NO PRUDE!" runs a screaming *New York Post* headline. Columnist Liz Smith is recounting what Tori Spelling, "the long-running virgin of *Beverly Hills 90210,*" told Movieline's Stephen Rebello when he asked, "Where's the wildest place you ever made love?" Tori answered, "An airplane! Which means I've reached the mile-high club. I'm terrified of flying . . . and on this particular flight I had two glasses of wine so I got a lot less self-conscious. The weird thing is, nobody even turned their head when we went into the bathroom. Maybe they were all drunk or something." Or maybe nobody cared. Poor Tori. She's reached the mile-high club, and nobody even cares. I think this must be her equivalent of my being-kissed-in-public problem.

After Katie Roiphe creeps out of the apartment of "not some-one . . . I should have been with at all," in her "clothes from the night before, rumpled, hair tangled, worrying as I passed the bald doorman that he would look at me in the bright fluorescence of the lobby and know," it occurs to her "with a surprising rush of disappointment, that no one cared. And even if they had known, they still wouldn't have cared."

Then in a 1998 *Glamour* "Sexual Ethics" column, Sara Eckel writes of a young woman named "Jennifer" who "dreaded informing her fuddy-duddy daddy that she was moving in with her boyfriend." She and her mother rehearsed a speech for months. "Finally, Jennifer took a nervous breath, dialed and broke the news. 'Well,' her father said after a pause, 'whatever saves you money.' 'I couldn't believe it,' says Jennifer. 'I wanted to say, 'Wait a second, don't you care? I just told you I'm living in sin!'"

In an earlier profile in *Elle,* Kathryn Harrison expressed her disappointment with the reaction that greeted her revelation she had had sex with her father: "I really expected if I told someone I was sexually involved with my father, that person would fall down dead." Much to the chagrin of all these ladies trying to pro-voke social disapproval, even incest isn't really scandalous any-more. Without the conventions of modesty, we are learning, we simply cannot be shocked.

Of course, we talk about sex all the time in the abstract. Every-one knows that they should be having a lot of it, that they shouldn't be embarrassed, and that they should, above all, be doing everything safely. But in the specific case, utter silence. When it comes to this particular man, and this particular woman, at this particular time, in this particular airplane bathroom, no one has a thing to say. Even if it's your father, no one has a thing to say. It is always smiles—or smirks—all around. If pressed, friends will say "as long as you're happy." If pressed, parents will say "as long as you're happy." It's almost as if, with respect to sex, we do not live in a soci-ety at all. We wouldn't want to "socially construct" anything. We have no common experiences, so we cannot advise—except for issuing these strange directives about plumbing, frequency, and safety, which manage to be at once vague and clinical. But when it comes to each case, we are all on our own. About what it all means, about where, if any place, it should be heading—utter silence.

"As long as you're happy." What does that mean? When I think of my earliest sexual awakenings, for instance, I had absolutely no idea what I was doing. As far as I was concerned, I crept up to my camp counselor's bedroom because I wanted someone I could talk to. In retrospect, I can see that I was attracted to him, but truthfully I don't think I realized this at the time, until he started to caress my hair. Not because I was so pure, though I was, but simply because I was plain confused. But that's what it means to be young, right? Everything is all mixed up. And there's nothing wrong with that. What's wrong is that there is no one anymore to help you untangle anything. Or to put it more accurately, the only people who will bother untangling you are usually the ones with a vested interest in untangling you in *their* direction.

"As long as you're happy." But when you're young and confused, when you want most to fit in, what exactly does happiness mean? What the young fear most, after all, is being lonely, finding out that we're not normal, that we won't "fit in." And it is an understandable fear. Even if you come from a strong family and have a good sense of worth, it is extremely difficult to insist on your right to be different. One has to be prepared to watch friends fade away, for strange looks, for constant wearing reminders of how "weird" one is—in some cases, for total ostracism. You hope that new friends will emerge, ones with whom you can be yourself, but when they do appear, it usually comes as an utter surprise.

Maybe the scary thing about adolescence, then, is that even though there are so many wonderful people in the world, and you are always bound to find someone, *somewhere,* who will accept you as you are, you can't know that for sure, when you're young. At the moment when you see you don't fit in, and you have to decide whether to force yourself to fit in, or start a new path all alone, as far as you're concerned you could be making a decision that means you will be alone for the rest of your life.

People say that adolescents exaggerate the importance of these earliest decisions. Indeed this has come to be one of the definitions of adolescence: that you suddenly perceive (wrongly) that everything is important. This giggly phone call which ties up the family line, or that boyfriend's odd indifference to you around his friends— it all matters terribly, when it's not supposed to, apparently.

I have to admit I have never understood this condescending definition of adolescence. I just don't see why it's an exaggeration to have a sense that the course of one's life will be determined by the decisions we make on these mundane matters. Why is it childish to think this is the stuff out of which we will discover who we are, what we hope for, who we want to become? It is exactly that. Do I fit in, or do I remain true to what I really feel—which is afraid, or embarrassed—and risk being left out?

Many teenagers commit suicide today because kids are just not taken seriously when they wonder this. Dr. Peter Jensen, chief of the child and adolescent disorders research branch of the National Institute of Mental Health, told *The New York Times* in 1997 that rates of both adolescent depression and suicide have risen over the last decade. "This is an urgent public health concern," he said. When children today find they don't fit in, they are given very little support. They therefore answer this am-I-the-only-one question wrongly. Yes I can't really talk to anyone. Yes, I can't really trust anyone. Yes, I'm all alone, and always will be. If they feel this and somehow manage not to kill themselves, then they usually end up killing their souls, or mutilating themselves in various ways to avoid confronting the fact that they're not being accepted as they are.

As adults sipping our wine, we can laugh at all this "melodrama," secure as we are in our circle of friends, and knowing as we do that someone always turns up. But when you're young there is no way of knowing this, and so it's a very serious question, whether you're going to be all alone or not. What this means is that when young people feel left out, they simply cannot distinguish happiness from their relief at not being left out. And that is why, when we're young, we depend on adults precisely to explain that this relief at not-being-left-out is not the same thing as happiness, and also to show us why, even if they were the same, that some things are more important than happiness, anyway.

But instead all we hear is this perverse "as long as you're happy." If I hear that one more time from one more adult, I'm going to have to . . . draw a comic strip. It would involve a serial killer about to be executed. He's on the electric chair, all strapped up, looking glum, and his divorced parents are in the doorway, waving enthusiastically at him—from separate sides of the doorway, of course—and smiling brightly. "Hi, Mom, hi Dad," he says, muffled through his mask, "Well, I guess this is it, huh?" His father steps forward. Can it be *concern*? It *is* concern. There can be no doubt from the eagerness with which father jumps to son's side. He gives a hearty reassuring pat on the orange jump-suited shoulder of the figure seated there, and says, "Don't worry, son—it's like we've been saying all along: As long as you're happy!"

Once in fifth grade, I asked my teacher for a safety pin—a button had fallen off my red-and-blue checkered skirt—and she whispered to me, *"Everything's in the bottom drawer."* So I opened the bottom drawer of her desk and discovered not safety pins, but all kinds of gels and jellies, sanitary napkins, and condoms. What was all this? Perhaps she misheard? This single drawer incident greatly perplexed me for about three weeks. Finally I decided I would settle the whole matter and conduct a simple test: again I asked for a safety pin, and again I was directed to this tampon-and-condom drawer. I was really confused. It was some time before I realized that she must have thought I couldn't ask for what I *really* wanted, and so she was just trying to be conscientious.

I loved my fifth-grade teacher dearly, and it's not fair to blame her for the prevailing cultural sensibility, but really, adults, sometimes when a child asks for a safety pin, all she really wants is a safety pin. In a different time, when the question was sexual, the answer was always prim and innocent: "Where do babies come from?" "The stork, dear." Now even when the question is innocent, the answer is always sexual: "May I have a safety pin?" "Of course you can have the tampons or condoms you really want."

When I was little a common school project was carrying around a raw egg. You had to refrigerate it at night, shlep it around with you during the day, and dress it up. Most importantly, though, you had to make sure it didn't break. If it broke, you were a bad parent. As I am writing this the current craze is handheld "virtual pets" from Tamagotchi, but the principle is the same. These creatures beep all the time, and their buttons must be pushed constantly in the correct combinations. The toys, reported *The New York Times,* are interfering with camp, with all the standard things children used to do, such as making friendship bracelets. They interfere, that is, with anything which would capture the child's imagination, encourage him to play with, say, *others.* Kids don't have time for friendship bracelets now—they have responsibilities. They have to push their alien's "Hungry and Happy" meters, over and over again. Unlike other toys, these virtual Tamagotchis cannot be turned off or put away; if you stop caring for them, then you fail at the game. You're a bad parent. A child in New Jersey, reported Jan Benzel, "gets so anxious over his creature's well-being that he shrieks, 'Mom, I can't take it anymore!'"

Is modern child's "play" really play, or practicing the same ritualized responsibility again and again? Everyone my age has a story about some egg they were required to shlep around. It was a silly project, and the Tamagotchi beeping aliens are silly toys, and one shouldn't extrapolate too much from trifles, but these things are popular for a reason: because they are a kind of allegory for what is expected of us. To be parents when we were still children.

Everyone calls my generation self-obsessed because we write about why we are on Prozac or why we are anorexic. But maybe there's a good reason why most kids my age can only write about how screwed up they've become. When you don't have parental support, there is simply no way a child can know that the problem is a sick culture. A child assumes the problem is with him.

Sociologist David Popenoe notes that between 1960 and 1990, the percentage of children living apart from their biological fathers doubled. And by the turn of the century, as many as "50 percent of American children may be going to sleep each evening without being able to say good night to their dads." Yet "almost all of today's fatherless children have fathers who are alive, well, and perfectly capable of shouldering the responsibilities of fatherhood."

In a 1998 issue of *Marie Claire*, recovering alcoholic Bonnie Root recalls,

> When I was 14, my boyfriend introduced me to crank, a cheap, chemical version of cocaine. I looked strung out—my hair was fried, my skin was bad, and still my parents never asked me what was wrong. I didn't really want to do any of this. I wanted my parents to say they loved me and were worried. That never happened . . . my parents were going through an ugly divorce. My mother was so upset, she could not see what I was doing. I was expelled in my freshman year and stayed home for two months. She never said anything. I finally told her that I wanted to go back to school.

Parents seem to think their children are so knowing and independent that they don't need mothers and fathers anyway, but in fact we are not. Very often we are faking it. At least that is the way it usually is at first, and then once we're knowing, that knowing becomes a kind of not-knowing, cutting off awareness of who we really want to be. Usually we're just dying for someone to kiss us good night, to care enough to tell us what the right thing to do is.

Our culture's message to young women used to be, "Hey you—what are you *doing?*" Now it says to us, "Hey you—what are you *not* doing?" Both questions are irritating to hear, but to the extent a culture is hardly ever neutral, and always attempts to influence one way or another, I think it is better that the question be the first. At least "Hey you—what are you *doing?*" expresses a concern for the young woman, whereas "Hey you—what are you *not* doing?" is just plain sick.

This inversion of the advice given to young women seems to be much the same in Britain. In the British *Vogue*, 28-year-old Lucinda Rosenfeld describes her unhappiness with living with her boyfriend. She initially fancied herself more sophisticated than her parents' generation who married "green with inexperi-ence," but comes to think that her generation's "mock marriages" are even worse. Their breakups—or "prolonged and painful mini-divorces"—aren't any easier than real ones, for she still cried "buckets of tears" after hers. A friend of hers agreed: "Right now I'm regretting having given over my late twenties to a man I didn't end up marrying." Our author decides, "I'd like to think that I won't be playing house again unless it's for ever." But her culture doesn't support her decision. As in America, "a formerly Bohemian life-style . . . has become the norm. . . . Indeed, to have reached 30 these days without having racked up a complicated romantic past is regarded as a little uncool." Instead of asking why a young woman would want to live with someone before mar-riage, parents now ask why a young woman *isn't* living with someone. If she's 18 and still a virgin, her own father will drive her to a hotel. *Stop whining, it's time for your deflowering. I discussed it already with your boyfriend.*

Whether it's the girl in *Glamour* who wanted her dad to put up a fight about cohabiting, Tori Spelling disappointed that no one cared she had sex in an airplane, or Katie Roiphe upset that the doorman didn't flinch when she left someone's apartment in the morning, the sad, incredulous question is the same: Don't you guys care about us at *all?* No, nobody seems to. Nobody says a word. "Sometimes I don't WANT you to MIND YOUR OWN BUSI-NESS." I have a friend whose religious mother wouldn't let her wear makeup until she was sixteen. When I tell any woman my age about this, they look at me bug-eyed—with envy. To have someone who cares about you so much!

Our mothers pined for liberation, and we are pining for inter-ference.

### SKIPPING OVER THE PILL

Nowadays, a girl can't get aspirin from her school nurse without parental permission, but in many states, she can get on the Pill or have an abortion. It is her decision alone.

I know a young unmarried woman who is not on the Pill. She would be mortified if anyone knew it, so she has to remain anonymous. But as luck would have it, we are very close, and so I happen to be privy to why she is not on the Pill.

My young friend—call her Ann—never gave the Pill any thought until her freshman constitutional law class, when her class read Justice Douglas's 1965 decision in *Griswold* v. *Connecticut,* establishing the right of marital privacy from one Connecticut law, and then learned that in the 1972 Supreme Court ruling *Eisenstadt* v. *Baird,* this particular right to privacy was extended to the individual—specifically, by overturning a Massachusetts law against distributing contraception to unmarried women. When Ann first heard of these cases, she found it terrifically funny that this could actually be an issue, whether people would allow single women contraception. How ridiculous, she thought. Did they want them to get pregnant? And she was also annoyed with the people who had made such laws: How dare they presume to tell women what to do? And to think that we only so recently, in 1972, figured out the way things should so obviously be! These questions were personal ones, not the sort of thing social policy should interfere in.

But that was before Ann had her own brush with birth control. Now she thinks things are more complicated.

A year and a half after that con-law class, Ann makes up her mind that she is going to lose her virginity, after all. She has just turned twenty, no longer a teenager, and she is sure she has found the right person. So before you could say, "Am I the world's oldest virgin?" Ann finds herself in the office of a gynecologist. But then an unexpected thing happened: she chickens out. Of course, had Ann read *Sex on Campus,* she would have known that "Shame, guilt, and fear are *not* emotions that belong in a gynecologist's office," but alas, the book was published too late for her to benefit from it. She had read Judy Blume's *Forever,* of course, so she knew the basic plot of what was *supposed* to happen: the female protagonist goes on the Pill and becomes a heroine. But Ann's experience at the gynecologist's turned out to be a little different—so depressing, in fact, that she would eventually end up not using the birth control provided.

Before the examination, Ann and the gynecologist have a little consultation. Immediately and without thinking, Ann breaks into a rivulet of gushing words over how excited she is, how wonderful her boyfriend is, how much she loves him, and how she is sure he is right for her, and boy, is she glad she waited! And then . . . then she completely freezes. Ann sees the expression on the gynecologist's face—one of polite condescension—and it occurs to her in a flash of horror that the good doctor isn't too terribly interested in how much she loves her boyfriend. How could she have thought otherwise? Ann is mortified. "Oh I'm so sorry what was I thinking of course you don't care, you're not here to—"

"No, it's *important* that I understand," the gynecologist says considerately, stealing a glance at her wristwatch.

"No, please, I'm so embarrassed—you're so kind to even pretend you're interested—"

"Now, remember, the first time it might hurt—"

"Oh, please," Ann pleads with her, "let's just not talk about this, okay, it's just too embarrassing for me."

"But we *have* to talk about it—" the gynecologist says, amused.

"You don't understand . . . perhaps I should explain," Ann blurts out. "See, this is all still very embarrassing for me, I mean—I'm, um, that is, um . . ."

"Yes, I understand," the gynecologist says soothingly. By this point she is looking at Ann as if at an alien. She is nodding but her eyes are wide and terrified. She seems to be to be afraid that Ann will infect her with her embarrassment.

The two soon travel to the next room, where Ann is examined. She must have done very well, because before she fled from the office the gynecologist thrusts into her palms, in addition to a prescription, lots of free samples of pill packages. "Plus it will also make your period regular!" was her final call to Ann.

It's humiliating to Ann how silly and girlish she is at 20, when one is supposed to be more sophisticated than that at that age.

Yet when a girl is deciding whether to have sexual intercourse for the first time, whatever her age, the same two forces are usually at war: her romantic hopes and curiosity on the one hand, and on the other, her natural embarrassment. I realize some say that embarrassment is socially constructed, and that's a part of it, but I don't think it's the main part. I would say the opposite—that embarrassment is natural but it can be socially *de*structed. For even though Ann lives in a society which tells her all the time not to be embarrassed, and even though she comes from a secular family, in which her parents never said anything like "don't have sex before you're married," she was still embarrassed at the gynecologist's. Why?

She was horrified by the discrepancy between her hopes and

the clinical nature of everything. Embarrassment is actually a wonderful signal, namely, that something isn't quite right. The sublime recoils from the clinical because it wants to inform it, to guide it and protect the girl. The animal side of her nature, of course, has the most immediate claim and tells the spirit to go away, that what it does is none of its business. So when the human soul meets the animal nature, which one will win? It all comes down to how much embarrassment you have left over. Embarrassment signifies that an important battle is going on.

Embarrassment is silly, but the fact is, it is also what makes girls strong. Ann's embarrassment protected her—if not from heartbreak, then at least from *more* heartbreak. Taught from day one that we should always give in to the animal, and that our embarrassment is a problem—*"now remember boys and girls, there is absolutely nothing to giggle about!"*—girls today have nothing to protect what is human in them. There is no battle going on like the one there was with Ann. Or rather, since we are now taught in school to be ashamed of the uniquely human rather than the animal, the battle was over before it began. Stripped of their natural embarrassment, girls are only more vulnerable: they just give in—again, and again.

Yet the human soul ends up reasserting itself, anyway, only since this time the disparity is between what they hoped for and what they got, the result is not embarrassment or hesitation, but usually misery—and that's when they start cutting themselves up. Misery because there is no longer anything they can do about it. At least when there is embarrassment or discomfort, that points to *not* doing something. Thus, Kelli, a 15-year-old patient of Mary Pipher's, asks her psychologist: "Did my mom tell you we were having sex?" When Dr. Pipher nods, the girl hastens to add, "It's no big deal," because she is, of course, "on the Pill." And yet, if it were really "no big deal," then what was she doing in Dr. Pipher's office to begin with? Answer: she was threatening to kill herself.

Anyway, when Ann returned home she shook out the bag on her bed and surveyed her windfall of little pink containers. She had not only five filled prescriptions, having filled them all at once to minimize embarrassment, but all those free samples besides. Plus as an extra bonus, it would make her period regular. That's what she had wanted her whole life, just to be "regular." A pamphlet was also in the bag, an advertisement for Ortho Tri-Cyclen. It informed her that the Pill can also "clear up your skin," "decrease the incidence of acute pelvic inflammatory disease—a condition which, if left untreated, can cause infertility," and also make "iron-deficiency anemia" less likely. She is definitely against acute pelvic inflammatory disease and iron-deficiency anemia. There seemed to be so many advantages to going on the Pill, and no disadvantages. Not to mention that it had to be right for her because, after all, the containers were pink, and pink was fun and feminine and cotton candy and everything nice. She popped her first pill with the thought usually accorded to popping an M&M. She was regular at last. Ann looked in the mirror to see what she looked like regular, and that's when she started to get depressed.

She even started crying. Wait, this wasn't regular. She called up her boyfriend: ". . . and don't you think it's kind of depressing that she doesn't even *care* how much I love you? Even *if* I love you? Or if you really love me? Don't you think that's kind of *weird?*"

"You're so funny," he said, affectionately.

"But there're all these *girls* all alone in that office, and nobody even cares if the person they're involved with really loves them, if he's right for them or *anything*. Everyone just wants to write a prescription for them and get paid for it. Don't you think that's *depressing?*"

"You're so funny," he repeated, somewhat less affectionately.

It was even funnier some months later, when the months passed and it became clear that he and Ann weren't right for each other. Now she had all these annoying pink containers rebuking her whenever she opened her underwear drawer. Should she keep them, in case she met someone she *did* want . . . ?

Well? It's an important question, and it's exactly the sort of question you can't really talk to anyone about nowadays, because it's nobody's business and we're all supposed to be independent. Ann had to decide what to do on her own. It reminded her of the time she bought Rollerblades, and they just stood there on her shelf for months, glaring at her, mocking her in their beady speedy way: *who are you kidding? You're not the Rollerblading type!* But on the other hand, they were so expensive; she had gone and made an *investment*. Should she keep them around . . . in case someday she became an entirely different person and woke up itching to Rollerblade?

And similarly, should she keep her Pinky Pills around . . . in case someday she became an entirely different person and woke up wanting to have lots of sex with everyone?

No, Ann decides, she would never come this close again, before marriage. She ended up throwing them all out. Screw regularity.

Ann is, it hardly needs pointing out, the exception. From her friends to the people she doesn't feel so friendly towards, from the magazines she reads to the advertisements on the billboards surrounding her, everyone and everything in Ann's culture seems to think the Pill is perfectly normal, perfectly "regular"—but to her it seems a little creepy. And frankly, I agree with Ann. The way I see it, for an unmarried woman the Pill—all contraception, for that matter—is essentially a conspirator in her self-deception. When she's about to go on it, she can think: "I'll be on the Pill! The container is pink! I'll be regular, too! Everything's going to be okay!"

But that's a lie. There's no guarantee of this. Preventing pregnancy *doesn't* make everything OK. Here is Representative Don Manzullo of Illinois, arguing against a house bill of September 1997 that gave every federal health clinic in the country permission to distribute condoms and birth-control pills to children as young as 13 without parental notification or consent:

> *In my district, a 13-year-old girl was molested by her 37-year-old teacher. The relationship went on for 18 months. He tired of using condoms, so he took her to the county health department, without the knowledge of her parents, to have her arm injected with a powerful drug, Depro-Provera. . . . The people who gave her the shots knew that she was being statutorily raped, but no report was made. . . . The girl became anorexic, and her parents finally asked what had happened. Today, she is in therapy five days a week.*

"What foils the male's tendency to random promiscuity is the woman," *Daily Mail*'s Douglas & Kate Botting report in "What Do Women Really See in Men?" "Here, the differences in the reproductive mechanisms of the two sexes are all-important. Male sperm are replenished at the rate of around 12 million per hour. By contrast, women are born with a finite number of eggs and will use just 400 in a lifetime. The act of sex demands a minimum biological investment from the male but can entail a maximum investment on the part of the female, involving a pregnancy lasting nine months and a child-caring period of several years." But what happens when there is no longer a risk of pregnancy?

At least when there is a risk of pregnancy, there is a physical corollary to the emotional risk—so you are careful. And because the women had to be careful, the men were careful too. Our bodies naturally protected our hearts. I'm not advocating that *Eisenstadt* v. *Baird* was decided wrongly. I'm just suggesting that things are more complicated than we will perhaps admit even to ourselves. If a woman is married, or planning never to get married, or divorced, or widowed, or has had such extensive sexual experience that these questions no longer have any meaning for her, then these are all different matters. What I'm talking about doesn't apply to them, and I don't mean to interfere with their lives. I'm talking about the young woman who hopes for marriage and is essentially waiting for "the right guy"; I think for her the Pill is seductive and, I would go as far as to say, dangerous, holding out the promise of sex without consequences, and without any "irregularities."

That's what I mean by calling it a tool of self-deception. It's like that Erl King from German legend, the one who whispers sweet words to children before snatching their souls. In Schubert's haunting adaptation of Goethe the Erl King sings seductively to the boy—*"Ich liebe dich,"* I love you, he coos to him, as father and son ride through the night. The boy cries "Father, Father—the Erl King is coming! Can you not see the Erl King?" but since the father can't hear the Erl King's melody, he won't believe his son and remains unconcerned. Finally when the ride ends, it's too late to save his son. In the father's arms *"das Kind war tot"*—his child is dead.

We don't believe our girls when they tell us what they hoped for. When they come crying to us in all sincerity or despair, we are annoyed with them and tell them, like Sharon Thompson, that "their distress" is "disproportionate." They would be better off, as she says, if they took "the romantic equation apart," "accept[ed] love as ephemeral." So we put her on the Pill, on Prozac, tell her to try harder, and by the end, it's her hopes that are dead. Then when she no longer cares about anything, we deem her "mature." If she's like me and still cares, then she is "immature."

Proof that my theory might be true is the viciousness usually directed against virgins from unmarried women who are on the Pill. Katie Roiphe found Beverly LaHaye's assistant "infuriating" for deciding to wait for sex. Isn't that an odd thing for someone to be infuriated about? Aren't there better things, such as, say, racism or mass starvation? Perhaps she finds earnestness so infuriating because it reminds her of the hopefulness she is trying to suppress in herself.

After I wrote an article on the daughters of women who lived the sexual revolution, a woman from California wrote me the saddest letter I had ever received in my life:

> *I remember from my college days in the late seventies and early eighties how insidious premarital sex among women was, because it essentially made women evil to other women. When I indicated to my female suite mates that I intended to remain a virgin until marriage, I was met with overt hostility—even to the point where, en masse, they trotted out their birth control devices and spoke about the glories of intercourse. Needless to say, resigned to the "reality" of my ostracism, I gave in and gave away my virginity to a boyfriend who deserted shortly thereafter. Premarital sex creates self-hatred in women. . . . Perhaps I am overstating my case. However, I have been through a lot of pain—the years of trying to patch together the wreckage of my self-esteem, the loss of innocence, the desire to feel clean and whole just out of my reach. Although I have had a few marriage proposals, none of the men who proposed were appropriate, and I am still unmarried at 37. I feel that if I had been allowed to be a virgin, I would have had a much healthier approach to "courtship." . . . A healthier society would protect women from premarital sexual experience.*

Why was it so important that this woman not be "allowed to be a virgin"? Maybe she was overstating her case to say that premarital sex creates "self-hatred" and "evil" in women. But it obviously creates *something* bad, for her suitemates to have so furiously ganged up on her. Many are in this woman's heart-wrenching position these days, but you only hear about them in whispers. So-and-so's sister—hey, what's going on with her? A pretty, lovely woman. Talented. Nice. Maybe too nice? Is that it? What's wrong with her, anyway? Or so-and-so's daughter. Maybe it's the men she's been involved with? What's wrong with men today? What's wrong with women today? It's the invisible American tragedy. No one wants to mention these women in public because it involves a kind of national taboo. *They* certainly can't speak up, because it would be decidedly uncool. If they did, people would sneer, so whaddaya want? To reinstate breach-of-promise suits? To even take notice of these women is to have one's own psychological makeup called into question: *I see, so you must have a fear of abandonment, is that it?*

Some will say that I'm trying to "oppress" women by suggesting that going on the Pill is not as easy and painless as our culture makes it out to be. Others will be irate and say that I am trying to restrict women's contraceptive options, even though I haven't said a word about legality or illegality. These are the forbidden questions. There are some things one simply is not permitted to talk about in polite American society anymore, and the Pill is one of them.

But this wall of ideology has not made our girls better off. To pretend that the female sexual drama is exactly the same as the male sexual drama is a sick-making lie. Each must discover on her own how very different it is. Since there will be no "interference," each assumes there is something wrong with her for being too emotional. What's truly oppressive to girls is presenting them with a false picture, one without any irregularities or complications. We tell them that the only risk is pregnancy or sexually transmitted diseases, but it simply isn't true. Maybe it's true if you're the sort of person who loves only yourself, because then you can never lose yourself completely in anyone else, but most girls are not as narcissistic as our culture trains them to be.

We are more vulnerable than you think.

### DIVORCE AND THE RETURN TO PRIVATE CLAIMS

I think the significance of divorce for my generation has been underestimated. Those who write about the ill effects of divorce usually write about the children of divorce—on their drug habits, or on the likelihood that they will get divorced too. Most critiques of divorce focus on this or that side effect, and only on the children of the rupture, as if divorce were an unpleasant consideration confined to its most immediate victims. But most of my friends whose parents are not divorced have essentially the same anxieties as children of divorced parents. What's rarely talked about is what it's like to grow up in a divorce culture even when your parents are not divorced. For even when they're happy, they always could get divorced; indeed, statistics say it's more likely that they will get divorced than stay together.

"Dear *Help!,*" writes one worried girl to the editor of *American Girl* in 1996, "My parents fight a lot. It always makes me scared that they're going to get a divorce. Mom will say, 'No, honey, we're fine.' But then I listen through the door to the basement or the laundry chute. What should I do?—*Upset.*"

Divorce is a living reality for all children. In author Marya Hornbacher's home, there was often talk of divorce, persistent "screaming fights in the kitchen about who would go to the grocery store, who was a bigger martyr." Her mother took "impromptu trips . . . out of town for inscrutable reasons." In a box of old papers Marya found a card she had written in preschool:

> On the cover, a stick-figure sad girl in purple pen, with the words: "to mom." Inside, the lines slant sharply downward: "DeAr mom. / I do Not Liek [scribble]. / It wen You Are / awae. I want You Back! / I can not sleep wen / Out you! Love, marya." At the bottom of the card, there is a purple heart . . . this particular disfigured heart is crying purple tears.

The fact is that my generation has grown up living in the constant awareness that we cannot depend on anyone but ourselves. Even when we're planning our weddings, it's never too early to start thinking about the inevitable. A 1996 issue of *New Woman* even offers us a "Newlywed's Guide to Divorce."

*Complete Woman* magazine conducted several polls in 1996 to find out if men believe "marriage is forever." Ed avers: "I trade my car in every four of five years no matter how much I like it to start with. So, I'd say if divorce didn't cost so much, every man would trade the old marriage in for a new one every so often." Tim is more tender-hearted: "It should be forever, but if things aren't working out, I'd bail."

We are constantly judged and reevaluated, even by our lovers, the ones with whom it was once thought one could rest. This omnipresence of divorce creeps into every interaction and is one of the clearest reminders that there is no longer any private and "safe" realm. Everything and everyone is up for grabs, and we always face the harsh world directly, unmediated by any enduring sentiment other than each out for him- or herself. "Nobody wanted me," as one 14-year-old girl put it simply, after her parents' divorce. So will anyone, then, want her? Perhaps not for very long. Even when we are lucky enough to be the exception and come from stable families, we are always, in a sense, on the run. No child can ever really rest in our culture of divorce. We have to be careful not to be sick, to be entertaining all the time. If we're too much of a burden, we could find ourselves all alone.

One of the major ways Western society overcame the practice of wife-beating was with an ideal that we seem to have now abandoned: the companionate marriage. In the companionate marriage, the chastisement doctrine—beating with a stick—was replaced with the legal notion of affective privacy. Like Thomas Reade, a Salisbury man, who in 1600 left all his property to his loving wife who "by her joint care, travail and industry hath supported and augmented my estate." Instead of the husband reigning supreme over the wife, love and domestic affection ("joint care") reigned supreme. Instead of violence, there was marital unity. Sometimes it seems as if we have reverted back to the chastisement doctrine— only this time marriage is taken to involve equal-opportunity chastisement. There is no longer to be any real marital unity, no forsaking of all others, just mutual scowling from separate outposts, lasting as long as ye both shall be able to stand it.

This is what makes me see sexual modesty among my peers as a return to the idea of having private claims, as a way of escaping from this mire of indeterminacy and insecurity. First, by not having sex before marriage, you are insisting on your right to take these things seriously, when many around you do not seem to. By reserving a part of you for someone else, you are insisting on your right to keep something sacred; you are welcoming the prospect of someone else making an enduring private claim to you, and you to him. But more significantly, not having sex before marriage is a way of insisting that the most interesting part of your life will take place *after* marriage, and if it's more interesting, maybe then it will last. And, the hope of modesty continues, if it lasts, maybe then you can finally be safe. Instead of living in dread, feeling slightly hunted, afraid someone will call us to account and abandon us, maybe then we can rest. At a time when everyone else seems to be giving up hope, a return to modesty represents a new start. Modesty creates a realm that is secure from an increasingly competitive and violent public one.

As Rosalind Miles reported in a 1996 issue of *Prospect,* "the marrying generation of today," those children of 60s parents, "disheartened and disgusted by their parents' divorces and degrading sexual *dégringolades,* currently display in their conversation, in their behavior, in their music and culture, a fierce faith in monogamous, exclusive, lifelong love and mutually faithful partnership which is likely to make anyone over 35 think of tooth fairies and Tinkerbell."

Take Maggie Kirn, who was born in 1975 and, much to her parents' horror, decided to get married at 19. Most people greeted her decision with words of tragedy. *"What about experimenting? What about youth?"* they wondered. In a way, she was just as shocked by her decision, she admits in a 1998 *Harper's Bazaar* essay:

> *Marriage wasn't part of my upbringing. My parents were living the sexual revolution when I was born. . . . They split up when I was one and have each been married three times, with each of their exes having their own exes and children. I belong less to a family tree than an enormous family hedge, sprawling outward, not upward. As a child, I absorbed the idea that marriage is a prison, that I'd never need a man, and that children were for 40-year-olds with established careers.*

And yet she fell "in love, and it just felt right." Their friends gave them such trouble about marrying early that her husband had to constantly tell people "It's not illegal." Maybe, she muses wickedly, "I was trying to rewrite my family history of divorce. Maybe I was rebelling against my hippie upbringing. Maybe I wanted to succeed where others before me had failed." There is a beauty to this story.

"Yes, We Still Want to Get Married . . . But Why?" asks *Cosmo* in 1995. The lead question on the cover of a 1997 issue of *Swing,* a magazine about life in your twenties, is "Can We End Divorce?"

The answer, I think, is yes, we can. But only if, like Maggie Kirn, we decide to value the things our parents didn't.

# Chapter 12

# BEYOND MODERNITY

> *In the new order [women] are isolated, needing men, but not able to count on them, and hampered in the free development of their individuality. The promise of modernity is not really fulfilled for women.*
>
> —*ALLAN BLOOM*, 1987

Oprah hosts a TV show in January 1998 on "NFL Stars Looking for Love." The football players are upset because their girlfriends want to marry them, sometimes even buy them things. "I want a woman who is more independent," one of them explains. The others agree. They don't want to be pestered about marriage: they are busy leading important lives. Oprah is very sympathetic: "Some women, they just don't know when to shut *up!*"

Independence, in this curious context, has come to mean having no expectations (or at least hiding them well) and doing whatever your boyfriend says. Independence entails, as Oprah unwittingly put it so well, the female *shutting up* about what she wants.

Today, the 92nd Street Y advertises with the slogan "Commit to Yourself Now." The tone suggests someone who made a terrible mistake and was punished. Now she has learned her lesson and will never repeat the error. From now on, she will never love anyone other than herself.

As it turns out, there is a significant difference between independence and freedom. Today we may all be independent, but are we really free in a society where we can only commit to ourselves? This unrelenting stream of injunctions to be independent seems to be a defense mechanism, furiously trying to mask, but not concealing, the sad truth that even if we wanted to depend on someone else we would be hard-pressed to find someone to really depend *on*.

But is the road back from independence even possible, given the way our society is now arranged?

Allan Bloom predicted that women will suffer more than men in modernity, because while men may be happy to be liberated from the old constraints, women still desire to have children. Was he right?

During my senior year in college, a kindly man alerted me that, as a woman, I have "basically two paths" I can take after graduation. On the one hand, "you could try to find someone to support you," or "you could be independent! Go out into the fray! Be on your own! Take care of *yourself!*"

I have a queer feeling in my stomach as I have to reassure him that, yes, I am well aware of my lavish options. How odd that a woman's position in modern life can be reduced to this. But of course, he's right. Only a woman can have this unique option. Yet he also put well, unintentionally, the flip side of this choice: only a woman can be made to feel that being herself is not enough. As the culture now puts the question, Do you want to be a drain on some poor man, one of those leeches, or do you want to be an eagle soaring above the clouds? Who could answer, I think I'll take the leech, please?

If you actually do want the love of a good man and many children, that is considered déclassé. When books that celebrate these traditional ideals are made into movies, the remnants of the *ancien régime* are carefully expunged, down the memory hole. When the movie version of *Little Women* came out in 1994, I rushed to see it. I waited for Marmee's line—"To be loved by a good man is the best and sweetest thing which can happen to a woman; and I sincerely hope my girls may know this beautiful experience"—but it never came. Now Marmee, played by Susan Sarandon, complained about "restrictive corsets" and "our confining young girls to the house, bent over their needlework." Someone had felt it necessary to "update" Marmee because the old Marmee had been oppressed, but was she really as oppressed as we imagine?

Working mothers with small children now say they work "because I have to." Why do so many women say that? If we have been freed from oppression and are supposed to be liberated, then how has it come to pass that so many women are forced to do what they do not want? We have come very close to Simone de Beauvoir's ideal, where "no woman should be authorized to stay at home to raise her children. Society should be totally different.

Women should not have that choice, precisely because if there is such a choice, too many women will make that one." In a different age we were forced to stay home, and now that men are no longer paid a family wage and no-fault divorce is an ever-present reality, we are just as often forced to have careers. Which is better? Perhaps there is always going to be social pressure for people to do one thing rather than another, and so why shouldn't it be directed at organizing one's life around the most meaningful things? Maybe our grandmothers weren't as stupid as we thought. The family, volunteer work, religion, shaping the hearts and minds of the next generation—maybe that all can't be reduced to just "shining floors and wiping noses," as Myriam Miedzian describes the lives of mothers who don't have careers.

Now that our mothers have pursued careers, have succeeded in them, we have learned that yes, indeed, women can work full time, but also that maybe that's not the most important thing, after all.

Brenda Barnes, president and CEO of North America operations at Pepsi-Cola, decided to step down in late September of 1997, pledging to devote herself "100 percent" to her husband and children. She changed her mind when her kids—ages seven, eight, and ten—kept pleading with her "to promise to be home for all of our birthdays." Around the same time, Elizabeth Perle McKenna, a young mother who gave up a six-figure salary as vice president of publishing for Hearst Book Group, came out with *When Work Doesn't Work Anymore: Women, Work and Identity,* which surveyed 1,000 women who felt similarly disaffected with corporate culture. All are now reshuffling their priorities.

On Mother's Day of the same year, Susan Jonas and Marilyn Nissenson published *Friends for Life: Enriching the Bond Between Mothers and Their Adult Daughters,* which reported that the biggest "undermining thing" in today's mother-daughter relationships was the fact that daughters are choosing to be more traditional wives. *Self* magazine remarks on this new trend, "It's interesting that most mothers feared their daughters were heading toward too much tradition."

But which, really, is the more misogynist view: the view that for all of world history women have been idiots, or the view that gives women more credit, and thinks we have only gone overboard in the blip of the past thirty years?

Those of our parents' generation tell us that we're too young and "optimistic," that we don't understand, that we just can't take back the sexual and motherhood revolutions. Well, why not? Do you have a monopoly on revolutions? Maybe you do, because we are finding that the price of this one is so high and the quality of what we are getting so poor. But maybe all you need is a little healthy competition. Maybe someone had to censor the best lines in *Little Women* because she has staked so much in her kind of life and now she is afraid that the competing view might be true. That it is too beautiful, resonates too well, and that if given the chance, young women would want to *take it all back*. So why not just hide the alternative from us?

Sorry, you can't fool us that easily. Even 11-month-olds know that an object continues to exist even after it disappears from view. It's called object permanence, and we don't have to read Piaget to know that just because we can't see something, that doesn't mean it isn't there, that it isn't beautiful and true. We have our own lives to lead, and one by one we are making our own choices.

## THE RELIGIOUSLY MODEST WAY

A vexed mother pens a 1997 Op-Ed about her rebellious son. From the tone, the reader gets the impression that her son has become an ax murderer, but then we learn what is really going on: "Powerless, we watched Adam transform himself from being a leader in liberal causes in college to studying with the campus Lubavitcher rabbi." Two years later, "Adam informed us in one of his calls that he was ready to buy a black hat and black jacket." Her reaction: "My stomach cramped at hearing those dreaded words. Had I lost my son to a sexist nineteenth-century society? . . . Rarely do I stop searching for clues to his becoming ultra-Orthodox, or a 'Torah-observing Jew,' as he would say. I struggle to identify mistakes I made as a mother. . . . Were we too lenient?"

It's always hard to pinpoint why someone becomes more religious. Yet it cannot be denied that many young secular men and women who return to more orthodox observance do so precisely for the attractions Miriam Stein, Adam's mother, considers "sexist"—that is, they want the fact that they are a man or a woman to guide and inform their lives. It may be sexist, but it is certainly not misogynist. Who is more of a threat to women, after all—a "nineteenth-century" man who is waiting for a wife to be devoted to, or a member of the Spur Posse who wins a contest because he "hooked up" with 60 girls? The so-called "nineteenth-century" men or women who return to religion because they find modern life empty do not do so because they want to oppress each other, but because they are looking for a way of life that transcends the ruthlessness of their surrounding culture.

Of course, followers of a religiously modest way often disagree as to which religion promotes the best understanding of modesty. For instance, Gila Manolson writes:

> *Having never been a practicing Muslim, I can't purport to know the reasoning behind Islamic female dress. Its practical effect, however, is to hide a woman's physical self almost entirely from view and, at the same time, make her appear nearly identical to all other women. While such a uniform certainly reduces her chance of being objectified, it also doesn't let her appearance reflect her inner beauty, or her individuality. This is antithetical to the Jewish concept of* tzniut. *The goal of tzniut is not to negate the female body, but to employ it for a purpose higher than self-display. Tzniut takes the powerful light of a woman's physical self and, rather than extinguishing it, uses it to radiate a message about her deeper identity.*

Yet as much as we tend to assume that women in Islamic countries are oppressed, *they* continue to insist that they are not. As Salma Shahabuddin from Montreal writes to *Vogue:*

> *As a 20-year-old Muslim woman who does not consider herself to be oppressed or repressed in the least, I found the article "Is The Veil Old Hat?," by Hadani Ditmar [Vogue's View, September], to be positively insulting, not to mention grossly inaccurate and totally misleading. Ms. Ditmars arrogantly dismisses the Islamic dress code as being the province of wild-eyed revolutionaries and 'fervent mullahs,' while disregarding the fact that fully one-fifth of the world's population is Muslim and is subject to this dress code. The Islamic dress code is based on the Islamic belief that sexual urges are a natural and normal part of the human experience, but that following these urges results in rampant adultery and fornication. In order to prevent our natural feelings for the opposite sex from overpowering our logic and dictating our behavior, it is prescribed that in public both men and women should cover themselves up.*

However particular religious understandings of modesty may differ, all are in agreement that modesty is inextricably entwined with holiness. Nan Pamer, for instance, notes that Jesus uses modest clothing as an allegory for the church to be ready for his coming: "Blessed is he that watcheth, and keepth his garments, lest he walk naked, and they see his shame." In his essay on modesty, Norman Lamm notes that when God reveals himself to Moses for the first time and calls to him out of the burning bush, Moses immediately covers his face because he is afraid to look at God. Also, in the sixth chapter of Isaiah, when Isaiah sees the fiery angels as they surround the throne of God, four out of six of the angels' wings are not functional, but for covering the angels' feet and face.

In the presence of the holy, one must cover up.

And yet it is not as simple as just that. Defenses of religious modesty are often surprising. Even when I interviewed women in my own community who were drawn to Judaism because the laws of *tzniut* appealed to them, I was often surprised by some of the reasons given for observing certain laws. Take "Susan," for instance: she is now 35, but when she started observing the laws of family purity in Judaism she was 29, she said. Were you drawn to these laws because you were a private person? I asked her. Because you didn't want to have sex before marriage? No, she said, because "when I was growing up, my parents would have a horrible fight at least once every month." I nodded politely, not sure I grasped the connection. Then she explained:

*Yeah, screaming, dishes flying, and stuff. 'I can't stand your father,' you know. Then they would make up, and for three weeks everything would be very kissy-kissy between them. No, sometimes they'd fight more than once a month, but usually it was once a month, like clockwork. Well, so when I first heard of Jewish modesty law, and heard about the no-sex-while-the-wife-is-menstruating rule, that's what I thought of first. My parents with their once-a-month fighting. The sheer brilliance of it! Having this time of separation, to create distance so that you can be reunited, but to have the distance created in a way other than by fighting? I would never have come up with that myself. I was kind of awed by the ingeniousness, you know, of all these rules. My husband and I started trying it, after four years of marriage.*

When were you married? I asked.

*Early, when I was 25. I was getting worried because we were starting to be like my parents. And it's the most amazing thing what it's done for our marriage—just this one simple rule. We have the mystery and the newness of a love affair, but we don't have to have affairs, and we don't have to fight. We still quibble, but I mean, who doesn't anyway?*

*The important point to me is that we don't fight the way we used to anymore, or the way my parents used to. You know, the kind of fighting that comes from getting bored? That we never have because we never take each other for granted. Because each month, there's this separation. I've heard people say that the no-sex-while-the-wife-is-menstruating rule is sexist, because it comes from thinking women are unclean, and I understand what they mean, but I think because they've never tried it, it's hard for them to see what's really going on. What could be sexist about having a wonderful marriage?*

Apparently, this is a very common reason for becoming more observant. Consider the following account from "Brenda," a woman in her late thirties: "though we do not follow a strictly [religiously] committed life-style, we were curious enough to try" Judaism's traditional rules of modesty. "For the first time in years, my husband makes a habit of calling me from work. It seems to happen precisely during the time when he can't touch me!"

Soon I began to wonder, like Susan—if Judaism is so smart about women and men, what else is it right about? I felt very stupid that this hadn't occurred to me before, but maybe these traditions have endured for thousands of years . . . for a reason?

When I reflect on all the women on Prozac, on all the men who don't open doors or give up their seats for women, but who will diligently perform their post-dumping checkups because it's expected of them; or on all our talk of "hang-ups" and "safe sex," I'm struck by how similarly everyone behaves and sounds. It's fascinating, but also a bit eerie, because ours is supposed to be a time of great freedom. And yet most people have ended up letting the culture they live in dictate their choices. I suppose this isn't an intrinsically bad thing—it just seems to be the way we are made. We're not isolated individuals, we need guidance, and we take the prevailing sensibility for our guide. Perhaps when it comes down to it, our daily choices are rarely generated from the self, much as we would like to think they are. Our choices are always "given" to us in some sense, and as long as they are going to be given, why not have them given to us by God, by traditions that hold warehouses of stored wisdom, rather than by Gallup polls?

A onetime antiwar protester and member of an Oregon commune, Judith Margolis, now "pursues the epitome of a busy modern life": she is an artist, college teacher, writer, wife, and mother. But Margolis is also one of the *ba'alei teshuvah*—those who, as adults, have chosen to practice Orthodox Judaism. A profile of her in the *Los Angeles Times* explains that "Margolis, 44, is not alone. Orthodoxy, rabbis say, is growing in Los Angeles . . ."

> *As part of their faith, Orthodox women must meet yet other religious requirements—some of which might seem to clash with elements of feminist thought and conduct. . . . Orthodoxy, for example, speaks of women's importance in running the home and family, not the office and the world. It limits their leadership roles in religious services. It details what are acceptable sexual and personal habits.*

And yet to one advertising executive, Susan Weintraub, these limitations are "about a dignified, disciplined way of being." As for Margolis, she finds more spiritual satisfaction in keeping the Sabbath than she ever found in political protests: "'by keeping the Sabbath, I take one day when I cannot be striving. . . . It's a day when I have to rest. It energizes me enormously.'" Her reasons for accepting the ancient laws of sexual modesty are also thoroughly modern:

> *Her career and marriage also has been helped, she said, by Orthodox laws that put some limits on intimate contact between married couples and requires wives to participate in a ritual bath or mikvah. "I think an artist needs a certain psychic privacy to be creative," she said. "A marriage is sometimes destructive to that because there is so much togetherness and merging of personalities. Orthodox practice . . . allows a person to have time alone. I experience myself. And that turns out to be supportive of creative work."*

Even the most sexist laws are earning the support of the formerly-secular:

> *Weintraub—fashionably attired recently in an oversized black jacket, two-piece black knit outfit, silver bracelets and black metal earrings— knows that Orthodox Jewry requires women to dress modestly and forbids them to swim with men. . . . "Modesty can also be translated as dignity. It's how you conduct yourself in business and with family and friends." She said she does not mind gender-based Orthodox rules, like one that in the synagogue separates the sexes with a wall. "My husband is very cute," she said. "If he were next to me, I'd be playing with his hair or something. I would be more involved with him than I should be for that period, which is supposed to be devoted to communing with the Almighty. I'm an intelligent woman. I can buy that."*

Not only does she not mind giving up a part of each week for religious purposes, she actually looks forward to it:

*"When you know every week that Friday and Saturday is a family day and that there is an order to it and a reason for it, the concept elevates your quality of living. . . . You spend time with family and friends talking about the Torah (the sacred Scriptures) and about what's meaningful." Her brief exposure to Orthodoxy has altered her life, she noted. "I started meeting people who were interesting and my life started changing. I started grappling with questions like: What am I living for? What is my purpose in life? What do I want to be remembered for? What is success? . . . [Orthodoxy] doesn't feel like there are rules and restrictions and . . . like I'm being suffocated. It gives me pleasure."*

In a 1996 *New York Times* article, Lena Williams explains a similar, but this time Christian, transformation. First there was the rebellion:

*Then came the radical 1960s and I, a self-avowed black power militant with a new Afro hairstyle that matched my new anti-establishment attitude, rebelled against the strictures of God, church and country. Hats were dismissed as symbols of oppression for women and status symbols of the black bourgeoisie. . . . "What does wearing a hat and shoes, too tight for comfort, and a starchy dress, have to do with my faith in God?" I once asked my mother in an unprovoked fit of defiance. She never answered me directly, choosing instead to "let go and let God," as she liked to say.*

After her adolescent rebellion, Ms. Williams soon discovered that "in a world of bandwagon fads and fleeting alliances, the black church remains a bastion of tradition." She is not the only one, either: ". . . many black women of a certain age, this one included, still do not enter a church for Sunday services dressed, as the elders might say, 'any old way.' And that means wearing a proper hat." Why?

*Call me a walking contradiction: a liberated woman tied to a symbol of submissive womanhood. But with custom comes assurance that grows with affirmation. After the furor of the 1960s and fickleness of the 70s, I came to see the wisdom of our elders' beliefs—that wearing fine clothes, from head to toe, was how mortals showed reverence to God. . . . I have plenty of company. On Sunday mornings all over*

*NewYork City, a parade of the millinery chic can be seen on street corners in Harlem, at bus stops in Bedford-Stuyvesant and in soul food restaurants after morning service. The millinery splendor not only expresses a personal esthetic, but a community's shared notion of social propriety and cultural values.*

Religious modesty sometimes makes people uncomfortable, though—and not always for the reasons one might expect. Consider the amusing discovery of Yasmin Alibhai-Brown in *The Independent:*

*Wearing the traditional Islamic "hejab" may not be what it seems. Two years ago, Shahida, a young Muslim college student in London, took on the hejab to assert her Muslim identity, much to the consternation of her middle-class Westernized family. Last month, she decided to give it up. Her reasons? Receipt of another anonymous letter from a young white student, declaring his lust for her in no uncertain terms. He wanted to rip her clothes off and possess her, he said, because she seemed so utterly unattainable. To her astonishment, a Muslim male student had also started whispering suggestive things to her as she walked past, all about how her modesty turned him on. This is not an isolated case. The veil draws to it and releases all sorts of contradictory meanings and heightened emotions which can shock even those who take the decision to wear it for rational and understandable reasons. After an article I wrote about Muslim women in Bosnia—photographed in hejab—I had five letters from white men telling me how intensely desirable they found women who covered themselves. Interviews on the subject I recently conducted with men in London were equally disturbing. . . . Haleh Afshar, an Iranian academic and writer, told me how a policeman wrote her a six-page letter begging for pictures of women in veils.*

It is not surprising, then, that even the totally secular have begun to incorporate modest dress in their daily lives. Modesty is powerful.

### THE RETURN TO MODEST DRESS

Reports the *International Herald Tribune,* "In 1996, no insider fashion audience is capable of getting hysterical at the sight of nipples and nether undergarments. We've seen it all before." And that is why it's the perfect time for modesty in dress to make a comeback. "Melanie," a woman who used to wear spandex, stilettos and skinny cigarette pants, tells the *Los Angeles Times* in 1997 that she "woke up one day and realized I looked like a hooker." No "Moral Majority finger wagging" made her revamp her wardrobe; she just realized she was attracting the wrong kind of man. "I think the nice guys were embarrassed by the way I dressed." Notes the *Los Angeles Times* reporter: "Many women may have similar attacks of modesty. After all, who wants to flash the boss boy at Ralph's every time you go in for a box of Cheerios?" One unmarried man who worked in Melanie's building didn't notice her until she wore a modest "rust double breasted pantsuit," and then he asked her out for dinner. "'You look really nice,'" he said shyly.

Through trial-and-error, Melanie stumbled upon what many cultures have known for thousands of years. Deborah Scroggins reiterates the Islamic case in the *Atlanta Journal and Constitution*:

> *In Turkey, Kuwait, and other countries where veils are not required, fundamentalist women speak of their "liberating modesty." . . . "Veiled women are much more attractive than unveiled women," said Ali Bulac, a Turkish Islamic writer. "One of the reasons sex died in the West was because they have no veils." The heavy Arab robes that infuriate Kuwaiti feminists thrill Islamic professional women in Afghanistan. [The hejab] "is one way to be equal," said Sakena Yacoobi, a young teaching instructor. She said the black veil is the Islamic equivalent of an American businesswoman's pinstriped, bowtied business suit.*

Tony Walker in Cairo reports that "Many parents have been perplexed by their daughters deciding to dress conservatively.":

> *Mona, a young university graduate who works at a foreign bank, began wearing traditional dress recently to the annoyance of her parents and brothers. She wears an ankle-length skirt without a belt and a veil to cover her hair. "My Islamic costume does not hinder my activities," she says. "I still go jogging early in the morning with a long T-shirt over my tracksuit . . . the way I dress has given me respectability."*

The trend is such that *The Des Moines Register* feels it necessary on October 30, 1995, to detail "the Types of Veils." An Egyptian web site brags that "veil wearing is actually a sign of independence for a woman. By covering her face and body (some wear long gloves so even their hands are covered) a woman gains control over the very commodity that is made cheap in the western world."

But not cheap for long, since the return to modesty in dress is happening not only in Islamic countries. In America the counterrevolution in dress seems to have started on or around July 17, 1989, when *Time* magazine announced we were "Back from the Bikini Brink." There we learned about the "tremendous trend toward modesty and conservatism." That same year, in the *Financial Times of London,* one woman recalled that "one of my friend's sisters had a calf-length skirt . . . and every week it would get lower until it touched the floor."

And, reported a 1991 issue of *Women's Wear Daily,* the demand for cover-ups has been rising higher each year. The article attributes the popularity of cover-ups to "changes taking place in the social climate." Observers at St. Tropez have noticed "that bathers on the whole were showing less skin" and that thongs "have lost a good deal of popularity."

Two of the biggest films in winter 1993, which were set in the late nineteenth century—Jane Campion's *The Piano* and Martin Scorsese's *The Age of Innocence*—quickly inspired changes in the world of fashion. According to the *Sunday Times,* shoe shops are now "full of high lace-up boots, the sort that once caused a young man's heart to flutter." Designer John Galliano points out that "after deconstruction, the only way forward is construction. Why disfigure the body with ugliness and ill-fitting clothes? We should be proud of our bodies. Romance, elegance, technique, and construction. All these things will go on to be very important," he predicts.

Ron Shamask, a New York designer who has become popular for making "subtlety . . . sexy," explains to *The Kansas City Star* that "you need coverage in order to show bareness" and that "sexuality isn't about nude bodies."

> One of the show favorites with both Shamask and Martin is a slinky long red evening gown with long sleeves and high neck by the designer Valentina, from the late 1930s. At the center front, across the midsection, is a vertical slash covered with modest lacing. "It is so sexy. It barely exposes anything," Shamask said.

As Dale Carolyn Gluckman, a costume spokeswoman for the Los Angeles County Museum of Art, put it, "Thanks to our interest in nostalgia as the century comes to a close, younger women are finding that a veiled hat can be very mysterious, and with all the period films we've had lately, they can see how a more conservative generation of women often used them as tools of seduction." Noted one Los Angeles *Daily News* reporter, "Thanks to the invention of blow-dryer and curling iron and women's lib, young women didn't want any part of their mothers' wardrobes." However, "Now that that period in our lives is over, we can wear them again—after all, it's our idea, not Mom's."

Still, hats aside, there is one hitch getting in the way of the counterrevolution.

### THE SURVIVAL VALUE OF IMMODESTY AND THE CARTEL OF VIRTUE

There is a certain survival value for a woman to suppress her natural modesty these days. There always was, to be sure. The story of Cordelia losing the kingdom because she refused to debase herself with cheap words is famous because it is one of the most basic human stories. But today the survival value of immodesty is higher than ever.

"In the halls of junior highs," finds Mary Pipher, "girls are pressured to be sexual regardless of the quality of relationships." Losing virginity "is considered a rite of passage into maturity," such that "girls may be encouraged to have sex with boys they hardly know." On the one hand, "they are worried that they will be judged harshly for their bodies and lack of experience." But "for the most part, girls keep their anxiety to themselves. It's not sophisticated to be fearful." So they take a deep breath and do what is expected of them—and usually at a very high cost.

As that girl in *New York* magazine, Liz, who was mutilating herself, put it: "To be a cool girl you kind of have to stab girlkind in the back." If she doesn't do it, she will typically be abandoned. As 14-year-old Marie from Cincinnati tells Lillian Rubin, "I was afraid, but I loved him. I knew how badly he wanted to do it, and there are so many girls who'll do it with him, so I finally decided it was okay."

Unfortunately, though the girls may have sex with a view to strengthening the relationship, their boyfriends don't often see it that way. "It was with a girl I had been going with in high school," reminisces 25-year-old Rob, also to Lillian Rubin. He is a Seattle graduate student, and in retrospect, admits: "I knew that she agreed to have sex with me because she wanted to solidify the relationship, but that's not where I was at all. She saw it as turning us into a solid couple, and I saw it as a coming of age and getting past something. It didn't have much to do with her or the relationship. I suppose even then I felt some guilt about using her like that, but, well, you know how it is."

"How it is" because of the survival value in immodesty, is that the balance of power has tilted markedly against girls. If a girl has sex with her boyfriend, there is a good chance she will be left alone, but if she doesn't, then she will *surely* be left alone. "I wanted to date but not have sex," 14-year-old "Christy" tells Mary Pipher. "It's hard to be popular without a boyfriend." But, on the other hand, all her dates "ended as wrestling matches." There is none of this "going steady" business, which, for all its stuffiness, allowed girls to have companionship and maybe even love without having to have intercourse. Now there is only a scary gamble: if you say no to enough guys, word may get around and people may start to think you are *really* weird. There is no longer any chance of "being sweethearts" with someone. If you don't do it, that's *It*. You're out of the game. You're out on the sidelines, you're benched. You're not allowed to play with anyone.

Adult women face the same dilemma. Sandy Denise from Manhattan wrote the following frustrated letter to *New York* magazine in 1998:

> *To the editor: I am so sick of the fact that every guy I meet expects that I should sleep with him on the first date. I am mortified on behalf of my peers who, when they hint to their boyfriends about marriage, find themselves dumped like garbage. Just when I thought there was no answer for a modern-day woman, I read your article "Looking for Mister Goldberg." I am shocked that there are young Orthodox Jewish men who have honorable intentions, date only to marry, do not lead a woman on, have no ulterior motives, do not even touch until after they are married—it's like you are speaking about people from Mars. And I am soooo jealous. Why aren't all men like this?*

Joseph Epstein wrote in his deeply wise 1974 book, *Divorced in America,* that "To the extent that divorce can be obtained with relative facility and with lack of social censure, to that extent is the ideal of permanence in marriage damaged. To the extent that divorce is used to solve other people's marital unhappiness, to that extent does living with one's own imperfect marital happiness come to seem less tolerable."

Our devotion to premarital sex, it must be admitted, has put us in a similar bind. To the extent premarital sex is accepted, to that extent is the idea of the necessity of marriage undermined. One fears saying it, because one doesn't want to sound like a prig, but the reality for the prigs and the anti-prigs is the same. To the extent that premarital sex is practiced and encouraged, to that extent will women who want to wait until marriage find it harder to meet men who will marry them without "trying them out" first, to have patience with someone with "hang-ups"—which is to say, hopes.

As Sara, 24, puts it:

> *I know at least five guys my age, living in New York who I know from school. Each is cohabiting with a different woman, and when I have lunch with them sometimes, it's always as friends, nothing more. Now, anyone who thinks that a man would dump someone who's having sex with him on a regular basis, and making breakfast for him, and who demands nothing in return from him, allows him to keep his "options open" in order to gamble on someone who will not have sex with him and wants a commitment first, well, they don't have a clue!*

Once women, as a group, forsake their natural power for an illusory one, it becomes difficult to reclaim that power individually: some kind of greater social sanction of that choice is required. One of my professors who didn't think modesty was a serious subject of inquiry memorably asked me why I couldn't "just be modest and shut up about it!" The answer is that modesty simply cannot be "just" a private virtue—a "personal choice"—in a culture where there is such a high survival value placed on immodesty. The choices some women make restrict the choices open to other women. Perhaps this is where liberalism failed, because it claimed society could be simply neutral about individuals' choices, and it never can. The direction of social pressure cannot be discounted. Here is Gila Manolson describing a common response to her lectures on sexual ethics:

> *In a more faltering voice . . . someone—let's call her Leah—will ask to speak to me privately after a class on Jewish dating. Once she's sure no one is listening, she'll confess, "I agree with everything you say. I*

*know most of my friends would, too. It all makes so much sense. It's
just that no one else I know is actually doing it. I don't know if I'm
strong enough to be the first one. Maybe if a group of us all started
together . . ."*

If you're still unconvinced about the "survival value" for
immodesty, just consider the words of a male advice columnist,
"Jim Dixon," in a 1997 issue of *Mademoiselle.* He is responding to
a woman who wrote in, worried that no man will have her
because she's still a virgin: "As for me," he expounds grandly, like
a king surveying his harem, "I prefer a woman with life experience, sexual and otherwise." Well, thanks for sharing, Jim.

Once the social pressure is on for women to have "life experience, sexual and otherwise," a cycle is then set in motion. More
women try to get this experience to fit in, but then the more
women who do, the more pressure there is in turn on other
women who do not, and the more likely it becomes that the
inexperienced woman *will,* in fact, be left alone. To a man who
says to a young woman, I prefer a woman with life experience,
sexual and otherwise, because I like a woman who knows how to
please me in numerous ways, and you probably will be a clingy
drag, so go out and learn a little more, honey, before I will condescend to have you pleasure me, the proper response, it seems to
me, is, That's nice, I happen to prefer a man who's not a jerk, so
goodbye.

But instead of saying goodbye, women are agreeing to this Jim
Dixon view of the world, and buying that depressing title I keep
seeing in bookstores, *203 Ways to Drive a Man Wild in Bed.* The
thought of this virgin reading Jim Dixon's response, her heart
sinking, the thought of her trotting out to the bookstore and
studying *203 Ways to Drive a Man Wild in Bed* is pretty dismal. In
a different time her innocence would have been valued and the
man would have been learning how to please *her.*

Formerly, a man who was impatient with women, with their
hang-ups or their inexperience, and just wanted to get right down
to business, would go to a prostitute. Or, to put it differently, when
men behaved like jerks, at least they compensated the women for
it. Today men expect to be able to treat all women like prostitutes,
only without just compensation, and the virgins are the ones who
are now stigmatized, told that no man will have them—just as the
prostitutes of old were once told that no man could ever love
them. Lest my position be confused with Andrea Dworkin, who

calls marriage "legalized rape," or with Dale Spender, who calls marriage "legalized prostitution," let me stress that I mean to make the exact opposite point: that after years of deriding the institution of marriage and the idea of enduring love, it is the single women who are treated like unpaid prostitutes.

Now, it is not pleasant to be left alone, and there are all sorts of good reasons why so many women accepted this new moral order. This is why the society you live in really does matter, because once society shifts what it values, if you persist in wanting something other than what it offers you and refuse to make concessions to it, there is a good chance you will be left behind. When a man leaves you because you won't sleep with him, particularly when you thought you were in love with him, this is hard to bear. And I can see the temptation to give up and live with someone so I won't be alone. But I have such strong feelings that in caving in to the Jim Dixon view of womanhood—that virginity is something to be gotten rid of, the sooner the better, and experience is what is to be valued—we have created a society of Jim Dixons. And then we all wonder why they won't "commit" to us. But why do we accept this misogynist's view of womanhood in the first place? Why are we agreeing that women are sexual objects, nothing more, and exist only to gratify men?

The more women who resolve to be alone rather than with Jim Dixon, the fewer Jim Dixons there will be. Or, to put it differently, I guess I'm advocating a return to the cartel of virtue.

In the past, women secured the chances of lasting love by forming a kind of cartel: they had an implicit agreement not to engage in premarital or extramarital sex with men. This made it more likely that men would marry and stay married to them. As with all cartels, to be sure, there were incentives for individual women to cheat or "chisel" on the agreement and have affairs out of wedlock. But in chiseling, something unexpected happened to these women, too. Most of the women I know who are living with men hope that these men will marry them. And most of the women I know who have had affairs with married men hope that the men will ultimately leave their wives for *them*—and when they do, they don't want little adulteresses romping around their new husband. What this means to me is that most women basically do want the same thing in this respect: the security of lasting love. Therefore, in chiseling, in breaking up this cartel of virtue, we spoiled things, ultimately, for ourselves.

This is why, if we are ever going to reduce the survival value

there is in immodesty, there must be not five or six women following this or that arbitrary rule, but a real cultural shift. We must
decide as women to look upon sex out of wedlock as not such a
cool thing, after all, and recreate the cartel of virtue.

Actually, it is already starting to happen.

### THE FUTURE OF MODESTY

Every day, it seems, another girl is assaulted in school. The day after
a 15-year-old girl was sexually assaulted at her Queens high
school, *The New York Post* reported: "A teacher at Martin Luther
King Jr. High School assigned an explicit sex poem titled *Climax-
in'* to his class full of 15-year-olds." It is, needless to say, rather hard
to prosecute boys who assault girls when their teachers are doing
more or less the same thing to them in the classroom.

Anne Roiphe writes in her latest book, *Fruitful,* that "in the
nineteen fifties . . . I was not afraid of being raped; I was afraid of
being talked about." She and other women of her generation
rejected the culture which valued modesty, because they didn't
want to be talked about. A culture which values modesty, after all,
had its disadvantages. Obviously you can't praise dressing modestly without, implicitly, condemning immodesty. And one must
grant that being talked about *is* unpleasant. It can feel oppressive.

But what is the alternative? We who have grown up in a culture of immodesty tend to find rape much worse than being
talked about. You can fear being talked about and still feel safe,
whereas if you fear rape and stalking, cannot safely walk in the
street alone, cannot be a 9-year-old girl in school without being
sodomized, you cannot feel safe. A culture which valued modesty
surely had its drawbacks, but now that we have experimented
with its opposite, we who have had our sex education in kindergarten and were assigned poems about orgasms instead of Shakespeare in school, we who have watched in horror as our
perpetrators of sexual assault get younger and younger—well, we
take a different view of things.

Still, even if we could agree it is desirable to return to a culture of modesty, would it even be possible? Don't notions of modesty and shame differ between cultures? Which style would we
opt for? In eighteenth-century France, deep décolletage was
allowed, but it was considered indecent to reveal the point of the
shoulder. The Indian woman is also reticent about revealing her
shoulders, but then the Chinese woman is shy about showing her

foot, and the Muslim woman, her face. And there is always Stendhal's native woman of Madagascar to reckon with, the one who
exposes all the things we cover up here, but would "rather die of
shame than expose her arms." What is one to make of her?

Stendhal concludes that therefore sexual modesty must be
mostly taught, a product of culture, but is this the only conclusion
one could reach about the woman from Madagascar? To me the
salient detail is not that she covers up a different part of her body,
but that even in Madagascar there is something a woman would
"rather die" than reveal. As Kurt Riezler pointed out in 1943, we
could not trace, discern, and compare that different manifestations
of shame were a fundamentally similar, even universal, attitude to
shame not presupposed:

> Anthropologists, in comparing cultures, find different tribes ashamed of
> different things. Obviously they could not make such comparisons
> unless they had a certain knowledge of an attitude called shame as dis-
> tinct from the contents of shame, the pudenda. . . . Habits are prod-
> ucts of yesterday's conditions. But how is it that each of the different
> stories has a chapter about shame?

Perhaps the same is true of modesty—another universal
instinct hidden within us, suppressed sometimes, but always ready
to show its face if we would only allow it. Frances Benton concluded as much in 1956 when she remarked that modesty was a
relative, but nonetheless universal, virtue:

> Specific rules about modesty change with the styles. Our Victorian
> ancestors, for instance, would judge us utterly depraved for wearing the
> modern bathing suit. Real modesty, however, is a constant and desir-
> able quality. It is based not on fashion but on appropriateness. A
> woman boarding a subway in shorts at the rush hour is immodest not
> because the shorts are in themselves indecent, but because they are worn
> in the wrong place at the wrong time. A well-mannered and self-
> respecting woman avoids clothes or behavior that are inappropriate or
> conspicuous.

Of course to us, that shorts rule seems as quaint as Victorian
bathing attire did to Frances Benton. And yet, this may be precisely why modesty is ripe for a return these days. There is simply
nowhere else to go in the direction of immodesty, only back.

Though no one wants to be accused of being "prudish," or "reactionary," or—worst of all—"not comfortable with her body," at the same time there is an emerging consensus that things have gone too far.

This is why a counterrevolution may be just around the corner.

When I returned to college after publishing an anti–coed bathroom article, I was positively overwhelmed with letters and e-mail messages from female students. Each began a different way—some serious ("I had to share a bathroom with four football players my sophomore year, and it was the most horrible year of my life"), others gleeful ("Dear Sister Chastity: *I can't stand it either!*"). But all eventually got to the same point, which was, I thought *I* was the only one who couldn't stand these bathrooms. One female student confessed that her doctor said she had contracted a urinary infection because she wasn't going to the bathroom enough. "I'm simply too embarrassed," she confided.

Even one girl who *liked* the coed bathrooms wrote me a gushing letter about my "bravery" for "speaking out," as if I had written an anti-Castro screed in Cuba, instead of just a piece about toilets in a free country. To appreciate how much these letters amazed me, one must understand that when I wrote this article I was absolutely sure that I was the only one who was uncomfortable with our coed bathrooms. Our college administration never requires our bathrooms to be coed—students are simply assigned to rooms their freshman year, boys and girls on the same floor, and then they all vote on whether it's "okay" for the floor bathrooms to be coed. Since the procedure was so democratic, and the votes in all the other freshman dorms always went the same way, I naturally assumed that the other students must like the idea of coed bathrooms. But as soon as I spoke up and started to receive these strange letters, each reporting the same "eerie" feeling, it became clear to me that in fact many college students were like me, uncomfortable with not having privacy, but not wanting to seem "uncool" by objecting. Students from various other colleges also wrote to tell me that this was happening all over the country, and wasn't it ridiculous? A few years later, *The New York Times* reported on the "open living arrangements that have been the vogue on campuses for years." Even secular Yale students weren't terribly pleased with today's dormitory arrangements: "Some quietly confessed that the permissiveness of residence life sometimes made them uncomfortable." Soon after, a *New York Times Magazine* profile found that to one young woman, "those same dormitories represent immorality itself, an arena of coed bathrooms, safe-sex manuals and free condoms, a threat to her very soul."

At my own college, the administration ended up changing its policy:

> *A Triumph for Modesty: Some incoming freshmen will have to deal with fewer awkward moments than their predecessors, as the College is planning to renovate the Fayerweather and East College dorms this summer, providing a second bathroom for each entry (read: one for each sex). . . . It appears that Wendy Shalit '97, whose article in* Reader's Digest *condemning the bathroom situation garnered Williams dubious distinction in the national spotlight, will finally be avenged.*
>
> —Williams Free Press, *May 19, 1998*

The grownups may be afraid to admit it, but clearly the children are rebelling. College students are refusing to live in coed dormitories, and the newest locker room trend among grade and high school students is refusing to shower after gym class. As Dirk Johnson explains in his "Students Still Sweat, They Just Don't Shower" report: "Students across the United States have abandoned school showers, and their attitudes seem to be much the same whether they live in inner-city high-rises, on suburban cul-de-sacs or in far-flung little towns in cornfield country." As he continues:

> *Modesty among young people today seems, in some ways, out of step in a culture that sells and celebrates the uncovered body in advertisements, on television and in movies. But some health and physical education experts contend that many students withdraw precisely because of the overload of erotic images . . . the reasons seem as varied as insecurities about body image [to] heightened sexual awareness.*

Or, to put it differently, in a different age, when young students were not endlessly bombarded with sexual images, showering could be innocent, a simple matter of proper hygiene. But now that everything has been sexualized, even the most harmless sphere becomes poisoned.

We all want to be cool, to pretend not to care, but our discomfort with immodesty keeps cropping up. In one episode of *Beverly Hills 90210*, America's most popular, and surely most immodest, teen TV drama, aspiring actress "Brenda" accepts a role that requires her to take off her clothes. When the critical moment arrives, though, she can't bring herself to strip. By the end, she muses, "On second thought, maybe masks aren't so bad after all."

Many young women today are having related "second thoughts." *Seventeen* magazine reports that teens are now demanding workshops on manners, of all things. As Alix Strauss explains, "Today's kids want to return to an era of courteousness. Plus, this is about more than just manners. It deals with improving your self-image and self-esteem."

Adults would be mistaken, though, if they thought this return to dignity and propriety is just for show. Today's young women aren't just learning their social graces, but changing their fundamental attitude about sex. For example, in a marked departure from their usual of-course-you-should-sleep-with-everyone pabulum, a 1997 issue of *Glamour* ran an article called "Casual Sex: Why Confident Women Are Saying No." The article explained the role played by oxytocin, the hormone produced during both sex and childbirth which many researchers suspect may be responsible for the bonding response in women. Biologically-based differences between the sexes? Yes. Essentialist? Yes.

Yet later on in the year, all three letters published in response to this piece were positive. Each woman sounded relieved to learn that there was nothing wrong with her for being emotionally attached to her sexual partners. "K.C." from Atlanta wrote that she felt as if the article "was written about me! I am involved in a relationship of sorts with a wonderful guy. From the beginning we established that for us, sex was that and nothing more—no strings attached. Now I am starting to get emotionally involved with him, whether I want to or not. *Glamour* readers, the phrase *casual sex* is the world's biggest oxymoron!" Another woman, Drew Pinkney in Detroit, said she found the article "fascinating. . . . Could this explain why we so often feel irrational attachments for lovers we barely know? Perhaps for women, casual, merely physical sex just isn't in our nature." These kinds of thoughts would have been unheard of in a women's magazine ten years ago.

Clearly modern woman still longs for courtship and romance to satisfy her erotic imagination, but she can only dream inside the world of romance novels and nineteenth-century period dramas. Why? Because outside of fantasy land, the fundamental prerequisite for courtship, a social sanction for modesty, has been denied her.

Thus, the most compelling rationale for a return to modesty is our discovery that our culture of immodesty isn't, finally, as sexy as we thought it was going to be. In an article entitled "Modesty Belles: Cover-all Glamour Dives into the Lead," the *Sunday Mirror* reports that "SIZZLING swimwear gets a girl noticed, but it's not always the most revealing style that sends temperatures soaring."

*We put eight of this year's hottest looks to the test and came up with some surprising results. It seems modesty now rules the waves. Today's beach belle prefers a style which leaves more than a little to the imagination. . . . Even the men on our panel of six judges chose a glamorous Forties-styles one-piece over a skimpy string bikini.*

But is our current interest in modesty and codes of conduct just a craze, or will today's young women succeed in changing the cultural climate? I think we may succeed, because there is enough dissatisfaction with the current state of affairs, as well as a recognition that the revolution our parents engineered hasn't worked. The most common complaint I hear from women my age is that there is no longer any "dating scene." Young people go out in packs, they drink, they "hook up," and the next day life returns to normal. I suppose you could find much depressing in this behavior—for starters, that there is not even a pretense of anticipation of a love that will last forever in the cold expression, "to hook up"—but there is also a lot about this behavior that should give us hope, and that is the fact that all of them have to drink to do it.

They aren't drinking wine to begin delightful conversation. They are drinking beer and hard liquor to get drunk—precisely to cut off delightful conversation and get "right to the point," as it were. That is the advertised purpose of most college parties, and this kind of drinking is really quite a stark admission: that in fact we realize we are not just like the lower animals, that our romantic longings and hopes should inform our most intimate actions, and that if the prevailing wisdom decrees "hook-ups" don't matter, that sex is "no big deal," then we must numb ourselves in order to go through with it. Thus we pay tribute to the importance of modesty by the very lengths to which we must go to stifle it.

Also, if our hook-ups didn't really matter, then why would we have our checkups? Why all this guerrilla etiquette gushing up from the quarters of the liberated? And why is the most pressing question in all the women's magazines still "how to overcome your hang-ups"?

These kinds of things give me hope that a restoration of a culture of modesty might not only be desirable, but possible. We're all modest already, deep down—because we're human—we just need to stop drinking so much, get off our Prozac, and come out of the closet about it. Like Modesty Anonymous. We would all admit that we are powerless over our embarrassment. That one blush was just never enough.

I'm not a happily married woman or spinster who now wants to spoil your fun. I'm writing because I see so much unhappiness around me, so many women settling for less, because I don't want to settle for less and because I don't think you should have to, either. In 1997, *Marie Claire* tells us about "Daisy Starr's one-night stand." She "knew Joe a bit from going into the bar/cafe where he works . . . we got to his house, we watched cartoons. . . . When I went home with him that night, I hadn't planned on having sex, but I guess I wanted it."

I don't want to have sex because "I guess" I want it. I want to wait for something more exciting than that, and modesty helps me understand why.

It is possible for a young woman to hope for something more, many of us do, and we hereby enter a plea that society permit us to hope for something more. But consider yourself forewarned: If you refuse to be cured of your sensitivity or your womanhood, if you start defending your right to your illusions, be prepared for people to tell you that you are silly and childish. Be prepared for some to make fun of you directly, and for others to be more sophisticated about it and try to reduce your hopes to various psychological maladies.

Don't believe them for a second.

Because the question has been thoroughly examined, in all of its boring detail, the data calibrated and recalibrated, multiple regressions have been performed, and in fact, not all modestyniks are abuseniks. It's actually quite within her rights for a young woman to want to be a woman.

Our culture's message to young women is, It's a free society, dearie, just one teensy footnote, by the way: *You'd better be having many hook-ups—or else! Shyness will not be tolerated! Hang-ups will not be tolerated! Rejection-sensitivity will not be tolerated! Go on Prozac! Lose your curves! Stop being a woman! Stop being a woman!*

But what would happen, I wonder, if women, instead of seeing their romantic hopes as "hang-ups" to get rid of, instead of being ashamed of themselves for being women, would start to be proud of their hesitation, their hopes, and their dignity? What would happen if they stopped listening to those who say womanhood is a drag, and began to see themselves as individuals with the power to turn society around?

Society might very well have to turn around.

# A MODEST CONCLUSION: INNOCENCE

> We were as twinned lambs that did frisk i'th' sun,
> And bleat the one at th' other. What we changed
> Was innocence for innocence: we knew not
> The doctrine of ill-doing, nor dreamed
> That any did. Had we pursued that life,
> And our weak spirits ne'er been higher reared
> With stronger blood, we should have answered heaven
> Boldly, "Not guilty", the imposition cleared
> Hereditary ours.
>
> —SHAKESPEARE, *THE WINTER'S TALE*

In her 1993 memoir *The Beginning of the Journey*, Diana Trilling describes the simple courtship she had with famed literary critic Lionel Trilling in the late twenties: they dated, they drank cocktails, they argued heatedly over politics. "On Bullfrogs and Alexanders. Lionel and I got to know each other well enough to decide to marry." Six months prior to their wedding, they went to bed together, she reveals, a fact that caused her deep shame at the time. Would her father find out? It was a radical act, a real risk, "a violation of convention." In her world, "necking was the chief premarital sexual activity." In any case, in six months they married, and after their fifty years together, Trilling concludes, "I have never met any man to whom I would rather have been married." Though they fought, of course, "over a long lifetime, we loved each other very much, . . . and there was never a time or situation in which we could not trust or count on one another."

And yet, and yet . . . after half a century with Lionel and some two decades as a widow, Diana wonders, was the hush-hush way her generation treated sex really right? "At seventeen," she writes, "I overheard my mother talking to a woman of a younger and more progressive generation than her own; she was explaining that the sexual ignorance—"innocence" was the word she used—in which she and her contemporaries reared their daughters was designed to preserve their illusions. Was she, I wonder, being honest?"

However reluctant Trilling may be to admit it, though, her illusions were for the most part fulfilled. She could always count on Lionel; she had "never met any man to whom I would rather have been married." Hers is an all-too-common refrain among women of a certain age. They generally take for granted the dating, the courtship rituals, the early marriage they enjoyed, and—what now almost never exists—the lifetime companionship, the simple trust one has with a spouse who was also one's first lover. To them, "innocence" is always in ironic quotes; it was a word their mothers used. They do not make the connection between this initial innocence and the lasting love that came after. They do not realize that those earnest, highly sublimated political conversations they had are impossible now because adolescents flatter themselves that they are getting right to the point by just having sex. They do not realize that if boys and girls argue seriously at all anymore, they will argue only about the girl's "hang-ups."

And so they wonder, as if trying on a new dress: Hmm . . . maybe I was oppressed? Maybe, in retrospect, the expectation that I be a virgin at marriage was calculated to cheat me out of a good time? They seem to fancy they are being worldly and up-to-the-minute by contemplating such daring thoughts. They have no idea how naïve they sound to the women who came after them, who drool over the kind of lifelong love Mrs. Trilling describes— over the kind of world that, at the end of her life, she was so prepared to toss into the garbage bin.

But that world was tossed away, and the pressure to keep girls' virginity was exchanged for something more sinister. One young woman tells Sally Cline:

> In our class, around thirteen or fourteen, there was terrible pressure on us to lose our virginity. Some of us didn't want to. We were kinda young I guess, there wasn't a real special reason. . . . [but] your virginity got to be a goddamn handicap so you had to give in and lose it. . . . After we'd all done it, we couldn't talk about losing it any more, or what it might be like, or even about fun stuff, going down cycle trails, going to the movies, cross country skiing, hanging out on the beach, all that good stuff. It was just all heavy dating talk. That's all we did, talked to each other about the guys. We even discussed their dicks. We stopped talking about us. At the time it seemed the regular thing to do, looking back you realize it was quite smart of them.

In a 1998 *Vogue* essay, Katie Roiphe tells a similar story, but from a different angle: Ten years ago, at 16, she had an affair with her 36-year-old teacher. The purpose of telling this story, entitled "The End of Innocence," is to prove that "*Lolita*-like affairs are not always about a predatory man and a victimized girl." Sure, there were some differences: "He drank a glass of brandy every night before going to bed, and I was more used to Bartles & Jaymes lime-flavored wine coolers." Mostly, though, she was in control, "had the power of youth." Also, the secrecy involved in having an affair with her teacher "made [her] feel important" and was "immensely flattering." But poignantly, by the end of the article, and despite her great efforts to prove otherwise, it doesn't seem like Roiphe's 16-year-old self was quite as happy as her 26-year-old self would prefer to remember:

> There may have been a darker side of this relationship that's been soft-ened and erased by time. There may be ways in which it haunts me that I am not even aware of. In the diaries I kept during those months, every account of the Older Man is obliterated with black paint, every kiss, every night by the fire, every phone call. The black paint reveals a level of shame and horror that I don't remember feeling. And it is true that after more than ten years, the smell of brandy makes me feel sick.

Losses of innocence, to be sure, are nothing new. What is new, however, and what does sadden me, is that it is now assumed we have no innocence to lose. The stories told today are no longer "My Loss of Innocence," but always something like "The End of Innocence" or like A. M. Homes's novel *The End of Alice*. When Sharon Thompson explains why she isn't sympathetic to the romantic girls who try to combine sex with love instead of hav-ing the casual sex they are supposed to be having, she writes, "fur-ther misgivings arise because the presumption of pure female innocence, which is the sine qua non of melodrama, has lost a lot of its viability in the wake of Freud and MTV." One mistakenly melodramatic "Victim of Love"—Thompson's favored moniker for a romantic girl—is 16-year-old Tracy, who is uncomfortable giving up her virginity to Don, because she feels she doesn't know him well enough:

> I had only dated him a couple of times. I figured, why should I rush into anything like that, because, first of all, I never went to bed with anyone before, and I was scared, and I was unsure of myself, and I fig-

*ured, why should it be with him? . . . I just want the person to care*
*enough and not to say, "I got what I wanted," and then just run out*
*on me, because that would hurt me a lot.*

If Freud or some music-video channel has annulled Tracy's innocence, she certainly doesn't seem to be aware of it.

Somehow adults have forgotten that we do, in fact, arrive in
this world innocent, no matter how knowing is the culture in
which we arrive. We still have to make decisions, such as if or
when we will go on the Pill, and when and with whom to lose
our virginity. No matter how knowing the culture, children
always have to be introduced to it, find their way in it, and the
way our culture treats its innocent is, it seems to me, quite brutal.
It's not that it tutors its innocent improperly; it simply denies the
possibility of innocence.

In March 1996, 11-year-old Susie Tucker and 57 other sixth-
grade girls were rounded up and given an order to disrobe in the
nurse's room of their Pennsylvania public school. When they
heard they were going to have to undress, many of the girls tried
to leave, "but a nurse in the waiting room blocked the door." It's
a drearily typical story:

> Inside the examining room, the girls were forced, one by one, to under-
> go a genital examination for which they had no prior warning. Susie
> cried. She asked permission to call her parents. So did others. But their
> pleas were refused. The girls, many of whom had never had a genital
> exam, did not know what the doctor was doing. But later, the parents
> were told that the doctor was looking for genital warts. "On a sixth-
> grader?" Susie's mother, Katie, asks.

On a sixth-grader. The medical staff told the girls, "Oh, you are
being such babies," and eventually they were quiet and submitted
to the examinations. When Susie returned home she felt humiliated, and said glumly to her father, an electrician: "Dad, you have
to kill someone for me." School officials, for their part, said they
were just conducting the examinations required by state law. The
next day in school, teachers wore blue ribbons in support of the
doctor and nurses who had performed the examinations.

So now we have a ribbon for the right to conduct genital
examinations on 11-year-olds? Sometimes the absurdity of our
culture gets the better of me. It's not hard to see why a new gen-

eration of girls is fantasizing about a world in which innocence actually exists.

In the wake of the Jessica Dubroff tragedy—when the media finally caught on to the absurdity of parents giving their 7-year-old daughter the "freedom" to fly a plane in a driving storm when she couldn't reach the pedals—*Time* magazine ran a very insightful piece entitled "Every Kid a Star." Author Elizabeth Gleick found that "pushed by parents to achieve or treated like tiny adults, some of today's children are paying the price." She wrote of all the baby beauty contests littering the country, of girls from six months to six years competing in categories like "personality" and "evening wear" for cars and Hawaiian cruises. In the article, a clinical psychologist in West Los Angeles notes that he is now starting to see "lots of adults in treatment who say 'I never had a childhood.'" Or as Marya Hornbacher put it a few years later, "If you grow up trying constantly to be an adult, a successful adult, you will be sick of being grown up by the time you're old enough to drink."

What, then, will become of this generation? Is all lost for us? Should we give up and get depressed? I think, on the contrary, that we have a lot to be optimistic about.

The most obvious connotation of sexual modesty is, of course, innocence. Yet I have been shying away from this aspect of it all along. I have defended modesty, essentially, in the most obscene way, but I did it because I had a hunch that this was the only way our culture would ever reconsider it. At least at first. But now that we have explored the aspects of modesty which are most counterintuitive, let's end by examining what is intuitively true about modesty.

At this point those who say that the woman who returns to modesty can only have been abused get very excited: now, they think, comes the *Aha!* moment, where I reveal that I really am an abusenik after all, and that's why I'm angling for innocence. Well, sorry to disappoint, but that's not it either.

For a woman can come from a loving family, as I do, and still find sexual modesty to be a compelling idea. If a young woman is sensitive and manages to escape being drugged by Prozac, she won't have to be sexually abused in order to feel abused by an essentially misogynist culture, a culture which sees all her romantic hopes as abnormal "hang-ups."

Because of the onslaught on childhood today, because of the

intrusion of sex educators and condoms and obscene lyrics into our earliest days, or because of parents who have abandoned their kids, many of us feel as if we never had a chance to be young. Sexual modesty is a virtue for us and, I predict, will become a virtue for increasing numbers of us because it's a way of affirming our essential innocence. It's a way of saying, At least maybe all this is not my fault. It may be a mess, but maybe *I* didn't do it, and what's more, maybe with my own life I can start anew.

So you may think our modesty projects should be called "An Outsider's View," because *you* think we're so provocative, but sometimes it's just you, professor. Sometimes it's really from the inside, and we really don't mean to be provocative all the time. And sometimes we would prefer not to have learned about AIDS in kindergarten. You may think that because of Freud, or because of MTV, our virginity doesn't mean anything, but some of us actually think Freud was wrong. And sometimes MTV might surprise you. One of the most popular videos for months, after all, was called "A Return to Innocence." Sometimes it comes as a relief to think—when everyone else is telling me how provocative I am, or have to be, or how many men I have to have—maybe, at least in my own life, before God, I could be just a little bit innocent?

And maybe then my children will be allowed to be children?

Who knows? Might as well try it, and see what happens.

After all, I don't see why our parents should get to have a monopoly on sexual revolutions.

# APPENDIX:
# SOME MODEST ADVICE

*You may differ, but it is interesting that people once had opinions on the subject. In some cases, we still do.*

🐚 ON *HOW TO DRESS WHILE TRAVELING,* from Alice-Leone Moats, *No Nice Girl Swears,* 1933 (p. 119):

"The main object, when traveling, is to remain inconspicuous at all times. That's why one's costume should be chosen with care and with as much attention to correctness as one would devote to riding clothes. As in these, simplicity and practicality are the most important features. A smart suit of some dark material, or a very plain dress under a coat, with a small brimmed hat (the object being to hide as much hair as possible and keep it in place) is the obvious choice. . . . You must look neat; therefore never pin on corsages, as they are not only incorrect with day clothes, but look too dismal when they start to droop after half an hour on a heated train."

🐚 ON *HOW TO WALK IN THE STREET: ALWAYS CURBSIDE, AVOID LADY-SAND-WICH,* from Emily Post, *Etiquette,* 1923 (p. 28):

"A gentleman, whether walking with two ladies or one, takes the curb side of the pavement. He should never sandwich himself between them."

🐚 ON *HOW TO DISTINGUISH BETWEEN BLUSHES,* from Søren Kierkegaard, *Either/Or,* 1959 (Volume I, p. 360):

"There are different kinds of feminine blushes. There is the coarse brick-red blush which romantic writers always use so freely when they let their heroines blush all over. There is the delicate blush; it is the blush of the spirit's dawn. In a young girl it is priceless. The passing blush produced by a happy idea is beautiful in a man, more beautiful in a young man, charming in a woman. It is a gleam of nightlight, the heat lightning of the spirit. It is most beautiful in the young, charming in a girl because it appears in her girlishness, and therefore it has also the modesty of surprise. The older one becomes, the more rarely one blushes."

🐚 ON *LIVING TOGETHER,* from "For Better or For Worse," George Bernard Shaw's preface to *Getting Married,* 1911:

"Young women come to me and ask me whether I think they ought to consent to marry the man they have decided to live with; and they are perplexed and astonished when I, who am supposed (heaven knows why!) to have the most advanced views attainable on the subject, urge them on no account to compromise themselves without the security of an authentic wedding ring."

❧ ON *HOW TO AVOID BEING PICKED UP,* from Alice-Leone Moats, 1933 (pp. 115–16):

"The only way to avoid being picked up is to develop the psychology of the averted eye. Never appear to see the people about you, and don't look directly at anybody. There are three ancient and tried ways of scraping up an acquaintance—offering a magazine, volunteering to open or close a window, and helping to lift a heavy suitcase. You have no choice but to accept these services with politeness, but you needn't put any inviting warmth into your thanks. There is a manner which is a mixture of civility and indifference that should put off the most insistent picker-upper, although every now and then one has the bad luck to encounter a pushing, thick-skinned individual who can only catch the point when you are out-and-out rude."

❧ ON *WALKING ARM IN ARM,* from Frances Benton, *Complete Etiquette,* 1956 (pp. 5–6):

"According to the older and stricter rules of etiquette, you shouldn't stroll along the streets arm in arm with any man except your husband, a relative, or your fiancé. Actually, however, most of us violate this rule nowadays, particularly in the evening. Perhaps all you have to remember about this subject is that you shouldn't thoughtlessly take the arm of a casual acquaintance, since the gesture implies familiarity. A woman may, of course, walk arm in arm with another woman with perfect propriety."

❧ ON *APPROPRIATE WORKPLACE TOUCHING—ONLY THE SHOULDER OR THE ARM!* from Janet Bailey in *Glamour,* April 1997:

"Touch in the workplace needn't involve sexual innuendo to be troubling. According to research at the University of Colorado at Boulder, the most objectionable nonsexual touches, as rated by employees, include: *Status reminders*—pats on the head, 'caretaking' hugs or other touches perceived as patronizing. *Order-giving touches*—'affectionate' touches accompanied by a request to do something (and therefore seen as annoyingly manipulative).... Of course, not all workplace touches are bad. 'The great majority are appropriate and enhance communication,' says Stanley Jones, Ph.D., the communication professor who did the research. Recognizing which touches are unwelcome still leaves room for friendly, congratulatory or supportive gestures. The safest way to make them: with brief contact on the shoulder, elbow or arm."

❧ ON *UNNECESSARY TOUCHING—NEVER THE SHOULDER NOR THE ARM!* from Frances Benton, 1956 (p.8):

"A well-mannered man avoids touching a woman unnecessarily. In helping a lady down from a bus or over an icy sidewalk, a certain amount of touching is necessary, but in ordinary conversation patting on the shoulder or squeezing the arm is wholly unnecessary. The line between friendliness and pawing is a very fine one."

*A MODEST RULE OF THUMB,* from an *Indianapolis News* editorial, October 10, 1995:

"Those who minimize the correlation between immodest dress and sexual promiscuity deceive themselves and others. . . . Perhaps a good rule of thumb is simply to wear clothing that complements one's whole personality rather than distracts from it."

*ON BEING KISSED UNAWARES,* from advice given by Mrs. Burton Kingsland in her column "Good Manners and Good Form," in the January 1908 issue of *The Ladies' Home Journal:*

"Q: If a young man should take a girl unawares by kissing her, what should she do?—BELLA"
"A: She should show her displeasure in a dignified way that leaves him in no doubt of it. She has reason to be displeased—for it is a liberty."

*ON WHAT KIND OF GIFTS TO ACCEPT FROM A MAN,* from Alice-Leone Moats, 1933 (p. 19):

"Flowers, books, and candy are considered the only presents which a lady may accept from a man. A jeweled bangle or some similar gift of trifling value may be received without fear of criticism, but expensive jewelry and wearing-apparel of any kind mean but one thing to this cynical world. There is only one way to pay for these, and few girls are so charming and lovely that they can forever defy the laws of economics and get something for nothing."

*ON WHAT TO SAY IF YOU NEED TO RETURN A GIFT,* from Frances Benton, 1956 (pp. 21–22):

"If such a gift is given, the girl should return it tactfully, saying something like, 'You're awfully kind to want to give me such a gift, but I'm afraid I couldn't possibly accept it.'"

*ON MODEST MARRIED BEHAVIOR,* from *The Canons of Good Breeding,* 1839 (pp. 87–88):

"It is in bad *ton* for a newly married couple, when going to an evening party, to enter the room together. Some older person, or some relative of hers, should take the bride in. It is in better taste that, on all occasions of appearing in public, the pair should not be exactly together. The recognition of that relation should as much as possible be confined to the fireside. It is not pleasant to see persons thrusting their mutual devotedness into the eye of society."

*ON PARASOL ELEVATION,* from Emily Post, 1923 (pp. 28–29):

"One should never call out a name in public, unless it is absolutely unavoidable. A young girl who was separated from her friends in a base-ball crowd had the presence of mind to put her hat on her parasol and lift it above the people surrounding her so that her friends might find her. Do not attract attention to yourself in public. This is one of the funda-mental rules of good breeding."

*ON GOING OUT WITH MARRIED MEN,* from Frances Benton, 1956 (p. 21):

"Although traditionally a single woman would never date a married man, this convention too has broken down somewhat in modern society. It is still a good rule, however, for nothing is misunderstood more quickly than going out repeatedly with the same married man."

*PUBLIC DISPLAYS OF AFFECTION WITH ONE'S BETROTHED,* from advice given by Mrs. Burton Kingsland in *The Ladies' Home Journal,* January 1908:

"Q: Will you answer a question that has greatly perplexed me? Is it prop-er to kiss one's betrothed in public?—ADDIE"
"A: No, it is exceedingly bad form. Such expressions of affection should be kept for private delectation."

*ON SYSTEMATIC SWEARING AND THE PROPRIETY OF SUBSTITUTING A SWEAR WITH "MY GOD!"* from Alice-Leone Moats, 1933 (p. 8):

"Although an occasional 'damn' passes unnoticed, any systematic swear-ing on the part of a woman comes as a shock. It is always ugly and par-ticularly, in moments of stress, vulgar. People who preface every sentence with 'My God' are worse. They're tiresome."

*ON THE BEST WORKING BEHAVIOR,* from Frances Benton, 1956 (p. 377):

"*Section 7:* Business Particulars for Women: TRY TO BE IMPERSONAL: . . . . The woman who is efficient and easy to work with is neither coyly and insistently feminine, nor does she aggressively try to be "one of the boys." She is a pleasant and poised worker, she tries to keep her personal prob-lems and emotional reactions out of her work, and she neither uses her femininity as a weapon, on the other hand, nor denies it, on the other."

*ON WHAT TO SAY IF YOU CATCH TWO BOARDERS PEEKING AT YOUR UNDER-WEAR AND SPECULATING ABOUT YOUR SEXUAL HISTORY,* advice given by Samantha Eggar to Cary Grant and Jim Hutton in *Walk, Don't Run* (1966):

"You've gone too far, and if you have any sense of decency, you'll leave in the morning."

*ON WHAT CONSTITUTES MODEST APPAREL,* from George Washington's *Rules of Civility and Decent Behavior,* 1748, Rule #52 (p. 41):

"In your Apparel be Modest and endeavor to accommodate Nature, rather than to procure Admiration keep to the Fashion of your equals Such as are Civil and orderly with respect to Times and Places."

🐚 ON *WHEN TO ASK A MAN IN,* from Alice-Leone Moats, 1933 (pp. 9–10):

"It all really comes down to what you mean by asking a man in. A girl who lives with her family has no reason to hesitate on doorsteps at night. Be it seven in the evening or four in the morning, her escort may march in for a drink or something to eat, safe in the knowledge that the family, awake or asleep, is always sufficient chaperon. The working girl or the girl who for some other reason lives alone is the one with the real problem to solve. Here are three rules that might prove helpful: Set the time limit at midnight, make sure the gentleman is sober; know your man—it is plain foolhardiness to ask a casual acquaintance in."

🐚 ON *WHEN TO GO TO A MAN'S APARTMENT,* from Alice-Leone Moats, 1933 (pp. 11–12):

"The key to the whole situation lies in the fact that you don't know when or by whom you will be seen coming in or going out. The most harmless visit can assume a naughty appearance, and certainly an acquaintance seeing you come out of a man's apartment in the early hours just before dawn will draw but one conclusion. Avoid stopping in for a drink after the theater, as the hour is a bit late, and it gives the young man ideas. Don't fall for the old line of having to go home for a long-distance call, and at the very mention of works of art run in the opposite direction. In any event, an innocent visit late at night seems rather silly, for it is taking a maximum risk for a minimum pleasure."

🐚 ON *HOW TO DISTINGUISH LOVE FROM LUST,* from Søren Kierkegaard, 1959 (Volume II, p. 21):

"What distinguishes all love from lust is the fact that it bears an impress of eternity."

🐚 ON *HOW TO ALLOW FOR FEMALE CHOOSING,* from Helena Rosenberg in *Self* magazine, January 1998.

"*8. Share less, assess more.* If you really want a husband, not just a convenient bed warmer, keep your legs crossed and your ears open. There will be plenty of time for wonderful sex later; the early stages should be reserved for getting to know a man, which includes ascertaining his marriageability. The best way to do that is without the distractions that come with sexual intimacy. If what you're feeling is 'real,' it's still going to be real later; add sex to the mix too quickly and it's easy to waste months or even years before coming to the conclusion that the relationship isn't going anywhere.

"*9. Don't cohabit unless you have a ring and a date.* Before you flog me for that politically incorrect instruction, let me finish the thought. Living with a man without an agreed-upon agenda is a foolish waste of time for a woman seeking marriage. You wouldn't give away months or years of your business knowledge or professional skills to someone on the off-chance that the recipient might hire you for a full-time position. Why would you be so selfless on the personal front?"

❧ *ON FALSE MODESTY,* from William Shakespeare, in *Much Ado About Nothing* (Act IV, Scene I, 1599):

"Would you not swear,/All that see her, that she were a maid,/By these exterior shows? But she is none: . . . /Her blush is guiltiness, not modesty."

❧ *ON WHY IT ISN'T CONSIDERATE TO SHOCK,* from Frances Benton, 1956 (p. 2):

"Another expression of our basic consideration for others is how we act in public. *Exhibitionism* is bad manners, not only because it is immodest but because it is inconsiderate. A lady or gentleman, therefore, does not wear outlandish clothes on a city street, or carry on an embarrassingly personal conversation in a crowded elevator. We don't spit our germs onto sidewalks, or cough our colds into other people's faces. Needless to say, it is not a pretty sight, either, to see someone combing his hair, picking his teeth, or cleaning his nails in public. It is not good manners—because it is not considerate—to do anything in public that might annoy, embarrass, disgust, or inconvenience other people."

❧ *A MODEST WARNING,* from Samuel Richardson, *Pamela,* 1740:

"My dearest child, our hearts ache for you; and then you seem so full of *joy* at his goodness, so *taken* with his kind expressions . . . that we *fear* you should be *too* grateful,—and reward him with that jewel, your virtue, which no riches, nor favour, nor any thing in this life, can make up to you. . . . Be sure don't let people's telling you you are pretty puff you up; for you did not make yourself. It is virtue and goodness only, that make true beauty. Remember that, Pamela—Your loving Father and Mother."

❧ *ON LOST MODESTY, CIRCA 1603,* from William Shakespeare, in *All's Well That Ends Well* (Act III, scene V):

"I hope your own grace will keep you where you are, though there were no further danger known but the modesty which is so lost."

❧ *ON HOW TO DRESS WHEN IN DOUBT,* from Emily Post, 1923 (p. 548):

"When in doubt, wear the plainer dress. It is always better far to be under-dressed than over-dressed. If you don't know whether to put on a ball dress or a dinner dress, wear the dinner dress. Or, whether to wear cloth or brocade to a luncheon, wear the cloth."

❧ *ON KEEPING YOUR EYES MODEST,* from Erving Goffman, *Behavior in Public Places,* 1963 (p. 84):

"*Civil inattention:* What seems to be involved is that one gives to another enough visual notice to demonstrate that one appreciates that the other is present (and that one admits openly to having seen him), while at the next moment withdrawing one's attention from him so as to express that he does not constitute a target of special curiosity or design."

🐦 ON *HOW TO WALK MODESTLY IN THE STREET,* from George Washington's *Rules of Civility and Decent Behavior,* 1748, Rule #53 (p. 41):

"Run not in the Streets, neither go too slowly nor with Mouth open go not Shaking yʳ Arms kick not the earth with yʳ feet, go not upon the Toes, nor in a Dancing Fashion."

🐦 ON *REACTING MODESTLY TO HOT FOOD,* from Frances Benton, 1956 (p. 30):

"*When food is too hot:* Don't spit it out! Just hastily swallow some water. (This is the only time you can take water with your mouth full.)"

🐦 ON HOW TO RECOGNIZE A SEXUAL EVENT, from Manis Friedman, *Doesn't Anyone Blush Anymore?* 1990 (p. 105):

"*Every* interaction between male and female should be recognized as a potentially sexual encounter. If the door is locked and a man and woman find themselves alone in the room, it becomes a sexual event. When we find ourselves in such a situation, we have to acknowledge that we are involved in a male–female relationship. Did we intend to become involved in that way? If not, why are we there?"

🐦 ON *HOW TO AVOID A SEXUAL EVENT,* from Manis Friedman, 1990 (p. 106):

"It is preferable that a man and woman who are not married to one another, and are not members of the same family, avoid being alone together in a closed room. They should avoid talking about intimate subjects. This doesn't mean they shouldn't be friends or coworkers. But they need to take into consideration that whenever a man and a woman have a friendship or a working relationship, it will have a potentially sexual component. For this reason they should follow certain precautions. They can be friends, they can work side by side, but they shouldn't go off alone on a canoe trip. They can discuss politics, art, business, or sports but should avoid topics that may initiate or strengthen feelings of sexuality."

🐦 ON WHAT TO SAY IF, DESPITE EVERYTHING, YOU STILL FIND YOURSELF A PAR-TICIPANT IN AN UNWANTED SEXUAL EVENT, from Manis Friedman, 1990 (p. 106):

"If their feelings get out of hand, they should break it off immediately. They should say, 'Wait a minute, we can't do this. Sorry.' In other words, they should do something to prevent sexual feelings when nothing sexual even ought to be taking place."

🐦 *ON WHAT TO SAY IF YOUR RABBI CATCHES YOU HIDING UNDER HIS BED AND LISTENING TO HIM HAVING INTIMATE RELATIONS WITH HIS WIFE,* from Rav Cahane (according to the Talmud, *Brachot 62A*):

"This too is Torah, which I need to learn!"

🐦 *ON WHAT TO SAY IF YOU'RE ON A NUDE CRUISE AND A FELLOW NUDIST OGLES YOU,* from Maxine Paetro in *New Woman,* May 1996:

"If you think you are being stared at, you might approach the other person in a friendly way and say something like, 'I notice you've been watching me. Is anything wrong?'"

🐦 *ON GLOVE DO'S AND DON'TS,* from Frances Benton, 1956 (p. 47):

"*Gloves:* You should wear gloves, or at least carry them, whenever you wear a hat. If you're a non–hat wearer, you should have gloves anyway for dressier occasions in the city. In the country, most people wear them only when needed for warmth. You normally take them off as soon as you come indoors. *You never eat in gloves.* Long evening gloves that are part of a whole costume may be pushed back over the hands (they are slit at the wrist for this purpose) for holding a cocktail glass or nibbling hors d'oeuvres, but they, too, must be completely removed at the dinner table.

White gloves must be kept meticulously clean, even if it means carrying an extra pair in your purse. It's better not to have them at all than to wear soiled ones.

Incidentally, a woman is never supposed to take off her gloves to shake hands, or apologize for not doing so.

Bracelets may be worn over gloves, particularly in the evening, but *rings should never be.* Leave your rings inside the gloves, where they belong."

🐦 *ON HOW TO DISCOVER WHO YOU REALLY ARE (ALWAYS USEFUL),* from Gila Manolson, *Outside/Inside,* 1997 (p. 19):

"In times such as ours, [modesty] is truly a lamp in the darkness. For [modesty] is infinitely more than what we wear—it is a way of being emerging from a deep vision of ourselves. It is inherent in potential within every one of us, male and female. . . . Most crucially, it is the key to all spiritual growth and, therefore, to the health of our society."

🐦 *AND TO RESOLVE THE ARM QUESTION, ONCE AND FOR ALL,* from advice given by Mrs. Burton Kingsland in *The Ladies' Home Journal,* October 1906:
:

Q. "Is it ever permissible for a man to take a woman's arm?"
A. "Not unless he is a policeman, and is guiding her to the lock-up! It is extremely provincial."

# NOTES

INTRODUCTION

p. 1      *"Modesty, which may be"*: Ellis (1910, p. 1).

p. 2      *dressing according to the standards: Dat Yehudit* are the standards of modesty adopted by Jewish communities, as distinguished from *Dat Moshe,* those laws of modesty mandated by the Torah. See Ellinson (1992, p. 119).

p. 4      *"A teacher of mine told me"*: Elizabeth Hayt, "Looking for Mister Goldberg," *New York* magazine, December 8, 1997.

p. 6      *After interviewing Beverly:* Roiphe (1997, p. 182).

p. 7      *The Marquis of Halifax:* Fletcher (1995, p. 387).

p. 7      *"perpetuate the public":* Ferguson (1993, p. 503).

p. 7      *Freud's view that girls:* Freud (1965, pp. 160–61):" Girls remain in [the Oedipus complex] for an indeterminate length of time; they demolish it late and, even so, incompletely. In these circumstances the formation of the superego must suffer; it cannot attain the strength and independence which give it its cultural significance."

p. 7      *"girls are having more trouble":* Pipher (1994, p. 28).

p. 7      *"Girls today are much more oppressed":* Pipher (1994, p. 12).

p. 7      *"the sexual license of the 1990's":* Pipher (1994, p. 208).

p. 7      *Her only clients who have escaped;* Pipher (1994, p. 92).

p. 8      *"we are all bad girls":* Wolf (1997, p. xxii).

p. 8      *"explore the shadow slut":* Wolf (1997, p. xvii).

p. 10      *a woman would never write:* "Ce qui fait que les femmes, quand elles se font auteurs, atteignent bien rarement au sublime . . . c'est que jamais elles n'osent être franches qu'à demi: être franches serait pour elles comme sortir sans fichu. Rien de plus fréquent pour un homme que d'écrire absolument sous la dictée de son imagination, et sans savoir où il va." Stendhal (1957, p. 67).

PART ONE. THE PROBLEM

CHAPTER ONE: THE WAR ON EMBARRASSMENT

p. 15      *"Every blush":* Hume (1985, p. 554).

p. 17      *Respect the Turtle:* Jean Hopfensperger, "Elementary Instruction: Board Expected to OK Sexual Harassment Curriculum," *Minneapolis Star Tribune,* October 9, 1993.

p. 17      *more than 4,200 school-age-girls:* Irene Sege, "A U.S. Survey Shows Wide Harassment of Girls in School," *Boston Globe,* March 24, 1993.

p. 18      *"school refusers":* Pipher (1994, pp. 69–70).

p. 18      *"Condom Line-Up":* Celeste McGovern, "Too Much, Too Soon," *Alberta Report,* March 14, 1994; Scott, *Children No More* (1995,

p. 121); Josh McDowell, "Sex, Lies and Truth," (Waco, TX: Word, 1986), video; NYC Board of Education's *HIV/AIDS Curriculum Guide: A Supplement to a Comprehensive Health Curriculum, Grades 7–9,* 1995, p. 186.

p. 18    *New Jersey's* Family Life *program:* Ellen Hopkins, "What Kids Really Learn in Sex Ed," *Parents* magazine, September 1993.

p. 19    *Schools in Fort Lauderdale:* Lona O'Connor, "Sex Ed Sparks Moral Battle: Parents Withdraw Kids from School," Fort Lauderdale *Sun-Sentinel,* April 17, 1997.

p. 19    *"I think that's too young":* Jomi S. Wronge, "Sex Education Gets a Boost," *Orange County Register,* July 3, 1997.

p. 19    New York City Board of Education: NYC Board of Education's *HIV/AIDS Curriculum Guide: A Supplement to a Comprehensive Health Curriculum, Grades K–6,* 1992, pp. 26–30.

p. 19    *Four Bronx boys:* "Four Boys Charged in Sodomy of Girl," *Daily News,* October 21, 1997.

p. 21    *"I'm SO embarrassed!":* Holyoke (1995, p. 39).

p. 21    *so many questions about embarrassment:* Holyoke (1997, p. 96).

p. 22    *"Sexually Healthy Adolescents":* Nancy C. DiMella and Cheryl A. Nelson, Newton Public Schools' *Student Workbook for Sexuality and Health: 9th Grade Sexuality and HIV/AIDS Education,* 1997, p. 4.

p. 22    *"refusing to take responsibility for their sexuality":* Lehrman (1997, p. 101).

p. 22    *"must take personal responsibility for her sexuality":* Paglia (1992, p. 53).

p. 24    *In 1997:* Alexander Sanger, "Sex Ed Is More Than Just Saying No," *Daily News,* July 18, 1997.

p. 24    *no increased condom use:* S. Kegeles, PhD. N. Adler, PhD., and C. Irwin, M.D., "Sexually Active Adolescents and Condoms: Changes Over One Year in Knowledge, Attitudes and Use," *American Journal of Public Health,* April 1988.

p. 24    *"It is time to stop kidding ourselves":* A. Stiffman, F. Earls, P. Dore, and R. Cunningham, "Changes in Acquired Immunodeficiency Syndrome-Related Risk Behavior After Adolescence: Relationships to Knowledge and Experience Concerning Human Immuno-deficiency Virus Infection," *Pediatrics,* May 1992.

p. 24    *The few studies that do:* In a 1991 study in *Family Planning Perspectives,* for example, it was found that instruction on contraception was significantly correlated with earlier initiation of intercourse. D. Kirby, R. Barth, N. Leland and J. Fetro, "Reducing the Risk: A New Curriculum to Prevent Sexual Risk-taking," *Family Planning Perspectives* 23 (1991), pp. 253–63. Even the Alan Guttmacher Institute, which supports contraceptive-based sex education, notes that teen pregnancy rates increased 23 percent from 1972 to 1990 and that fully one third of the 20 million STD infections reported annually in the United States struck teens—all during the years when comprehensive sex education became widespread.

CHAPTER TWO: POSTMODERN SEXUAL ETIQUETTE, FROM HOOK-UP TO CHECKUP

p. 26    *"Here, I think, is a task":* Brecher (1969, p. 326). Edward Brecher was a key figure in popularizing the work of Alfred Kinsey (*Sexual*

*Behavior in the Human Male,* 1948, and *Sexual Behavior in the Human Female,* 1953) and William Masters and Virginia Johnson (*Human Sexual Response,* 1966).

p. 26    *"debilitating sexual disease":* Brecher (1969, p. xv).

p. 27    *never "I'll always love you":* Bloom (1987, p. 122).

p. 27    *"with sex and utilities included":* Bloom (1987, p. 106).

p. 27    *"In recent decades":* Elliott and Brantley (1997, pp. 49–55).

p. 28    *"Dating takes a lot of time":* The University of Michigan quotes were recorded by David Gelernter (1997, p. 92).

p. 29    *"Your Hook-up Points":* O'Neill (1972, p. 168).

p. 29    *A 1993 study of college women:* R. J. Ogletree, "Sexual Coercion Experience and Help-Seeking Behavior of College Women," *American Journal of College Health,* Vol. 41 (January 1993).

p. 30    *"Will I ever see you again?":* Elliott and Brantley (1997, p. 56).

p. 30    *Consider the following advice:* Allison Glock, "Dr. Sooth," *GQ* magazine, December 1997.

p. 31    *"Even when love goes badly:"* Thompson (1995, p. 285).

p. 31    *"Once the breakup has taken place":* Lesley Dormen, "Breaking Up: A Protect-Your-Heart Plan: How to Minimize Pain and Prep Yourself for New Love," *Glamour,* December 1997.

p. 32    *"My girlfriend talks":* **Cosmopolitan,** 1998.

p. 32    *"But if you follow our timetable":* Daryl Chen, "Can You Be Friends with Your Ex?" *Mademoiselle,* April 1998.

p. 34    *"let no half courtesy continue":* Advice on how to snub those who have wronged you, given to readers of the *American Code of Manners* (1880), and Clara Sophia Jessup Moore's *Sensible Etiquette* (1878), as cited in Kasson (1990, p. 145).

p. 34    *"The best predictor":* Psychologist Carl Hindy, *YM,* January 1998.

p. 37    *"Diving Area":* The "Pool of Love" test, *YM,* Spring 1998.

p. 38    *"God help my baby":* Roiphe (1996, p. 8).

p. 38    *how one "becomes" a woman:* Beauvoir (1952), p 733: "What is extremely demoralizing for the woman who aims at self-sufficiency is the existence of other women . . . who live as parasites." P. 540: "The great danger which threatens the infant in our culture lies in the fact that the mother to whom it is confided in all its helplessness is almost always a discontented woman: sexually she is frigid or unsatisfied . . . she has no independent grasp on the world or on the future. She will seek to compensate for all these frustrations through her child." P. 693: "Every woman in love is more or less a paranoiac."

## CHAPTER THREE: THE FALLOUT

p. 39    *"Where the Victorians":* James Atlas, "The Not-So-Proper Victorians," *New York Times,* March 3, 1997.

p. 39    *In Orthodox Judaism:* Talmud, *Nedarim* 20B.

p. 39    *"American legislators":* Tocqueville (1966, p. 603).

p. 40    *all 50 states have anti-stalking:* "In the Mind of a Stalker," *New Woman,* February 1996.

p. 40    *"Given the law":* Jeffrey Toobin, "Stalking in L.A." *New Yorker,* February 24 & March 3, 1997.

p. 40    *a recent survey:* Pipher (1994, p. 206).

p. 40    *In another study:* Hattemer and Showers (1993, p. 31).

p. 41    *"is a totally devastating":* Paglia (1992, pp. 64–65), reprinted from an October 1991 interview published in *Spin* magazine.

p. 41    *Christopher Archer:* Lefkowitz (1998, p. 417).

p. 41    *"The schools pass out":* Pipher (1994, p. 70).

p. 41    *"two of the suspects":* Norimitsu Onishi, "4 Charged with Rape in Queens," *New York Times,* May 21, 1997.

p. 41    *Koss found that 15.3%:* Mary Koss, Christine Gidycz, and Nadine Wisniewski, "The Scope of Rape: Incidence and Prevalence of Sexual Aggression and Victimization in a National Sample of Higher Education Students," *Journal of Consulting and Clinical Psychology* 55:2 (1987), pp. 162–70.

p. 42    *"Have you ever":* Neil Gilbert, "Realities and Mythologies of Rape," *Society,* May–June 1992, pp. 4–5.

p. 42    *Most conservative:* Roiphe (1993, p. 52); Sommers (1994, pp. 212–13); Mary Matalin, "Stop Whining!" *Newsweek,* October 25, 1993.

p. 42    *The main finding:* Wilson (1995, p. 113); Mary Koss, "Hidden Rape," in Ann Wolbert Burgess, ed., *Rape and Sexual Assault II* (New York: Garland, 1988), p. 16.

p. 42    *"God forbid":* Fletcher (1995, p. 338).

p. 43    *astonishing House of Lords case:* A 1976 case, as cited in Feinberg and Gross (1995, pp. 459–61).

p. 44    *"if women want equality in society":* Bonnie Erbe, *To the Contrary,* April 7, 1996.

p. 46    *Sara McCool:* Carlip (1995, p. 42).

p. 46    *but "what do young":* Carlip (1995, p. 41).

p. 47    *"That modesty is a charm":* Trollope (1950, p. 221).

p. 47    *Consider the 1909 man:* Mrs. Burton Kingsland, "Good Manners and Good Form," *The Ladies' Home Journal,* May 1909.

p. 47    *"hate it when":* Cosmopolitan, April 1997.

p. 47    *"What do you do":* Mrs. Burton Kingsland, "Good Manners and Food Form," *The Ladies' Home Journal,* March 1905.

p. 49    *"My husband and I":* De Angelis (1997, p. 189).

p. 49    *the number of strip clubs:* Juliann Garey, "Dancing as Fast as They Can: Why Strippers Are Suddenly Everywhere," *Glamour,* January 1996.

p. 50    *"Yawn":* William Grimes, "Now, the Ennui of Outrage," *New York Times,* May 4, 1997.

p. 50    *"could lead viewers"* Steiner (1996, p. 50).

p. 51    *"I think that young girls":* Cathleen Medwick, interview with A. M. Homes, "Virgin Territory," *Mirabella,* March/April 1996.

p. 51    *Her boyfriend had explained:* Jennifer Silver, "Caught with a Centerfold: No More Porn—I'm No Prude, But I've Got My Pride," *Mademoiselle,* January 1997.

p. 53    *According to psychologist:* James B. Allen, Douglas T. Kenrick, Darwyn E. Linder, Michael A. McCall, "Arousal and Attraction," *Journal of Personality and Social Psychology* 57:2 (1989), pp. 261–70. Also Douglas T. Kenrick, Sara E. Gutierres, and Laurie L. Goldberg, "Influence of Popular Erotica on Judgments of Strangers and Mates," *Journal of Experimental Social Psychology* 25:2 (1989), pp. 159–67.

p. 53    *"The feminists fear":* Posner (1992, p. 374). Irving Kristol's famous article, which outlines the corruption-of-morals charge, originally appeared in "Pornography, Obscenity and the Case for Censorship," *The New York Times Magazine,* March 28, 1971. (Of related interest is Walter Berns's "Pornography vs. Democracy: The Case for Censorship," *The Public Interest,* Winter 1971.)

p. 53    *"what is* needed": Paglia (1992, p. 259).

p. 54    *A high school girl:* Nancy Jo Sales, "Sex and the High School Girl," *New York* magazine, September 29, 1997.

p. 54    *"Why not, since everyone seems to think":* Hornbacher (1998, p. 70).

p. 55    *"They let me go":* Hersch (1998, pp. 176–80).

p. 56    *"the separation of the* niddah": Abramov (1988, p. 101).

p. 56    *If she chose to greet:* Kasson (1990, p. 143).

p. 57    *"I've been dating":* Letters are from *Mademoiselle,* May 1997 and July 1996 issues.

p. 57    *"the rest of the night crying":* "The First Time: One Girl's Personal Account," *The Lion's Roar,* March 10, 1994.

p. 57    *1995 Sex in America:* Conducted in 1992 by the National Opinion Research Center at the University of Chicago, and surveyed 3,500 men and women ages 18–59.

p. 57    *"deadness":* Pipher (1994, p. 48).

p. 57    *"to set limits":* Pipher (1994, p. 183).

p. 57    *"Casey":* Pipher (1994, p. 194).


CHAPTER FOUR: NEW PERVERSIONS

p. 58    *"My anorexic body":* Hornbacher (1998, p. 229).

p. 59    *"brag of the careless use":* Hornbacher (1998, p. 126).

p. 59    *Heidi:* Pipher (1994, p. 169).

p. 59    *"When I was starving":* Knapp (1996, p. 130).

p. 60    *"If I was at my ideal":* Hesse-Biber (1996, pp. 60, 83).

p. 60    *"Oh shame! where is thy blush?":* *Hamlet,* Act III, scene iv.

p. 61    *Yale's official response:* "Dormitory Life Is Essential to a Yale Education," *New York Times,* September 11, 1997.

p. 62    *"There is nothing the matter with girls":* Martin (1899, p. 98).

p. 63    *"My husband and I":* "Harriet Lerner's Good Advice," *New Woman,* April 1997.

p. 63    *"Cayenne":* Pipher (1994, p. 35).

p. 64    *"more androgynous":* Pipher (1994, p. 18).

p. 64    *"romantic ideals":* A. L. Erickson, *Women and Property in Early Modern England* (London, 1993), p. 7.

p. 64    *A 1994 survey:* "Teens Talk About Sex: Adolescent Sexuality in the 90's: A Survey of High School Students," commissioned by Rolonda in association with SIECUS, pp. 6, 21, 25, 41. Interviewing was conducted April 11–25, 1994, with 503 high school students from across the United States. *Sexuality education may be lacking:* section E of Chapter Three.

p. 64    still *"condition[ing] sexual consent":* Thompson (1995, p. 39).

p. 64    *Deana:* Thompson (1995, p. 37).

p. 64    *"Tracy":* Thompson (1995, p. 43).

p. 64    *"having serial expectations":* Thompson (1995, p. 274).

p. 64    *"Liza":* Thompson (1995, p. 242).

p. 64    *"bids for sympathy":* Thompson (1995, p. 41).

p. 65    *just as the ideal young woman:* Brathwait (1631, frontispiece).

p. 65    *the bodily harm:* Orenstein (1994, p. 89).

p. 65    *Tammy:* Pipher (1994, p. 159).

p. 65    *"Are you sexually involved":* Pipher (1994, p. 160).

p. 66    *"Now it's a frequent":* Pipher (1994, p. 157).

p. 66    *"Romantic love":* Kierkegaard (1959, Vol. II, p. 22).

p. 66    *"sexual love":* Kant (1963, p. 163).

p. 67    *"My mom was telling":* Merle Ginsberg, interview with Natalie Portman, "Natalie's World," *W* magazine, November 1997.

p. 67    *"Many races":* Ellis (1910, pp. 8–10, 12–14).

p. 69    *When subject:* Ellis (1910, p. 75).

p. 69    *"Yes, it is possible to look":* Ellen Fein and Sherrie Schneider, "Living the Rules: The New Relationship Etiquette," *Cosmopolitan,* April 1997.

p. 69    *"Even fears for a child's":* Frances O'Rourke, "War of the Wardrobes," *Irish Times,* August 5, 1996.

p. 70    *"The world's absolute-worst dress":* Knapp (1996, p. 160).

p. 70    *dared by one of her friends:* Jenna McCarthy, "Slut for a Day," *Mademoiselle,* February 1997.

p. 71    *"confess that actually leaving the house":* Brenda Polan, "Revealing Truth Behind the Wonderbra," *Daily Mail* (London), September 4, 1992.

p. 72    *"The further role shame":* Riezler (1943, p. 462).

p. 72    *Nervous "Sandy" tells: Cosmopolitan,* January 1996.

p. 73    *"TV has turned more realistic":* Caryn James, "Straying into Temptation in Prime Time," *New York Times,* August 10, 1997.

p. 73    *genes that are doing all the cheating:* Robert Wright, "Infidelity: It May Be in Our Genes," *Time,* August 15, 1994.

p. 73    *"Affairs can support a marriage":* Eric Alterman, "Affairs of the Heart," *Elle,* November 1997.

p. 74    *"just keep them as pets":* Becky Garrison, interview with Helen Gurley Brown, "The Little Lady Who Started a Great Big Revolution," *Women's Quarterly,* Autumn 1997.

p. 74    *as Laura Gowing points out:* Scholar Laura Gowing explains that "women occupied a very particular place in the negotiation of sexual guilt and honour" in early modern London. By positioning themselves as the arbiters of what was honorable, women regulated sexuality in their local communities with "a verbal and legal authority" that would best serve their interests. As cited in Fletcher (1995, p. 268).

p. 75    *"Ever since I was a kid":* Interview with Holly Joan Hart, "Holly by the Bay," *Playboy,* April 1998.

p. 76    *"was rebelling against being a girl":* Lardner (1995, p. 49).

p. 76    *"We wanted all the children to be independent":* Lardner (1995, p. 163).

p. 77    *"just like everyone else does":* Lardner (1995, p. 166).

p. 78    *"Cayenne":* Pipher (1994, p. 32).

p. 79    *"I'm so determined":* Interview with Alicia Silverstone, *Premier* magazine, July 1997.

p. 79    *"Are You Normal?": Women's Own,* December 1995.

## PART TWO. THE FORGOTTEN IDEAL

CHAPTER FIVE: FORGIVING MODESTY

p. 87    *I did some research:* "Perspective on Language: What Ever Happened to S-X?," *Los Angeles Times,* July 22, 1993; Judith Butler, *Gender Trouble: Feminisms and the Subversion of Identity,* New York: Routledge, Chapman and Hall, 1990, p. ix.

p. 89    *"There is also the use of 'modesty'":* Schueler (1997, p. 467).

p. 89    *"At the same time it is hard":* Schueler (1997, p. 483).

p. 90    *49% of women wish:* "How Many Men Have You Slept With?" *Glamour,* March 1998.

p. 90    *The response to this article:* "The Men You've Slept With," Letters from Readers in *Glamour,* May 1998.

p. 90    *men say they would sleep:* Buss, *Evolution of Desire,* as cited in Lehrman (1997, pp. 115, 214).

p. 91    *"Equality means":* Margaret Atwood, speech to the American Booksellers Association, 1993, as cited in Katherine Dunn, "Call of the Wild," *Vogue,* June 1995.

p. 91    Kate Potter: "When Did You Last Have Sex?" *Marie Claire,* September 1997.

p. 92    *"Women Who Have Sex with":* Sexlife magazine, Vol. 2, 1997.

p. 93    *Donald Kratz:* Joe Kita, "The 5 Things That Scare Him Most About You," *Cosmopolitan,* October 1997.

p. 94    *"A woman once bought me":* "What's the Best (or Worst) Gift a Woman Ever Gave You?" *Glamour,* December 1997.

p. 95    *"Below is a generic":* "20 Ways to Get Him to Do What You Want Him to Do, Even When He Doesn't Want to Do It," *Cosmopolitan,* April 1997.

p. 95    *"WHO SAYS YOU CAN'T ENJOY":* ad for upcoming article in January issue by Louise Bernikow, *Cosmopolitan,* December 1995.

p. 95    *"Lucy" tearfully confessing:* Gloria Brame, "Cosmo Questionnaire," *Cosmopolitan,* December 1995.

p. 96    *"Without modesty":* Ellis (1910, p. 82).

p. 96    *"All peoples":* Riezler (1943, p. 461).

p. 96    *"And if we consider Modesty":* Allestree (1673, 1:14). According to Ruth Bernard Yeazell, there is some confusion over whether Allestree was indeed the author of this guide or whether his biographer, Bishop Fell, was its author.

p. 97    *"in reality, only an outrage":* Renooz (1898, p. 86): "cette pudeur dont on lui fait un mérite et qui n'est, en réalité, qn'un outrage fait à son sexe."

p. 97    *"Do not adorn yourself outwardly":* I Peter 3:3–4.

p. 97    *More recently:* Sunday Gazette Mail, May 15, 1994.

p. 98    *As Stuart Cloete put it:* Cloete (1943, p. 138). *Congo Song* was a novel primarily about relations between the sexes, a sort of updated version of Conrad's *Heart of Darkness.*

p. 98    *"ARE YOUR HANG-UPS SABOTAGING YOUR LOVE LIFE?"* Cover of *Cosmopolitan,* October 1997.

p. 101    *"Loving modesty":* Brathwait (1631, p. 228).

p. 101    *"That secret inscreened beauty":* Brathwait (1631, p. 50).

p. 101    *"Modesty is the choycest"*: Brathwait (1631, p. 169).

p. 101    *"Array your selves"*: Brathwait (1631, p. 6).

p. 101    *"Those, whose spotless affections"*: Brathwait (1631, p. 93).

p. 101    *"Conceits. . . . sweetly tempered"*: Brathwait (1631, p. 52).

p. 102    *"If there bee any that provideth not"*: Brathwait (1630, p. 154).

p. 102    *"the Voluptuous Libertine"*: Brathwait (1630, pp. xvii, 340).

p. 102    *Mill's distinction between external*: Mill (1979, p. 27).

p. 102    DeMay *v.* Roberts: NW 146, Mich. 1881.

p. 103    *In 1837*: Robert Ebisch, "Paying Lip Service to That Historic Romantic—the Kiss," *Chicago Tribune,* February 14, 1986.

p. 103    *Then most conservatives*: George Will, "Sex Amid Semicolons," *Newsweek,* October 4, 1993.

p. 104    *the woman must give willingly*: Kierkegaard (1959, Vol. I, p. 424).

p. 104    *one truly loves only once*: Kierkegaard (1959, Vol. II, pp. 91–95).

p. 104    *Indeed, Havelock Ellis's 1899*: Ellis (1910, p. 1). Initially his *Studies in the Psychology of Sex* began with his essay on "sexual inversion," but Ellis placed the modesty essay first when the former arrangement didn't go over well with the public or the Crown.

p. 105    *"The following week"*: Flaubert (1995, p. 5).

CHAPTER SIX: THE GREAT DECEPTION

p. 106    *"Another school sex case"*: Henri E. Cauvin, *Daily News,* October 17, 1997.

p. 106    *"We Sweat, We Swagger"*: Anna Seaton Huntington, "What Women Athletes Are Really Like," *Glamour,* January 1996.

p. 106    *Of the many so-called "fictions"*: Yeazell (1991, p. x).

p. 106    *that woman's prerogative*: Kasson (1978, p. 143).

p. 107    *"It is a mark of high breeding"*: "A Gentleman" (1836, p. 60).

p. 107    *men's assumption*: Langelan (1993, p. 249).

p. 107    *"The discovery"*: Dworkin (1974, p. 174).

p. 107    *"deconstruct the stereotypes"*: Amy Gross, "Femininity '96: The New Heroes," *Elle,* May 1996.

p. 109    *"But in order"*: Hume (1967, p. 570). Freud adopted this view, in 1918, but he applied it more specifically to virginity in "The Taboo of Virginity."

p. 109    *Popular prejudices*: Rousseau (1967, p. 167): "Préjugés populaires! Me crie-t-on. Petites erreurs de l'enfance! Tromperie des lois et de l'éducation! La pudeur n'est rien. Elle n'est qu'une invention des lois sociales pour mettre à couvert les droits des pères et des époux, et maintenire quelque ordre dans les familles. Pourquoi rougirions-nous des besoins que nous donna la Nature? . . . Pourquoi, les désirs étant égaux des deux parts, les démonstrations en seraient-elles différentes? Pourquoi l'un des sexes se refuserait-il plus que l'autre aux penchants qui leur sont communs? Pourquoi l'homme aurait-il sur ce point d'autres lois que les animaux?"

p. 110    *"upon a very ticklish"*: Mandeville (1724, p. 49).

p. 110    *Many have suggested*: Bloom (1987, p. 102). In the *Charmides,* 160e–161b, Socrates argues that the kind of self-control that "makes a man feel shame and be bashful" is a good thing, but is not necessarily the same thing as modesty (*Early Socratic Dialogues,* p. 186).

p. 111   *"I am persuaded that":* Wollstonecraft (1992, p. 230).

p. 111   *"unnatural coldness of constitution":* Wollstonecraft (1992, p. 238).

p. 111   *"The reserve I mean":* Wollstonecraft (1992, p. 236).

p. 111   *"most improved their reason":* Wollstonecraft (1992, p. 229).

p. 111   *"love will teach [women] modesty":* Wollstonecraft (1992, p. 238). Another interesting and little-remarked-upon fact about this essay is its attack on the Jews and their observance of modesty laws: "that regard to cleanliness, which some religious sects have perhaps carried too far, especially the Essenes, amongst the Jews, by making that an insult to God which is only an insult to humanity." This only reflects Wollstonecraft's misunderstanding of Judaism, for the woman who goes to the *mikveh* is required to be clean—even to remove her nail polish—*before* immersion precisely because the laws of modesty concern not cleanliness, but holiness. The point of the *mikveh* ritual is not to cleanse a woman who is unclean, but to imbue the sexual relations between husband and wife with sacredness. (The Essenes were a brotherhood of Jews of the 2nd century B.C. to the 2nd century A.D.)

p. 111   *"outrage":* Renooz (1898, p. 86): "Je répondrai à cela que la pudeur c'est la honte masculine attribuée à la femme ... cette pudeur dont on lui fait un mérite et qui n'est, en réalité, qu'un outrage fait à son sexe."

p. 112   *A "mythic celebration":* Dworkin (1976, pp. 27, 105).

p. 112   *"The act of prevailing":* Stoltenberg (1989, p. 19).

p. 112   *"they are not comparable":* Rousseau (1979, p. 358).

p. 112   *"To be rapable":* MacKinnon (1989, p. 178).

p. 113   *"Clearly, women like":* Lehrman (1997, p. 99).

p. 114   *the husband's sexual obligation: Shulchan Aruch, Orach Chaim* 240:1.

p. 114   *The conjugal [women's sexual] rights:* Maimonides, *Mishneh Torah, Hilchot Ishut* (The Laws of Marriage), Chapter 14.

p. 115   *Rashi:* Bereshit 3:16. "Rashi" (1040–1105) is the abbreviated name of Rabbi Solomon Yitzhaki or ben Isaac.

p. 115   *Bernard Mandeville:* as cited in Fletcher (1995, p. 394).

p. 115   *The Elizabethan musician:* As cited in L. Stone, *The Family, Sex and Marriage in England 1500–1800* (London: 1977), p. 495.

p. 115   *Leslie H. Farber:* Heather Horne, Letter to the editor, *Commentary,* August 1972.

p. 116   *"Are pictures of naked men sexy?": New York Post* woman-on-the-street interview, December 29, 1997.

p. 116   *Jayne Napier:* "When Did You Last Have Sex?" *Marie Claire,* September 1997.

p. 117   *"The desires are equal!":* Rousseau (1967, p. 170): "Les désirs sont égaux! Qu'est-ce à dire? Y a-t-il de part de d'autre mêmes facultés de les satisfaire?" Incidentally, Ruth Bernard Yeazell says that this passage refers not to female fear of rape, but to male fear of impotence, which is interesting. See Yeazell (1991, p. 26).

CHAPTER SEVEN: CAN MODESTY BE NATURAL?

p. 118   *"With regard to the modesty":* Rousseau (1967, p. 170): "A l'égard de la pudeur de sexe en particulier, quelle arme plus douce eût pu donner cette mêmes Nature à celui qu'elle destinait à se défendre?"

p. 119   *There is everything to gain:* Stendhal (1957, p. 62): "Pour une femme au-dessus du vulgaire, il y a donc tout à gagner à avoir des manières fort réservées. Le jeu n'est pas égal."

p. 119   *"The witness acknowledged":* Neil A. Lewis, "Accuser Is Criticized in Army Sex Case," *New York Times,* July 2, 1997.

p. 120   *if we should seek to raise:* Rousseau (1979, p. 363).

p. 121   *"Sherry," 30:* "When Men Go Gross," *Cosmopolitan,* April 1997.

p. 121   *Advice columnist Blanche Vernon: Mademoiselle,* February 1996.

p. 121   *Howard Stern is the first to admit:* "Interview with Howard Stern," *Cosmopolitan,* March 1997.

p. 122   *"While walking across":* Mike Royko, "Women Skirting the Real Issue," *Chicago Tribune,* May 23, 1986.

p. 122   *"his body beautifully":* Alvarez (1991, p. 96).

p. 123   *"you look like you've gotten":* Alvarez (1991, p. 103).

p. 124   *"I'm really flat":* "Hall of Shame," *YM,* Spring 1998.

p. 124   *"Whenever I get embarrassed":* Holyoke (1996, p. 7).

p. 125   *"We know likewise":* France (1926, p. 146). Anatole France lived from 1844 to 1924, and he did not want *Under the Rose* to be published during his lifetime.

p. 125   *the "faithful wife of Susa":* From Xenophon's *Cyropaedia.*

p. 125   *Paul says is symbolized:* I Corinthians 11.

p. 125   *what parts of the body must be covered:* Sura XXIV.

p. 126   *"in Sanskrit":* Riezler (1943, p. 461).

p. 127   *"There will always be certain differences":* Beauvoir (1952, p. 766).

p. 127   *"Her modesty is in part":* Beauvoir (1952, p. 400).

p. 127   *in a society that trivializes:* Beauvoir (1952, p. 410).

p. 127   *"The girl is not so much":* Kant, *Bemerkungen,* as cited in Hull (1996, p. 304).

p. 128   *In public, Charles repeatedly:* Tannen (1990, p. 219).

p. 128   *"women's feelings that they should not boast":* Tannen (1990, p. 223).

p. 128   *"to recommend that women learn":* Tannen (1990, p. 224).

p. 129   *"Why should men and women":* Crider et al. (1993, p. 160). Study is referred to as "Deci, 1975."

p. 130   *A fascinating 1993 study:* Ahn et al. (1993, p. 740).

p. 132   *"You meet a person who is":* Lamm (1997, p. 5).

p. 132   *so many studies:* D. Orr, M.D., et al., "Reported Sexual Behaviors and Self-Esteem Among Young Adolescents, *American Journal of Diseases of Children,* January 1989.

p. 132   *"having pride in yourself":* Faith Perkins, *Orlando Sentinel Tribune,* June 19, 1990.

p. 133   *the virtue of pride is derived from prude:* Daly (1987, p. 156).

p. 134   *"I'm bad at keeping secrets":* Holyoke (1996, p. 6).

p. 135   *"TOTALLY SHAMELESS GIRLS":* Cover of *XXX Exposure,* Vol. 10 (1997).

p. 136   *"No previous baggage":* Personals ad in *New York* magazine, August 18, 1997.

p. 136   *"Be not immodest":* Washington (1989, p. 44). The 15-year-old George Washington copied down these rules from a French Jesuit Rules of Civility and Decent Behavior (1545).

p. 136   *shame arises naturally:* Straus (1966, p. 220): "The public sphere is only found among humans. . . . Incidentally, what we call the private sphere is a delimited public sphere and not the polar opposite to 'public,' which we call 'immediate.'"

p. 138   *In 1998, a* New York Press: Amy Sohn, "Female Trouble," *New York Press,* May 27–June 2, 1998.

p. 138   *"make them think you're one of the guys":* Nancy Jo Sales, "Sex and the High School Girl," *New York* magazine, September 29, 1997.

p. 141   *couples who live together:* In a 1992 Wisconsin study of more than 13,000 adults, couples who had cohabited prior to marriage reported "greater marital conflict and poorer communication" than those married couples who had never cohabited. (Elizabeth Thomson and Ugo Colella, "Cohabitation and Marital Stability: Quality or Commitment?" *Journal of Marriage and the Family* 54 [1992], pp. 259–67.) A 1991 study had found that marriages that began as cohabiting couples had a 50 percent higher divorce rate than those that did not. (Larry L. Bumpass. James A. Sweet, and Andrew Cherlin, "The Role of Cohabitation in Declining Rates of Marriage," *Journal of Marriage and the Family* 53 [1991], pp. 913–27.)

p. 141   *"Art dealer":* New York Post, November 7, 1997.

p. 142   *In the 1890s, she found:* Brumberg (1997, p. xxi).

p. 142   *"What is extremely demoralizing":* Beauvoir (1952, pp. 733 and 540).

p. 142   *"Since housewifery":* Ferguson (1989, p. 217).

p. 142   *"the eternal element in love":* Kierkegaard (1959, Vol. II, p. 22).

p. 143   *"Her charity":* Stoltenberg (1989, p. 23).

## CHAPTER EIGHT: MALE CHARACTER

p. 145   *Should the Titanic disaster happen today:* "Should a Woman's Life Be Spared Before a Man's? 66% Say No," *Glamour,* May 1998.

p. 145   *a Manhattan beautician claimed:* "Did Flirty Finest Miss W. Side Sighting?" *New York Post,* July 18, 1997.

p. 146   *"demand chivalry":* Lehrman (1997, p. 101).

p. 146   *Yeazell eloquently notes:* Yeazell (1991, p. 84). Yeazell also points out that when the anti-Pamelists, as they would become known, wanted to "smear" the idea of this heroine's sexual inexperience, they sneered about Pamela's "skill in intrigue." (See also Fielding's *Shamela.*) Of course, if one accepts this interpretation of modesty—that it works best when the woman is most ignorant of its operation—this would seem to exclude the possibility of modesty being moral—at least in the Kantian terms I outlined earlier. It may be more moral for modesty to be the product of rational struggle, but then in Richardsonian terms, it would also to that degree be less beautiful.

p. 146   *"an overprotective manner":* Sally Satel, "It's Always His Fault," *Women's Quarterly,* Summer 1997.

p. 147   *(Genesis 9:21–27):* "Noah, the tiller of the soil, was the first to plant a vineyard. He drank of the wine and became drunk, and he uncovered himself within his tent. Ham, the father of Canaan, saw his father's nakedness and told his two brothers outside. But Shem and Japheth took a cloth, placed it against both their backs and, walking backward, they covered their father's nakedness: their faces were turned the other way, so that they did not see their father's nakedness. When Noah woke up from his wine and learned what his youngest son had done to him, he said, 'Cursed be Canaan/The lowest of slaves/Shall he be to his brothers.' And he said, 'Blessed be the LORD/The God of Shem;/Let Canaan be a slave to them./ May God enlarge Japheth,/ And let him dwell in the tents of Shem;/ And let Canaan be a slave to them.'"

p. 147    *Later in Exodus (28:42–43):* "You shall also make for them linen breeches to cover their nakedness; they shall extend from the hips to the thighs. They shall be worn by Aaron and his sons when they enter the Tent of Meeting or when they approach the altar to officiate in the sanctuary, so that they do not incur punishment and die. It shall be a law for all time for him and for his offspring to come."

p. 147    *Additionally, both male and female:* Both *yichud M'deoraisa,* forbidden by Torah law, and *yichud M'derabonon,* forbidden by rabbinic ordinance, refer to man/woman seclusions, i.e., a man may not be alone with a girl older than three years of age and a woman may not be alone with a boy more than nine years of age.

p. 148    *"Full manhood was unattainable":* Fletcher (1995, p. 97).

p. 148    *Thomas Ricketts, for example:* Fletcher (1995, p. 270).

p. 148    *"Talking About Women":* Benton (1956, p. 8).

p. 149    *"Why do guys tell":* "Q & A," *YM,* January 1998.

p. 149    *"The woman who":* Ellis (1910, p. 5).

p. 150    *"Honor, in the chivalric code":* Fletcher (1995, p. 126).

p. 150    *"An insult to a woman's chastity":* Cecilia Morgan, "In Search of the Phantom Misnamed Honour," *Canadian Historical Review,* December 1995.

p. 150    *"God forbid":* as cited in Fletcher (1995, p. 338).

p. 151    *"A man of character":* "More Men Get Alimony, and More Women Get Mad," *Wall Street Journal,* July 30, 1997.

p. 151    *"Gossip reduces the other":* Barthes (1978, p. 185).

p. 151    *"You shouldn't spend the next day":* "Men's Sexual Strategies," *Marie Claire,* September 1997.

p. 151    *"One day, over brunch":* Jennifer Moses, "Keep It To Yourself!" *Glamour,* September 1997.

p. 154    *"In lifting his hat":* Post (1923, p. 23). More recently, the wolf whistle is still considered by many women to be the most acceptable and least "harassing" of street greetings precisely because it is not a direct attempt at engagement but an impersonal way of conveying appreciation. (See D. Larsen, "Do You Like to Be Whistled At?" *San Francisco Chronicle,* July 3, 1961.)

p. 154    *"Walking with a Woman":* Benton (1956, p. 9).

p. 155    *"prostitution":* John Taylor, "Are You Politically Correct?" *New York* magazine, January 21, 1991.

p. 155    *"women are incapable":* Marilyn Frye, "Oppression," anthologized in Paula S. Rothenberg, *Racism and Sexism: An Integrated Study* (New York: St. Martin's Press, 1988), p. 41.

p. 155    *"protection rackets":* Nancy M. Henley, *Body Politics: Power, Sex and Nonverbal Communication* (New York: Touchstone Books/Simon & Schuster, 1986), p. 63.

p. 155    *"The entire ritual structuring":* Kasson (1990, p. 133).

p. 155    *"these traditions don't make much sense":* Holyoke (1997, p. 17).

p. 156    *"The genocidal mentality":* Dijkstra (1996, p. 444).

p. 156    *"The idea of the male sex":* Stoltenberg (1989, pp. 29–30).

p. 156    *"enough elongated tissue":* Stoltenberg (1989, p. 31).

p. 156    *"born into a physiological continuum":* Stoltenberg (1989, p. 28).

p. 156    *"genital tubercle":* Stoltenberg (1989, p. 27).

p. 156    *Testosterone supplements: Wall Street Journal,* July 26, 1997.

p. 157    *"On their first date":* "Vows," *New York Times,* May 18, 1997.

p. 158    *Judge Daniel R. Moeser:* "Decision Denying Motion to Dismiss" a complaint that ladies' night violates sec. 101.22(9) 1 and 3 of a Wisconsin statute, in *Novak and Luscher v. Madison Motel Associates,* Dane County, WI, Branch 11, Case No. 93-CV-1005. July 30, 1993.

p. 158    *sexual stereotyping:* This is found on pp. 6–7 of Judge Daniel R. Moeser's "Decision Denying Motion to Dismiss." Here he is citing Heidi C. Paulson, who authored *Ladies' Night Discounts: Should We Bar Them or Promote Them?* (1991).

p. 159    Tigner *v.* Texas: 310 US 141, 147 (1940); *Goesaert v. Cleary:* 335 US 464 (1948).

p. 160    *at Johns Hopkins the women's basketballs:* Walter Olson, "Reasonable Doubts," *Reason,* February 1998.


## PART THREE. THE RETURN

### CHAPTER NINE: AGAINST THE CURING OF WOMANHOOD

p. 163    *"When I meet women who are over 55":* Alex Kuczynski, interview with Gloria Steinem, "Bosom Foes Together Again," *New York Times,* May 3, 1998.

p. 163    *"There is nothing the matter":* Martin (1899, p. 98).

p. 164    *In a 1995 issue:* Lynn O'Shaughnessy, "Is Prozac the Prescription for Happiness?" *American Woman,* September/October 1995.

p. 164    *Donald Klein's research:* Kramer (1993, pp. 70–77, 91).

p. 165    *"If you can 'set a floor' ":* Kramer (1993, p. 89).

p. 165    *Enter Gail:* Kramer (1993, p. 94).

p. 165    *"if Lucy" " can be spared":* Kramer (1993, p. 70).

p. 165    *" 'easy blushers' ":* Kramer (1993, p. 100).

p. 165    *"hunger for approval":* Kramer (1993, p. 98).

p. 165    *"Sonia":* Kramer (1993, p. 238).

p. 166    *"even asked men to dance":* Kramer (1993, p. 147).

p. 166    *pamphlet on teen dating violence:* By "Sousa, Bandcroft, and German."

p. 166    *"Prozac does not just brighten":* Kramer (1993, p. 270).

p. 166    *In a brilliant 1997 Op-Ed:* Jenny McPhee, "A Feminist Redefined," *New York Times,* March 4, 1997.

p. 166    *"Stand tall":* Helena Rosenberg, *Self,* January 1998.

p. 167    *"As vivid and exciting":* Christopher (1997, p. 197).

p. 167    *"Equality…means":* Margaret Atwood, speech to the American Booksellers Association, 1993; as cited in Katherine Dunn, "Call of the Wild," *Vogue,* June 1995.

p. 167    *"a great moralist":* Beauvoir (1966, p. 40).

p. 167    *"all the insipidity":* Beauvoir (1966, p. 11).

p. 167    *"whipping a few girls":* Beauvoir (1966, p. 8).

p. 168    *"Why should all emotionally vulnerable":* Kramer (1993, p. 90).

p. 168   *When on two successive:* Roger Kimball, "A Syllabus for Sickos," *Wall Street Journal,* November 5, 1997.

p. 168   *As the singer explains:* M. P. Dunleavey, "Is *Bitch* a Compliment?" *Glamour,* February 1998.

p. 169   *Camille Paglia may be right:* Paglia (1990, 1994).

p. 169   *"an excess of general intensity":* Hornbacher (1998, p. 6).

## CHAPTER TEN: MODESTY AND THE EROTIC

p. 171   *"Samuel G. Freedman's article":* Letter to the editor, *New York Times Magazine,* June 21, 1998.

p. 171   *every year, another study:* Edward O. Laumann, John H. Gagnon, Robert T. Michael, and Stuart Michaels, *The Organization of Sexuality: Sexual Practices in the United States* (Chicago: University of Chicago Press, 1994), pp. 363–65; William R. Mattox, Jr., "What's Marriage Got to Do With It?" *Family Policy 6:* 6 (February 1994); Robert J. Levin and Amy Levin, "Sexual Pleasure: The Surprising Preferences of 100,000 Women," *Redbook,* September 1975, pp. 51–58.

p. 172   *"the most virtuous women":* Balzac (1901, p. 46).

p. 172   *The "Cannon Coaster" ride:* Kasson (1978, p. 43).

p. 172   *"affairs can support a marriage":* Eric Alterman, "Affairs of the Heart," *Elle,* November 1997.

p. 173   *"Black nylon":* Carol J. Williams, "In Bosnia, Islam Has Many Faces," *Los Angeles Times,* May 29, 1994.

p. 173   *"The number of dates":* Elizabeth Hayt, "Men's Sex Strategies," *Marie Claire,* September 1997.

p. 173   *"The largest association of nudists":* Jennifer S. Lee, *Wall Street Journal,* August 11, 1997.

p. 173   *"Breasts point up":* Maxine Paetro, "Nude Cruise," *New Woman,* May 1996.

p. 173   *Even a man who assumed:* Aaron Gell, "Is Topless a Turn-on?" *Mademoiselle,* June 1995.

p. 174   *A recent complainant:* "Dear Abby," *New York Post,* August 3, 1997.

p. 174   *In contrast, in Malaysia:* Jean J. Boddewyn and Heidi Kunz, "Sex and Decency Issues in Advertising: General and International Dimensions," *School of Business at Indiana University Business Horizons,* September 1991.

p. 174   *the "modesty piece":* Mackrell (1986, p. 23).

p. 174   *"unveiled and surprisingly":* Hadani Ditmars, "Is the Veil Old Hat?" *Vogue,* September 1997.

p. 175   *"Despite an ascetic life":* Elizabeth Hayt, "Where Lingerie Sells to the Orthodox," *New York Times,* January 11, 1998.

p. 177   *coed wrestling team:* "Increasing in Number, Women Stake Out Turf on the Williams Wrestling Team," *Williams Record,* November 19, 1996.

p. 178   *"Not long ago, a group of teenagers":* Friedman (1990, p. 101).

p. 179   *"Now that we live together":* Blanche Vernon, "Sex Q & A," *Mademoiselle,* March 1998.

p. 179   *"HELP! I'm a healthy":* Letter to "Ask E. Jean," *Elle,* September 1997.

p. 180   *guilty of dancing the turkey trot:* James R. Peterson, "The End of

Innocence: Part II, 1910–1919; Playboy's History of the Sexual Revolution," *Playboy*, February 1997.

p. 183 *"Therefore shall a man"*: Genesis 2:24.

p. 183 *"THINK YOU KNOW"*: David Hochman, "7 Sex Secrets He'll Never Tell . . . But We Will," *Mademoiselle*, November 1995.

p. 183 *"When I was young"*: Roiphe (1997, p. 48).

p. 186 *"An excess of modesty"*: Stendhal (1957, p. 66): "L'excès de la pudeur et sa sévérité découragent d'aimer les âmes tendres et timides, justement celles qui sont faites pour donner et sentir les délices de l'amour." The footnote: "J'ai vu les femmes les plus distinguées et les plus faites pour aimer donner la préférence, faute d'esprit, au prosaïque tempérament sanguin."

p. 187 *"Let's face it"*: Jenny Lombard, "How to Stay Single FOREVER," *Cosmopolitan*, June 1994.

p. 188 *"Being a virgin definitely"*: Cline (1993, p. 170).

p. 188 *John Lange published:* Fletcher (1995, p. 49).

p. 188 *"Out you green-sickness"*: *Romeo and Juliet*, Act III, scene v.

p. 188 *"I haven't found someone"*: Rubin (1990, p. 68).

p. 188 *"Few men want"*: Gordon Harvey, "Men on Your First-Time Sex Techniques," *Cosmopolitan*, June 1998.

p. 191 *a "lascivious" philosophy:* Wollstonecraft (1992, pp. 188–89, 234, and 238).

p. 192 *the "Genital Appropriation Era":* Cline (1993, p. 169).

p. 192 *holding back on intercourse:* Valarie Frankel, "Almost Sex," *Mademoiselle*, October 1996.

p. 192 *"Virtue," " chimerical and imaginary"*: Beauvoir (1966, p. 52).

p. 193 *"no aphrodisiac"*: Beauvoir (1966, p. 28).

CHAPTER ELEVEN: PINING FOR INTERFERENCE

p. 194 *"I'll never forget the night . . ."*: Eric Tisdale, "My Girlfriend's Father— What a Man!" *Glamour*, June 1998.

p. 196 *"A woman arriving"*: Benton (1956, p. 101).

p. 196 *"Where's the wildest place"*: "Tori's Sure No Prude!" *New York Post*, August 4, 1997.

p. 197 *"not someone"*: Roiphe (1997, p. 189).

p. 197 *"dreaded informing"*: Sara Eckel, "Sexual Ethics: Not in Front of My Parents!" *Glamour*, January 1998.

p. 197 *"I really expected"*: Kathryn Harrison profile, *ELLE*, April 1997.

p. 199 *Dr. Peter Jensen:* "Use of Antidepression Medicine for Young Patients Has Soared: To Bolster Market, Makers Seek FDA Sanction," *New York Times*, August 10, 1997.

p. 200 *The current craze is handheld:* *New York Times*, August 31, 1997.

p. 201 *between 1960 and 1990:* David Popenoe, *Wilson Quarterly*, Spring 1996.

p. 201 *"When I was 14"*: Bonnie Root, *Marie Claire*, February 1998.

p. 202 *"green with inexperience"*: Lucinda Rosenfeld, "Viewpoint: Mock Marriage," British *Vogue*, February 1998.

p. 203 *"Shame, guilt, and fear"*: Elliott and Brantley (1997, p. 182).

p. 205 *"It's no big deal"*: Pipher (1994, p. 199).

p. 207 *"What foils the male's tendency"*: Douglas Botting and Kate Botting,

"What Do Women Really See in Men?" London *Daily Mail,*
September 12, 1995.

p. 210  *"Dear Help!":* Holyoke (1996, p. 25).

p. 211  *"screaming fights in the kitchen":* Hornbacher (1998, 32).

p. 211  *even when we're planning our weddings:* "Newlywed's Guide to
Divorce," *New Woman,* February 1996.

p. 211  *"Nobody wanted me":* Pipher (1994, p. 137).

p. 212  *"by her joint care":* Fletcher (1995, p. 230).

p. 212  *"the marrying generation of today":* Rosalind Miles, "Current Affairs,"
*Prospect,* January 1996.

p. 213  *"Marriage wasn't part":* Maggie Kirn, "Teen Bride," *Harper's Bazaar,*
February 1998.

p. 213  *"Yes, We Still Want to Get Married . . . But Why?":* Cosmopolitan,
November 1995.

p. 213  *"Can We End Divorce?":* Swing, November 1997.

## CHAPTER TWELVE: BEYOND MODERNITY

p. 214  *"In the new order":* Bloom (1987, p. 114).

p. 215  *"no woman should be authorized":* Betty Friedan, interview of Simone
de Beauvoir, as cited in Sommers (1994, p. 257).

p. 216  *just as often forced to have careers:* See Arendell (1986, pp. 152–53):
"The sixty women interviewed had been repeatedly penalized
within the law for having been primarily wives and mothers and not
wage earners. Although husbands and wives apparently have equal
access to obtaining a legal divorce, in practice even that equality is
mythical. In being treated by the law as if they were social and economic equals, these women were put at a profound disadvantage,
and the inequities of the traditional marital arrangement were
obscured. They lost their primary source of income and were given
nearly total responsibility for their dependent children and themselves."

p. 216  *"shining floors and wiping noses":* Miedzian (1991, p. 4).

p. 216  *Brenda Barnes:* Kathy Bishop, "Balancing Act II; It's Family That
Matters," *New York Post,* September 30, 1997.

p. 216  *a young mother who quit:* Elizabeth Perle McKenna, *When Work
Doesn't Work Anymore: Women, Work and Identity* (New York
Delacorte, 1997).

p. 216  *"interesting that most mothers feared":* Self, May 1997.

p. 217  *"Powerless, we watched":* Miriam Stein, "Rarely Do I Stop Searching
for Clues to His Becoming Orthodox," *Forward,* December 26,
1997.

p. 218  *"Having never been":* Manolson (1997, p. 39).

p. 218  *"As a 20-year-old Muslim":* Salma Shahabuddin from Montreal,
Letters to the Editor, *Vogue,* December 1997.

p. 218  *"Blessed is he":* Pamer (1990, p. 35), quoting Revelations 16:15.

p. 219  *when God reveals himself:* Lamm (1997, p. 3). *Va-yaster Mosheh panav
ki yarei me'habit el ha-Elokim* (Shemot).

p. 220  *"Brenda":* Abramov (1988, p. 99).

p. 220  *Judith Margolis:* Gary Libman, "Modern Women Explain Return to
Orthodoxy," *Los Angeles Times,* February 7, 1989.

p. 222  *"Then came the radical 1960s":* Lena Williams, "In Defense of the Church Hat," *New York Times,* May 12, 1996.

p. 223  *Consider the amusing discovery:* Yasmin Alibhai-Brown, "Cloak of Modesty: Sexy Accessory or Symbol of Oppression?" *Independent,* December 22, 1994.

p. 223  *"In 1996, no insider":* Sarah Mower, "It's What's Underneath That Counts in Milan's Transparency Scene," *International Herald Tribune,* October 12, 1996.

p. 224  *"Melanie":* Mimi Avins, "In L. A. You Can Get Away with Anything But Do You Really Want To?" *Los Angeles Times,* February 23, 1997.

p. 224  *"In Turkey, Kuwait":* Deborah Scroggins, "Women of the Veil," *Atlanta Journal and Constitution,* June 28, 1992.

p. 224  *"Many parents have been perplexed":* Tony Walker, "Arab Women Clothe Fashion Trends with the Veil of Modesty," *Financial Times Limited,* June 16, 1989.

p. 224  *An Egyptian web site brags:* http://www.scriptorium.org/odyssey/week8/DailyGrind02.html.

p. 225  *"changes taking place":* Soren Larson, "Cover-ups Leave the Beach," *Women's Wear Daily,* September 17, 1991.

p. 225  *"after deconstruction":* Nilgin Yusuf, "Modern Romance," *Sunday Times,* November 14, 1993.

p. 225  *Ron Shamask:* Jackie White, "The Daring Is in the Wearing, Not the Baring," *Kansas City Star,* April 21, 1996.

p. 225  *"Thanks to our interest in nostalgia":* Barbara De Witt, Fashion Editor, "Hat Trick: Spring Styles Brimming with Fun for the Head," *Los Angeles Daily News,* March 27, 1997.

p. 226  *"In the halls of junior highs":* Pipher (1994, p. 207).

p. 226  *reminisces 25-year-old Rob:* Rubin (1990, p. 51).

p. 227  *"I wanted to date":* Pipher (1994, p. 204).

p. 227  *"I am so sick of the fact":* Letter to the editor, *New York* magazine, January 19, 1998.

p. 227  *"To the extent that divorce":* Epstein (1974, p. 98).

p. 228  *"In a more faltering voice":* Manolson (1997, p. 82).

p. 229  *"As for me":* Jim Dixon, "Men Q & A," *Mademoiselle,* August 1997.

p. 230  *"legalized rape":* Dworkin (1976, p. 27).

p. 230  *"legalized prostitution":* Spender (1982, p. 341).

p. 231  *"in the nineteen fifties":* Roiphe (1996, p. 128).

p. 231  *In eighteenth-century France:* Laver (1969, p. 9).

p. 232  *Stendhal concludes:* Stendhal (1957, p. 61): "Une femme de Madagascar laisse voir sans y songer ce qu'on cache le plus ici, mais mourrait de honte plutôt que de montrer son bras. . . . Il est clair que les trois quarts de la pudeur sont une chose apprise."

p. 232  *"Anthropologists, in comparing":* Riezler (1943, p. 457).

p. 232  *"Specific rules about modesty":* Benton (1956, p. 3).

p. 234  *"those same dormitories":* Samuel G. Freedman, "Yeshivish at Yale," *New York Times Magazine,* May 24, 1998.

p. 234  *refusing to shower after gym class:* Dirk Johnson, "Students Still Sweat, They Just Don't Shower," *New York Times,* April 22, 1996.

p. 235  *"Today's kids want to return":* Alix Strauss, "Mind Your Manners," *Seventeen,* December 1997.

p. 235  *in a marked departure:* Lynn Harris, "Casual Sex: Why Confident

Women Are Saying No," *Glamour,* September 1997; letters from the
November 1997 issue.

p. 236   *"SIZZLING swimwear gets a girl noticed":* "Modesty Belles: Cover-all
Glamour Dives into the Lead," *Sunday Mirror,* July 10, 1994.

p. 237   *"Daisy Starr's one-night stand": Marie Claire,* June 1997.

## A MODEST CONCLUSION: INNOCENCE.

p. 239   *"We were as twinned lambs":* Shakespeare, *The Winter's Tale,* Act I,
scene ii, Polixenes to Hermione.

p. 239   *"On Bullfrogs and Alexanders":* Trilling (1993, p. 14).

p. 239   *"necking was the chief":* Trilling (1993, p. 16).

p. 239   *"I have never met any man":* Trilling (1993, p. 2).

p. 240   *" 'In our class' ":* Cline (1993, p. 170).

p. 241   *"There may have been a darker":* Katie Roiphe, "The End of
Innocence," *Vogue,* January 1998.

p. 241   *"further misgivings arise":* Thompson (1995, p. 41).

p. 241   *"I had only dated him":* Thompson (1995, pp. 20–21).

p. 242   *"Inside the examining room":* Joe Maxwell, "A Cinderella Nightmare,"
*World,* August 17/24, 1996.

p. 243   *"pushed by parents to achieve":* Elizabeth Gleick, "Every Kid a Star,"
*Time,* April 22, 1996.

Abramov, Tehilla. *The Secret of Jewish Femininity: Insight into the Practice of Taharat Hamishpachah.* Southfield, MI: Targum Press, 1988.

Agonito, Rosemary. *No More "Nice Girl."* Holbrook, MA: Adams Publishing Company, 1993.

Ahn, Alicia; Bates, Cynthia; Brown, Heather; Daubman, Kimberly A.; Preston, Camille; and Heatherington, Laurie. "Two Investigations of 'Female Modesty' in Achievement Situations." *Sex Roles* 29 (1993): 739–54.

Ahn, Alicia; Daubman, Kimberly A.; and Heatherington, Laurie. "Gender and the Self-Presentation of Academic Achievement." *Sex Roles* 27 (1992): 187–204.

[Allestree, Richard.] *The Ladies Calling.* Oxford: n.p., 1673.

Alvarez, Julia. *How the Latina Girls Lost Their Accents.* New York: Penguin Books, 1991.

*The American Code of Manners.* New York: W. R. Andrews, 1880.

Anon. *The Canons of Good Breeding.* Philadelphia: Lee and Blanchard, 1839.

Arendell, Terry. *Mothers and Divorce.* Berkeley: University of California Press, 1986.

Balzac, Honoré de. "The Physiology of Marriage." *The Works of Honoré de Balzac.* Vol. 33. New York: Thomas Y. Crowell, 1901.

Barthes, Roland. *A Lover's Discourse: Fragments.* Trans. Richard Howard. New York: Hill and Wang, 1978.

Beauvoir, Simone de. *The Second Sex.* Trans. and ed. H. M. Parshley. New York: Alfred A. Knopf, 1952.

——. "Must We Burn Sade?" Introduction to *120 Days of Sodom and Other Writings,* by the Marquis de Sade. Trans. Austryn Wainhouse and Richard Seaver. New York: Grove Press, 1966. (Essay originally published in the December 1951 and January 1952 issues of *Les Temps Modernes* as "Faut-il brûler Sade?")

Benton, Frances. *Complete Etiquette: The Complete Modern Guide for Day-to-Day Living the Correct Way.* Co-edited by the General Federation of Women's Clubs. New York: Random House, 1956.

Bloom, Allan David. *The Closing of the American Mind.* New York: Simon & Schuster, 1987.

——. *Love and Friendship.* New York: Simon & Schuster, 1993.

Bonald, Louis de. *On Divorce.* Trans. and ed. Nicholas Davidson. New Brunswick, NJ: Transaction Publishers, 1992 (original publication 1801).

Brathwait, Richard. *The English Gentleman.* London: Printed by John Haviland, and . . . sold by Robert Bostock . . ., 1630.

——. *The English Gentlewoman.* London: Printed by B. Alsop and T. Fawcet, for Michaell Sparke . . ., 1631.

Brecher, Edward M. *The Sex Researchers.* Boston: Little, Brown, 1969.

Brown, Peter. *The Body and Society: Men, Women, and Sexual Renunciation in Early Christianity.* New York: Columbia University Press, 1988.

Brumberg, Joan Jacobs. *The Body Project: An Intimate History of American Girls.* New York: Random House, 1997.

Buss, David M. "Sex Differences in Human Mate Preferences: Evolutionary Hypotheses Tested in 37 Cultures." *Behavioral and Brain Sciences* 12 (1989): 1–49.

———. *The Evolution of Desire: Strategies of Human Mating.* New York: Basic Books, 1994.

Carlip, Hillary. *Girl Power: Young Women Speak Out!* New York: Time Warner Books, 1995.

Carroll, Lewis. *Alice's Adventures in Wonderland.* New York: Dodge Publishing Company, 1907.

Christen, Yves. *Sex Differences: Modern Biology and the Unisex Fallacy.* Trans. Nicholas Davidson. New Brunswick, NJ: Transaction Publishers, 1991.

Christopher, Nicholas. *Somewhere in the Night: Film Noir and the American City.* New York: Free Press, 1997.

Cline, Sally. *Women, Passion & Celibacy.* New York: Carol Southern Books, 1993.

Cloete, Stuart. *Congo Song.* Boston: Houghton Mifflin 1943.

Cohen, David. *Law, Sexuality, and Society: The Enforcement of Morals in Classical Athens.* Cambridge: Cambridge University Press, 1991.

Colin, Virginia L. *Human Attachment.* New York: McGraw-Hill, 1996.

Cotton, Nancy. *John Fletcher's Chastity Plays: Mirrors of Modesty.* Lewisburg PA: Bucknell University Press, 1973.

Crider, Andrew B.; Goethals, George R. II; Kavanaugh, Robert D.; Solomon, Paul R. *Psychology, Fourth Edition.* New York: HarperCollins, 1993.

Dahl, Tove Stang. *Women's Law: An Introduction to Feminist Jurisprudence.* Oslo: Norwegian University Press: 1987.

Daly, Mary. *Webster's First New Intergalactic Wickedary of the English Language.* New York: HarperCollins, 1987.

De Angelis, Barbara. *Ask Barbara: The 100 Most-Asked Questions About Love, Sex, and Relationships.* New York: Delacorte Press, 1997.

Dijkstra, Bram. *Evil Sisters: The Threat of Female Sexuality and the Cult of Manhood.* New York: Knopf, 1996.

Dworkin, Andrea. *Woman Hating.* New York: Dutton, 1974.

———. *Our Blood: Prophecies and Discourses on Sexual Politics.* New York: Harper & Row, 1976.

———. "Renouncing Sexual Equality." *Letters from a War Zone.* Chicago: Lawrence Hill Books, 1993.

Ellinson, Rabbi Getsel. *Serving the Creator: A Guide to the Rabbinic Sources.* Woman and the Mitzvot, Vol. 1. Trans. Rabbi Mendell Lewittes and Avner Tomaschoff. Jerusalem: Ahva Press, 1986.

———. *The Modest Way.* Woman and the Mitzvot, Vol. 2. Trans. Raphael Blumberg. Jerusalem: Ahva Press, 1992.

Elliott, Leland, and Brantley, Cynthia. *Sex on Campus: The Naked Truth About the Real Sex Lives of College Students.* New York: Random House, 1997.

Ellis, Albert. *Sex Without Guilt.* New York: Lyle Stuart, 1958.

Ellis, Havelock. "The Evolution of Modesty." *Studies in the Psychology of Sex,* Vol I, 3rd ed. Philadelphia: F. A. Davis, 1910 (first published in 1899).

Emerson, Everett H., *English Puritanism, from John Hooper to John Milton.* Durham, NC: Duke University Press, 1968.

Epstein, Joseph. *Divorced in America: Marriage in an Age of Possibility.* New York: Dutton, 1974.

Erler, Mary, and Kowalesky, Maryanne, eds. *Women & Power in the Middle Ages.* Athens, GA: University of Georgia Press, 1988.

Evdokimov, Paul. *The Sacrament of Love.* Trans. Anthony P. Gythiel and Victoria Steadman. Crestwood, NY: St. Vladimir's Seminary Press, 1995.

Eyer, Diane E. *Mother-Infant Bonding: A Scientific Fiction.* New Haven: Yale University Press, 1992.

Farber, Leslie H. *Lying, Despair, Jealousy, Envy, Sex, Suicide, Drugs, and the Good Life.* New York: Basic Books, 1976.

Fein, Ellen, and Schneider, Sherrie. *The Rules: Time Tested Secrets for Capturing the Heart of Mr. Right.* New York: Warner Books, 1996.

Feinberg, Joel, and Gross, Hyman, eds. *Philosophy of Law,* 5th ed. Belmont, CA: Wadsworth Publishing Company, 1995.

Ferguson, Ann. *Blood at the Root: Motherhood, Sexuality and Male Dominance.* London: Pandora Press, 1989.

————. "A Transitional Female Sexual Morality." Anthologized in *Feminist Frameworks: Alternative Theoretical Accounts of the Relations Between Women and Men.* New York: McGraw-Hill, 1993.

Firestone, Shulamith. *The Dialectic of Sex: The Case for a Feminist Revolution.* New York: Morrow, 1970.

Flaubert, Gustave. *A Simple Heart.* New York: Penguin Books, 1995.

Fletcher, Anthony. *Gender, Sex and Subordination in England 1500–1800.* New Haven: Yale University Press, 1995.

Fordham, Jim and Andrea. *The Assault on the Sexes.* New Rochelle, NY: Arlington House, 1977.

Fradkin, Hillel. "God's Politics—Lessons from the Beginning." *The Best of This World.* Ed. Michael A. Scully. Lanham, MD: University Press of America, 1986.

France, Anatole. *Under the Rose.* Trans. J. Lewis. New York: Dodd, Mead, 1926.

Freud, Sigmund. *Civilization and Its Discontents.* Trans. and ed. James Strachey. New York: Norton, 1961.

————. *New Introductory Lectures on Psycho-Analysis.* Trans. and ed. James Strachey. New York: Norton, 1965.

Friedman, Manis. *Doesn't Anyone Blush Anymore?* Ed. J. S. Morris. Minneapolis, MN: Bais Chana Press, 1990.

Gallagher, Maggie. *Enemies of Eros: How the Sexual Revolution Is Killing Family, Marriage, and Sex and What We Can Do About It.* Chicago: Bonus Books, 1989.

Gelernter, David. *Drawing Life: Surviving the Unabomber.* New York: Free Press, 1997.

"A Gentleman." *The Laws of Etiquette.* Philadelphia: Carey, Lee and Blanchard, 1836.

Gilmore, David D. *Manhood in the Making: Cultural Concepts of Masculinity.* New Haven: Yale University Press, 1990.

Goffman, Erving. *Behavior in Public Places: Notes on the Social Organization of Gatherings.* New York: Free Press, 1963.

Green, Katherine Sobba. *The Courtship Novel, 1740–1820: A Feminist Genre.* Lexington: University Press of Kentucky, 1991.

Grene, Marjorie, and Mendelsohn, Everett, eds. *Topics in the Philosophy of Biology.* Dordrecht, Holland: D. Reidel Publishing Company, 1976.

Gurstein, Rochelle. *The Repeal of Reticence: A History of America's Cultural and Legal Struggles over Free Speech, Obscenity, Sexual Liberation, and Modern Art.* New York: Hill and Wang, 1996.

Ḥanbal, Ibn, and Rāhwayh, Ibn. *Chapters on Marriage and Divorce.* Trans. Susan A. Spectorsky. Austin: University of Texas Press, 1993.

Hansen, Joseph; Reed, Evelyn; and Waters, Mary-Alice. *Cosmetics, Fashions and the Exploitation of Women.* New York: Pathfinder Press, 1986.

Harrison, Kathryn. *The Kiss.* New York: Random House, 1997.

Hart, Clive, and Stevenson, Gilliland. *Heaven and the Flesh.* New York: Cambridge University Press, 1995.

Hattemer, Barbara, and Showers, Robert. *Don't Touch That Dial.* Lafayette, LA: Huntington House, 1993.

Heller, Rebbetzin Tziporah. *More Precious Than Pearls: Selected Insights into the Qualities of the Ideal Woman, Based on Eshes Chayil.* Jerusalem: Feldheim Press, 1993.

Hersch, Patricia. *A Tribe Apart: A Journey into the Heart of American Adolescence.* New York: Ballantine Books, 1998.

Hesse-Biber, Sharlene. *Am I Thin Enough Yet?: The Cult of Thinness and the Commercialization of Identity.* New York: Oxford University Press, 1996.

Hill, Gareth S. *Masculine and Feminine: The Natural Flow of Opposites in the Psyche.* Boston: Shambhala Press, 1992.

Holyoke, Nancy. *Help! An Absolutely Indispensable Guide to Life for Girls!* Illustrated by Scott Nash. Middleton, WI: Pleasant Company Publications, 1995.

————. *More Help! From the American Girl Library.* Illustrated by Scott Nash. Middleton, WI: Pleasant Company Publications, 1996.

————. *Oops! The Manners Guide for Girls.* Illustrated by Debbie Tilley. Middleton, WI: Pleasant Company Publications, 1997.

Hornbacher, Marya. *Wasted: A Memoir of Anorexia and Bulimia.* New York: HarperCollins, 1998.

Hrdy, Sarah Blaffer. *The Woman That Never Evolved.* Cambridge: Harvard University Press, 1981.

Hubbard, Ruth. *The Politics of Women's Biology.* New Brunswick, NJ: Rutgers University Press, 1990.

Hull, Isabel V. *Sexuality, State, and Civil Society in Germany, 1700–1815.* Ithaca, NY: Cornell University Press, 1996.

Hume, David. *A Treatise of Human Nature.* Ed. L. A. Selby Bigge. Oxford: Clarendon, 1967 (originally published in 1739).

————. "On Impudence and Modesty." *Essays: Moral, Political and Literary.* Indianapolis: Liberty Fund, 1985. This essay originally appeared in the first edition of *Essays, Moral and Political* (Edinburgh: A. Kincaid, 1741), but after 1760 the essay was withdrawn.

Irigaray, Luce. *An Ethics of Sexual Difference.* Trans. Carolyn Burke and Gillian C. Gill. Ithaca, NY: Cornell University Press, 1993.

James, Henry. *The American Scene.* Bloomington: Indiana University Press, 1968.

Johnson, Samuel. Entry "modesty," from *A Dictionary of the English Language,* Vol. II. New York: AMS Press, 1967 (originally published in 1755).

Jung, C. G. *Aspects of the Feminine.* Trans. R.F.C. Hull. Princeton, NJ: Princeton University Press, 1982.

Kant, Immanuel. *Lectures on Ethics.* Trans. Louis Infield. New York: Harper and Row, 1963.

Kasson, John F. *Amusing the Million: Coney Island at the Turn of the Century.* New York: Hill and Wang, 1978.

———. *Rudeness & Civility.* New York: Hill and Wang, 1990.

Keen, Maurice. *Chivalry.* New Haven: Yale University Press, 1984.

Kierkegaard, Søren. *Either/Or.* Trans. Walter Lowrie. 2 vols. New York: Anchor Books, 1959.

Kimmel, Michael. *Manhood in America: A Cultural History.* New York: Free Press, 1996.

Knapp, Caroline. *Drinking: A Love Story.* New York: Dial Press, 1996.

Kramarae, Cheris, and Treichler, Paula A. *A Feminist Dictionary.* London: Pandora Press, 1985.

Kramer, Peter D. *Listening to Prozac: A Psychiatrist Explores Antidepressant Drugs and the Remaking of the Self.* New York: Penguin Books, 1993.

Lamm, Maurice. *The Jewish Way in Love and Marriage.* New York: Harper & Row, 1980.

Lamm, Norman. *A Hedge of Roses: Jewish Insights into Marriage and Married Life.* New York: Philipp Feldheim, 1966.

———. "Tzeniut: A Universal Concept." *Haham Gaon Memorial Volume.* Ed. Rabbi Marc Angel. Jerusalem: Sepher-Hermon Press, 1997.

Langelan, Martha J . *Back Off!* New York: Fireside/Simon & Schuster, 1993.

Lardner, George. *The Stalking of Kristin.* New York: Atlantic Monthly Press, 1995.

Lasch, Christopher. *Women and the Common Life: Love, Marriage, and Feminism.* Ed. Elisabeth Lasch-Quinn. New York: Norton, 1997.

Laver, James. *Modesty in Dress: An Inquiry into the Fundamentals of Fashion.* Boston: Houghton Mifflin, 1969.

Lefkowitz, Bernard. *Our Guys.* New York: Vintage Books, 1998.

Lehrman, Karen. *The Lipstick Proviso: Women, Sex & Power in the Real World.* New York: Doubleday, 1997.

Levin, Michael. *Feminism & Freedom.* New Brunswick, NJ: Transaction Publishers, 1987.

Lewis, C. S. *The Four Loves.* New York: Harcourt Brace, 1960.

Liu, James J. *The Chinese Knight-Errant.* Chicago: University of Chicago Press, 1967.

MacKinnon, Catharine A. *Toward a Feminist Theory of the State.* Cambridge, MA: Harvard University Press, 1989.

Mackrell, Alice. *Shawls, Stoles, and Scarves.* London: Batsford, 1986.

Mandeville, Bernard. *A Modest Defence of Publick Stews; or, an Essay upon Whoring, as It Is Now Practis'd in These Kingdoms.* London: Moore, 1724.

Manolson, Gila. *The Magic Touch: A Candid Look at the Jewish Approach to Relationships.* Jerusalem: Har Nof Publications, 1992.

———. *Outside Inside: A Fresh Look at Tzniut.* Jerusalem: Targum Press, 1997.

Martin, Edward Sandford. *The Luxury of Children: & Some Other Luxuries.* New York: Harper & Brothers, 1899.

Miedzian, Myriam. *Boys Will Be Boys: Breaking the Link Between Masculinity and Violence.* New York: Doubleday, 1991.

Mill, John Stuart. *Utilitarianism.* Indianapolis: Hackett Publishing Company, 1979.

Mitchell, Juliet, and Rose, Jacqueline, eds. *Feminine Sexuality: Jacques Lacan and the école freudienne.* New York: Norton, 1982.

Moats, Alice-Leone. *No Nice Girl Swears.* New York: St. Martin's Press, 1983. (Originally published in 1933.)

Moore, Clara Sophia Jessup. *Sensible Etiquette of the Best Society, Customs, Manners, Morals and Home Culture.* Philadelphia: Porter & Coates, 1878.

Nasaw, David. *Going Out: The Rise and Fall of Public Amusements.* New York: HarperCollins, 1993.

North, Helen. *Sophrosyne: Self-Knowledge and Self-Restraint in Greek Literature.* Ithaca, NY: Cornell University Press, 1966.

Odenwald, Robert P., M.D. *The Disappearing Sexes: Sexual Behavior in the United States and the Emergence of Uni-Sex.* New York: Random House, 1965.

O'Neill, Nena and George. *Open Marriage: A New Life Style for Couples.* New York: M. Evans, 1972.

Orenstein, Peggy. *Schoolgirls: Young Women, Self-Esteem, and the Confidence Gap.* In Association with the American Association of University Women. New York: Doubleday/Anchor Books, 1994.

Paglia, Camille. *Sexual Personae.* New York: Vintage Books, 1990.

———. *Sex, Art, and American Culture: Essays.* New York: Vintage Books, 1992.

———. *Vamps & Tramps: New Essays.* New York: Vintage Books, 1994.

Pamer, Nan. *Modesty: A Fresh Look at a Biblical Principle.* Hazelwood, MO: Word Aflame Press, 1990.

Plato. *Early Socratic Dialogues. Charmides.* Trans. Donald Watt. New York: Penguin Books, 1987.

Pipher, Mary. *Reviving Ophelia: Saving the Selves of Adolescent Girls.* New York: Ballantine Books, 1994.

Poovey, Mary. *The Proper Lady and the Woman Writer: Ideology as Style in the Works of Mary Wollstonecraft, Mary Shelley, and Jane Austen.* Chicago: University of Chicago Press, 1984.

Posner, Richard A. *Sex and Reason.* Cambridge: Harvard University Press, 1992.

Post, Emily. *Etiquette: In Society, in Business, in Politics and at Home.* New York: Funk & Wagnalls, 1923.

Renooz, Madame Celine. *Psychologie Comparée de l'Homme et de la Femme.* Paris: Bibliothèque de la Nouvelle Encyclopédie, 1898.

Ribiat, Rabbi Dovid. *The Halachos of Yichud.* Jerusalem: Feldheim, 1996.

Richardson, Samuel. *Pamela: Or Virtue Rewarded.* New York: Norton, 1958. (First published in 1740).

———. *Clarissa: Or The History of a Young Lady.* New York: Viking Penguin, 1985 (first published in 1747–48).

Riezler, Kurt. "Comment on the Social Psychology of Shame." *American Journal of Sociology* 48 (January 1943): 457–65.

Roiphe, Anne. *Fruitful—Living the Contradictions: A Memoir of Modern Motherhood.* New York: Penguin Books, 1996.

Roiphe, Katie. *The Morning After: Sex, Fear, and Feminism on Campus.* Boston: Little, Brown, 1993.

———. *Last Night in Paradise: Sex and Morals at the Century's End.* Boston: Little, Brown, 1997.

Rothman, Sheila M. *Woman's Proper Place.* New York: Basic Books, 1978.

Rousseau, Jean-Jacques. *Lettre à M. d'Alembert sur son Article Genève.* Paris: Garnier-Flammarion, 1967.

———. *Emile: Or On Education.* Trans. Allan Bloom. New York: Basic Books, 1979.

Rubin, Lillian, B. *Erotic Wars: What Happened to the Sexual Revolution?* New York: Farrar, Straus & Giroux, 1990.

Schueler, G. F. "Why Modesty Is a Virtue." *Ethics* 107 (April 1997): 467–85.

Scott, Brenda. *Children No More: How We Lost a Generation.* Lafayette, LA: Huntington House, 1995.

Shanley, James Lyndon. *A Study of Spenser's Gentlemen.* Evanston, IL: Northwestern University Press, 1940.

Singer, Irving. *The Nature of Love: Courtly and Romantic.* Chicago: University of Chicago Press, 1984.

Sommers, Christina Hoff. *Who Stole Feminism? How Women Have Betrayed Women.* New York: Simon & Schuster, 1994.

Spender, Dale. *Women of Ideas and What Men Have Done to Them.* London: Routledge and Kegan Paul, 1982.

Steiner, Wendy. *The Scandal of Pleasure: Art in an Age of Fundamentalism.* Chicago: University of Chicago Press, 1996.

Stendhal. *De l'Amour.* Édition Établie et Commentée par Henri Martineau. Paris: Le Divan, 1957 (first edition published in 1822).

Stoller, Robert J. *Presentations of Gender.* New Haven: Yale University Press, 1985.

Stoltenberg, John. *Refusing to be a Man: Essays on Sex and Justice.* Portland, OR: Breitenbush Books, 1989.

Straus, Erwin. "Shame as a Historiological Problem." In *Phenomenological Psychology.* New York: Basic Books, 1966.

Tannen, Deborah. *You Just Don't Understand: Men and Women in Conversation.* New York: Morrow, 1990.

Thackeray, W. M. *Mr. Brown's Letters to a Young Man About Town.* New York: D. Appleton and Company, 1852.

Thompson, Sharon. *Going All the Way: Teenage Girls' Tales of Sex, Romance, and Pregnancy.* New York: Hill and Wang, 1995.

Tocqueville, Alexis de. *Democracy in America.* Trans. George Lawrence, ed. J. P. Mayer. New York: Harper & Row, 1966.

Trilling, Diana. *The Beginning of the Journey: The Marriage of Diana and Lionel Trilling.* New York: Harcourt Brace, 1993.

Trollope, Anthony. *An Autobiography.* Eds. Michael Sadleir and Frederick Page. New York: Oxford University Press, 1950.

Ward, Peter. *Courtship, Love, and Marriage in Nineteenth-Century English Canada.* Québec: McGill-Queen's University Press, 1990.

Washington, George. *Rules of Civility & Decent Behavior in Company and Conversation.* Introduction by Letitia Baldrige. Mount Vernon, VA: The Mount Vernon Ladies' Association, 1989 (originally written down, it is thought, around 1748).

Willis, Ellen. *No More Nice Girls: Countercultural Essays.* Hanover, NH: Wesleyan University Press, 1992.

Wilson, John K. *The Myth of Political Correctness: The Conservative Attack on Higher Education.* Durham, NC: Duke University Press, 1995.

Wolf, Naomi. *The Beauty Myth: How Images of Beauty Are Used Against Women.* New York: Doubleday. 1992.

———. *Promiscuities: The Secret Struggle for Womanhood.* New York: Random House, 1997.

Wollstonecraft, Mary. *A Vindication of the Rights of Woman.* Ed. Miriam Brody. New York: Penguin Books, 1992 (originally published in 1792).

Wurtzel, Elizabeth. *Bitch: In Praise of Difficult Women*. New York: Doubleday, 1998.

Yeazell, Ruth Bernard. *Fictions of Modesty: Women and Courtship in the English Novel*. Chicago: University of Chicago Press, 1991.

Zion, William Basil. *Eros and Transformation: Sexuality and Marriage, An Eastern Orthodox Perspective*. Lanham, MD: University Press of America, 1992.

# ACKNOWLEDGMENTS

Some anecdotes in this book have appeared in previously published articles, including "A Ladies' Room of One's Own," *Commentary*, August 1995; "The Death of Girlhood," *The Weekly Standard*, April 29, 1996; "Diversity's Limits," *City Journal*, Autumn 1997; "Daughters of the (Sexual) Revolution," *Commentary*, December 1997; and "Sex Ed's Dead End," *City Journal*, Spring 1998.

I am extremely grateful to Neal Kozodoy of *Commentary* who, when I wrote him my freshman year asking to be an intern, invited me to write for the magazine instead. If I hadn't started writing, I would probably never have made the discovery that there were other women with similar thoughts—each wondering whether she wasn't "the only one." Surely Neal had better things to do than be bothered by some college freshman he had never met, but he pretended he didn't.

Without the good advice of Liz and Hillel Fradkin throughout my high school and college years I would not be the same person—which arguably may not be a good thing—but still I feel very lucky for their friendship.

I have benefited greatly from my conversations with Stephanie Bourdin, Astrid Johanson, Maya Kaplan, Andrea Lieberman, and Jo Procter. Adam Bellow I thank for having faith in this particular idea from the beginning and for being so encouraging. My editor Chad Conway and editorial director Elizabeth Maguire were endlessly patient and helpful. In addition I profited greatly from the advice of my agent, Cynthia Cannell, who guided me through the mysterious world of book publishing.

Other helpful suggestions were made by Mary Daly, Michael Joyce, Irving Kristol, Myron Magnet, Joseph McAlhany, Michael Medved, Walter Olson, Daniel Polsby, and James Taranto. I am particularly grateful to two writers I never met: Ruth Bernard Yeazell and Anthony Fletcher, for their fascinating work on the drama of modesty.

I had many wonderful professors at Williams, but I am most grateful for the wisdom of Trudi Abel, Elaine Beretz, Kristin

Carter-Sanborn, Stephen Fix, Robert Jackall, Gary Jacobsohn, E. J. Johnson, Jeff Weintraub, and especially that of Michael J. Lewis. None of them, needless to say, should be held remotely responsible for any of the conclusions I have reached in this book, but all took my ideas seriously, even when they disagreed with me.

But I also want to thank the professor who did not address my ideas, and constantly attacked me personally. One thing he criticized me for was being "incapable of separating [my] ideas from [my] personal life." It may surprise him to know that I think he was right about me—that I do have this tendency—but I'm not sure why it is necessarily such a bad thing. To me the whole point of philosophy is to inform your life, and it's discussing these questions in a detached way that seems grotesque. For if ideas are to have no bearing on your life, then why bother discussing them in the first place?

"You are so expert in the art of talking in Perfectly general terms without letting yourself be moved by it," said Kierkegaard in *Either/Or*—and was Kierkegaard not a philosopher? If we're expected only to think, and never actually to *believe* or be moved by anything, then perhaps our time would be better spent in a soup kitchen. I didn't major in philosophy to philosophize, but to find out how *I* should live, so I'm particularly grateful for your feedback because it pointed me in the right direction. If I hadn't had you pointing so explicitly at what I wasn't allowed to be, I don't know—and I mean this in all sincerity—if I would have discovered who I was.

Most of all I am fortunate to have been born to the best parents and grandparents in the world, who—although they might not agree with everything I write—are always understanding. My sisters Mina and Ruthie not only were a constant source of encouragement, but more important, taught me in early childhood what I now see as a formative lesson: all the fun that could be had when we girls are left alone in our bathrooms.

Finally, without the expertise of Dr. Jeffrey Katz at Brigham and Women's Hospital in Boston, Dr. Mathew Lee at the New York University Medical Center, and Drs. Jeffrey Ngeow, Stephen Paget, and Arthur Yee at the New York Hospital for Special Surgery, none of this—nor much of anything else, for that matter—would have been possible. My debt to them is inexpressible.

# INDEX

*A RETURN TO MODESTY: Discovering the Lost Virtue* by Wendy Shalit is a fascinating and provocative exploration of the flip side of the sexual revolution, a world in which young women are forced to feel shame for their sexual inexperience and romantic longings. Shalit is a fresh new voice who courageously challenges many of the basic assumptions of modern American society and the relations between men and women.

### DISCUSSION QUESTIONS

1. How does Wendy Shalit define modesty? Do you agree or disagree with her definition? How is modesty different from prudery? What does modesty mean to you?
2. Do you think our society values modesty? What about civility?
3. The author links early sex education with the increased demystification of sex. At what age do you think children should be introduced to the topic of sex? Should parents supply their children with birth control options when they reach puberty? What, if any, effect has sex education had on your own views about sex?
4. Do you agree with David Hume that the risk of pregnancy makes women sexually more vulnerable? If so, wouldn't the Pill take care of that vulnerability? Or are women more sexually vulnerable for other reasons?
5. Does one have to be sexually adventurous to be fully liberated? To be mature?
6. What is the role of imagination and mystery in love and desire?
7. Wendy Shalit states that "in a society that respected the power of female modesty, the men were motivated to do what women wanted." Do you agree or disagree with this statement? Why?
8. Do you think Simone de Beauvoir was right to predict that a society which doesn't appreciate modesty will be one with more violence against women?
9. Modesty in dress is an important issue in the book and the author gives evidence that women who dress modestly earn more respect from men. She also writes about a young Mus-

lim woman who gave up her veil because men found it too alluring and provocative. What do these examples say about the origins of modesty? Do you believe modesty is natural or socially constructed?

10. The author frequently looks to the past—from the 1950s to as far back as the 3rd century B.C.—to define a standard of modesty for today. What historical trends and events come to mind when you think of the evolution of modesty?

11. Wendy Shalit says that she wrote this book in part because modesty cannot be a private virtue in an immodest world. What do you think she means by this? Do you agree or disagree?

12. Do men play a role in helping women maintain their modesty? How do women encourage modest behavior on the part of men? What do you think of the author's views about the relationship between the sexes?

13. Using her grandparents as an example, the author calls for a return to traditional courtship rituals. What would be the benefits and disadvantages of reintroducing these rituals into modern society? Which traditional and modern rituals do you feel strongly about?

14. Does equality mean that men and women must behave the same?

15. How do your personal experiences relate to Wendy Shalit's argument? How do you feel about unisex bathrooms? The role of pornography in our society? The role of the media in the evolution of modesty?